RICHARD RORTY

SUNY Series in Philosophy
George R. Lucas, editor

RICHARD RORTY

Prophet and Poet of the New Pragmatism

By
David L. Hall

State University of New York Press

Published by
State University of New York Press, Albany

For information, address the State University of New York Press,
State University Plaza, Albany, NY 12246

Production by Christine Lynch
Marketing by Theresa A. Swierzowski

Library of Congress Cataloging-in-Publication Data

Hall, David L.
    Richard Rorty : prophet and poet of the new pragmatism / by David
L. Hall
        p.   cm. — (SUNY series in philosophy)
    Includes index.
    ISBN 0-7914-1771-9 (hard : alk. paper). — ISBN 0-7914-1772-7
(pbk. : alk. paper)
        1. Rorty, Richard. 2. Pragmatism—History—20th century.
I. Title. II. Series.
B945.R524H35 1994   76324
191—dc20   93-18515
                                                            CIP

10 9 8 7 6 5 4 3 2 1

DEDICATION

To the students in my twentieth century philosophy class
whose spirited praise (and censure) of Richard Rorty
prompted me to write this book.

CONTENTS

ABBREVIATIONS

CIS   *Contingency, Irony, and Solidarity* (Cambridge: Cambridge University Press, 1989)

CP   *Consequences of Pragmatism* (Minneapolis: The University of Minnesota Press, 1982)

Papers (1)   *Objectivity, Relativism, and Truth* [Philosophical Papers, Volume 1] (Cambridge: Cambridge University Press, 1991)

Papers (2)   *Essays on Heidegger and Others* [Philosophical Papers, Volume 2] (Cambridge: Cambridge University Press, 1991)

PMN   *Philosophy and the Mirror of Nature* (Princeton: Princeton University Press, 1979)

ACKNOWLEDGMENTS

I am grateful to Cambridge University Press for permission to quote from the following copyrighted works: *Contingency, Irony, and Solidarity* (Cambridge: Cambridge University Press, 1989); *Objectivity, Relativism, and Truth* [Philosophical Papers, Volume 1] (Cambridge: Cambridge University Press, 1991); and *Essays on Heidegger and Others* [Philosophical Papers, Volume 2] (Cambridge: Cambridge University Press, 1991).

I wish to thank Roger Ames, my collaborator in things Chinese, who abandoned our *Anticipating China* manuscript long enough to allow me to write this book. The fact that he was engaged in completing his fine translation of Sun Tzu's *Art of Warfare* makes his absence even more forgivable. A draft of this book was completed while a guest in the Ames' household. My thanks to Roger, Bonnie, Clifford, Jason, and Austin for my summer shelter. I appreciate Richard Rorty's kindness in providing several of his unpublished essays, and his apparent willingness to abide this sort of scrutiny. Bill Eastman, director of SUNY Press has, as always, provided imaginative goad-ance and omnivorous solicitude throughout this project. Several anonymous readers for SUNY Press offered spirited critiques of the penultimate draft of my manuscript. I hope some of these will be able to endure a second trip though my work in order to see just how helpful their remarks turned out to be. I am pleased to thank more personally the three readers whose names I know—Alasdair MacIntyre, George Allan, and George Lucas. The presence of my student assistant, Irene Payan, greatly added to the pleasures of the early stages of this project; I have lamented her absence during the final stages. Thanks to Carl Jackson, Dean of Liberal Arts, John Bruhn, Vice President for Academic Affairs, and President Diana Natalicio, whose flexible and imaginative approach to university administration has consistently produced an environment conducive to my scholarly work.

Finally, to Stephanie, catalyst and comfort . . .

PRETEXT:
THROUGH THE LOOKING GLASS

Few contemporary thinkers own the paradoxical presence of Richard Rorty. Panned by the reviewing establishments of New York and London, Rorty's erudite and rather demanding works are selling in quantities large enough to suggest that many of the same philosophical colleagues who scorn him in public are crawling under their covers late at night, armed with flashlights, avidly poring over the pages of his books.

Philosophers, habitually smug in their belief that their discipline is surely unassailable, are publicly affronted by Rorty's attack upon the integrity and autonomy of the philosophic task, while many of them have begun to struggle privately with a vague feeling that the jig, in fact, is up. Analytic thinkers, chagrined by what they take to be Rorty's treasonous betrayal, must take up their cudgels in defense of their own clearly waning cause. Further, most American thinkers of the pragmatic persuasion, who have longed for a prophet to lead them out of the doldrums of pragmatism,[1] see Rorty coming in a blaze of glory but feel they should, perhaps, be lost to history rather than be led by this self-anointed usurper of the pragmatic privilege. Proponents of liberal democracy and *Ideologiekritik* stand uneasily together against what they take to be a conservative assault upon *principled* political discourse, though they see well enough that such discourse invites a plethora of counterdiscourses each of which grounds its alter's lightening and steals its thunder. Meanwhile, those outside the Academy, lured by the commotion, look bemusedly on, wondering what all the fuss is about.

A relatively disinterested party might suspect that much of the antagonism toward Rorty is tinctured by self-contempt and *ressentiment*. It is as if the black sheep of the family had just broadcast a scandalous secret all but he had conspired to suppress. There is a true irony in the fact that the American thinker who has sought to engage his philosophic community more than any other of his contemporaries should have his embraces spurned by so many of those he has addressed. This phenomenon certainly advertises the depressed condition of contemporary philosophy. This condition is doubtless born from the intransigently provincial character of alternative philosophic ideologies. We seem able to escape the throes of relativism and incommensurability only so long as we refuse to venture outside of our closed shops.

Rorty's defenders, where they can be found, are no less tainted. Konstantin Kolenda's highly complimentary exposition and commentary[2] is almost completely lacking in critical bite. Rorty's thought is laid out "like a patient etherized upon a table," with a consequent numbing effect upon the reader. Rorty is much admired in literary critical circles, but here many of his strongest proponents are untrained in philosophical discourse and thus have attached themselves to his conclusions, for the most part ignoring the substantive arguments that render these conclusions plausible. Further, one suspects that the critic, Harold Bloom, a serious champion of the Rortyan cause, is merely seconding Rorty's use of his ideas. Such mutual admiration leads to an incestuous solidarity that, as much as anything else, reveals the isolation of Rorty's thinking.[3]

Rorty's importance is signalled in large measure by the complex motivations for positive and negative responses to his work on the part of philosophers, critics, and the lay public. Had he been content to stick with defending the thesis of his *Philosophy and the Mirror of Nature*, he would have found no dearth of philosophers anxious to engage his thought. For when Rorty said in that work, "it is pictures rather than propositions, metaphors rather than statements which determine most of our philosophical convictions,"[4] and then proceeded to say that "the picture which holds traditional philosophy captive is that of the mind as a great mirror,"[5] he challenged analytic philosophers to recognize their dependence upon mirroring metaphors. As a consequence, he found himself seriously engaged in conversation with those who still found value in traditional epistemology but were willing to move toward its reform.

But beginning with *Consequences of Pragmatism* and moving through *Contingency, Irony, and Solidarity* and the two volumes of his *Philosophical Papers*, Rorty has begun to venture beyond the tradition constituted by the model of *speculum mentis* to explore the effects of strictly literary uses of metaphors as causal agents in intellectual discourse. He has thus turned away from his role as the arch internal critic of the philosophic tradition and has moved through the looking glass. Standing now behind the mirror of nature, he is seen by many of his philosophical colleagues to be . . . beyond the pale.

Rorty's initial attack upon the epistemological tradition, serious as it was, at least provided a dialectical foil for the old guard and the new defenders of the traditional philosophy. His later, more constructive, proposals have constituted another sort of enterprise altogether—one which has bewildered those on the other side, the *reflective* side, of the glass.

My attempt to follow Rorty through the looking glass, and to assess what he finds there, is motivated by my belief that though he has indeed moved beyond the strictly philosophic pale, his thinking nonetheless focuses important tendencies within contemporary intellectual culture that may one day succeed in extending the pale. There is some evidence that this is already taking place among the younger generation, as well as among the philosophically unsophisticated of our intellectual culture. For this reason, I have sought to write a book that would be accessible not only to philosophers, but to those outside the strictly philosophic community as well. I believe that it will be useful to communicate Rorty's ideas beyond the philosophical society, since many of the issues he is currently addressing are of importance to the widest areas of liberal democratic societies. For example: Rorty's transvaluation of the priorities of the public and private spheres and of the relations of philosophy and literature to these spheres could affect our choice of modes of political socialization as well as the use of our leisure time. Likewise, his discussions of the role of a "poeticized science" in contemporary society could have significant applications to the orientation of our school curricula, as well as to the funding of scientific and humanistic research. Once merely a philosopher's philosopher, Rorty has the potential to become a somewhat eccentric, perhaps overly shy and shuffling, Philosopher Laureate of American society.

I began to see how Rorty's thinking might be interesting beyond the restricted community of philosophical sophisticates while using his *Philosophical Papers* in an undergraduate philosophy course. I was truly surprised to discover how accessible these essays turned out to be to my students, many of whom were taking their first course in philosophy. I believe that this was so in part because the philosophically naive are less likely to suffer from what Richard Bernstein calls "Cartesian Anxiety"—the feeling that "*either* there is some support for our being, a fixed foundation for our knowledge, *or* we cannot escape the forces of darkness that envelop us with madness, with intellectual and moral chaos."[6] Rorty's "anti-foundationalism" seems less scary to those untutored by Descartes. Ironically, therefore, the "nonphilosophical," those burdened neither by the objectivist, ahistoricist inclinations of the analytic tradition, nor by the debilitating effects of Cartesian Anxiety, will find Rorty's message somewhat easier to grasp.

Despite all my efforts, nonphilosophical readers of this work may still feel too much is being demanded of them. Rorty's narratives often presuppose a rather detailed understanding of the history of philosophy. I have not had the space to provide all of the most helpful background materials. In addition to my discussion of Rorty's doctrines in the text, therefore, I have added an "Epitext" which offers additional assistance to the general reader by keying the argument of the book to important essays selected from the two volumes of Rorty's *Philosophical Papers*. I have also provided, among other things, a list of the most important "heroes" and "villains" of Rorty's narratives. I believe that occasional resort to the "Epitext" will be helpful in expanding my readers' understanding of Rorty's pragmatism.

There are a number of difficulties in trying to follow Rorty though the looking glass. The most significant lies in the fact that he has a genius, abetted by some sophisticated rhetorical devices, for isolating his thinking from critical assault. There is little to be gained from attempting to micro-manage, fine-tune, disassemble, or deconstruct the account Rorty provides. The best one can do is to judge the relative attractiveness of Rorty's views by recourse to alternative visions.

Rorty has offered some helpful, if somewhat playful, guidance to his potential critics by distinguishing three types of critical response.[7] The "third rate" critic attacks the original thinker on the basis of the rhetorical consequences of his thought and defends the status quo against the corrupting effects of the philosopher's rhetoric. "Second rate" critics defend the same received wisdom by semantic analyses of the thinker which highlight ambiguities and vagueness in his terms and arguments. But "first rate" critics "delight in the originality of those they criticise . . . ; they attack an optimal version of the philosopher's position—one in which the holes in the argument have been plugged or politely ignored."[8] This "robustly external" criticism "consists in showing the inability of the philosopher under study, even at his best, to do what the critic thinks needs to be done."[9] First rate critics construct a dramatic narrative which contextualizes the thinker under critique in such a manner as to show that "the philosopher has not understood the pattern of the past and the needs of the present as well as, thanks to the critic, we now do."[10]

Rorty's term for the sort of narrativism employed by first-rate critics is "recontextualization." This procedure, which substitutes for the pragmatic method of "inquiry," advantages the critic by allowing him to set the ground rules for engagement. Rorty employs this method in his own assessments of historical and contemporary thinkers. This manner of inviting gadflies into his parlor is vintage Rorty.

I must say that I find Rorty's always graceful allemande with those he engages one of the more pleasing features of his mode of thinking. I have, consequently, sought to employ the method of recontextualization in a manner that would qualify me as one of Rorty's first-rate critics. My treatment of Rorty, therefore, will require the juxtaposing of elements of his thinking with alternative metaphors and narratives with the aim, not of refutation, but simply of eliciting approval or disapproval. The act of recontextualization will involve isolating important themes in Rorty's thought and then placing them in the context of alternative views. These themes will include his nominalist historicism, his new version of pragmatism, his belief in the radical disjunction of private and public life, his critique of the role of science in society, his liberal ironism, and his anti-methodological stance. These acts of recontextualization will involve a minimum of dialectic, since a corollary of Rorty's view that the motor of philosophical discourse is metaphor rather than statement is that, apart from their rhetorical function, arguments per se are of little use. Making this distinctly unmethodological procedure seem something more than irresponsible posturing, on my part as well as Richard Rorty's, is one of the tasks of the following exposition.

I would be tempted to say that I have tried to be an honest expositor of Rorty's thinking were that not, on Rorty's terms, to condemn my project with the faintest of praise. For Rorty endorses Harold Bloom's view that only through a "strong misreading" may the poet and critic appropriate the creative thinking of others. I would be remiss, therefore, if I did not attempt, here and there, a strong misreading of Rorty as a means of establishing his importance as a thinker.

The need for strong misreadings and recontextualization lies in the fact that, as I have said, Rorty's philosophy is closed to rational analysis, critique, or dialectic. I agree with Rorty that we are forever outside one another's discourse, and that language, therefore, is not a medium of communication open to rational analysis but a "tool." From the perspective of understanding, one person's language is little more than a vague supplement to the language of another.

Often, especially in the first three chapters, I will exhaust quite a few pages in providing alternative contexts for Rorty's arguments. These efforts would certainly be extraneous to the purposes of straight exposition or dialectical critique. Given the peculiar character of Rorty's thinking, however, this is the fairest procedure both for Rorty and his readers. For only in this way will the true strengths and weaknesses of his narratives stand out.

The use of recontextualization throughout this work will require what might at first appear to be the needless repetition of Rorty's narratives. I urge the reader to recognize that, though the narrative context might seem familiar, *what is contextualized is not.* When José Ortega y Gasset claimed that philosophy is like the flight of a gyrfalcon circling toward its prey,[11] he highlighted a general fact about one important way of doing philosophy. In Rorty's case, with each retelling of a narrative, the argumentative circle is tightened and we come closer to the center of his thinking. Readers who approach this work expecting the usual forms of exposition and critique, therefore, might well be initially confused. My advice is to keep in mind Ortega's metaphor of the tightening circles of the falcon's centripetal flight.

The first chapter of this book is a good illustration of the employment of these tightening circles. Here I shall provide several examples of the stories Rorty tells of the fate of philosophy in modern culture. Woven together these form a Grand Narrative which provides the most general context for Rorty's philosophic conclusions. After highlighting the principal elements of Rorty's Grand Narrative, I shall be concerned to contextualize that account by appeals to other possible narratives.

Chapter 2 addresses directly the lineaments of Rorty's version of pragmatism. Here I will contextualize Rorty by appeal to the classical tradition of American thinkers (Edwards, Emerson, Peirce, James, Dewey, and so forth) with which his thought has some sympathy. In chapter 3 I will, again through the process of recontextualization, suggest a somewhat different reading of irony from that which grounds Rorty's narrative strategies.

Chapter 4, entitled "Excursus ad Hominem," may require special comment. Though an explicitly ad hominem approach would be ruled out of court with respect to most thinkers, Rorty's dependence upon metaphors rather than statements, pictures rather than arguments, and global interpretations rather than internal analyses of the thinkers he employs, means that the persuasive dimension of his thinking is stressed above that of the strictly logical. As a consequence, his own thinking skirts the edges of ad hominem argumentation, often wandering rather far into that questionable territory. Thus Rorty not only tempts, but invites, his expositors to treat him in the same manner.

In the final chapter of this work I have provided an explicit discussion, and critique, of Rorty's "method" of recontextualization. Though it might seem more logical to provide an explanation of methodology first, I believe that a characterization of Rorty's novel method before a consideration of the reasons he feels traditional methods to be irrelevant to his purposes, and before an actual demonstration of that method in discussing Rorty's thought, would have been unproductive.[12]

I really haven't any opinion as to the final import of my treatment of Rorty except to say that, though I began with the hope that I might serve as amicus curiae, siding neither with the prosecution nor the defense, I soon found myself hopping back and forth between exuberant praise and testy complaint. It is a sign of Rorty's potential importance that, with respect to his most central commitments, half-measures of either praise or blame seem insufficient.

Though my remarks may seem to wander here and there in Rorty's rather broadly conceived corpus, I shall throughout attempt to remain focused upon one of the issues disputed among his critics and would-be disciples as well—namely, his justification for calling himself a pragmatist. Specifically, I intend to address Rorty's endeavor to "adapt pragmatism to a changed intellectual environment,"[13] seeking to understand the manner in which his professed nominalist historicism reshapes the American pragmatic tradition.

I should indicate here why I shall not consider a question that remains of great concern to many of Rorty's readers—namely, the difference between the "early" and the "late" Rorty. It has long been the fashion to divide the thought of many of this century's major philosophers into early and late phases.[14] That fashion has been extended, unjustifiably I think, to Richard Rorty's work. I believe it a mistake to parse Rorty's thinking into analytic and post-analytic (or "postmodern") phases. Thus, I believe Richard Bernstein incorrect when he claims that Rorty's recent writings constitute "the discourse of a one time 'true believer' who has lost his faith."[15]

No one reading the introduction to Rorty's *Linguistic Turn*[16] with any care could fail to see a continuity between his views in 1967 and his 1979 *Philosophy and the Mirror of Nature*,[17] the work that purportedly begins the revolution in his thinking. In the former volume Rorty focuses upon the "rethinking of certain epistemological difficulties which have troubled philosophers since Plato and Aristotle." He notes that the traditional "spectatorial" account of knowledge is "the common target of philosophers as different as Dewey, Hampshire, Sartre, Heidegger, and Wittgenstein."[18]

It is not just his sympathetic mention of Dewey, Heidegger, and Wittgenstein as critics of the spectatorial theory that suggests continuity with his later work. Of equal significance is his persistent recourse to metaphilosophical discussions, for the resort to self-conscious taxonomic operations is a principal characteristic of Rorty's entire philosophical career.[19]

In the following pages, therefore, I shall not be interested in assaying a Rortyan *Kehre*. I hold there to be little evidence that Rorty ever was a "true believer," that he ever had any philosophical faith (at least a first-intentional one) to lose. I believe Rorty was, from the beginning of his mature intellectual life, conditioned by the same Unhappy (Self) Consciousness of the metaphilosopher his thought now advertises and that he has managed to escape the more serious rigors of that hovering mode of reflection only by gradually, but inexorably, yielding himself up to the most tenaciously refined nominalism ever to grace (or stain) the pages of modern intellectual history.[20]

If there was no *Kehre*, there would seem no reason to concentrate, as I shall, upon Rorty's post-*Mirror* writings. My doing so has less to do with any possible break in his constructive writings and more to do with the fact that Rorty has begun to target a new audience. This change of audience is significant. For it alters the stress of Rorty's arguments in such a way as to recontextualize certain of his primary beliefs. Rorty's earlier works were evangelical appeals addressed to those whose sins were darkest—the analytic philosophers. His recent writings, though they still presuppose a rather detailed understanding of the post-Kantian philosophical tradition, are addressed to fellow members of a putative community, the invisible Church of the New Pragmatism. Rorty's interests are slightly less prophetic now and more apologetic. He has found his voice and the message[17] he has been preaching all along, muffled until now by his critical rhetoric, is made unmistakably clear to those who have ears to hear.

The message of the Church of the New Pragmatism is meant to appeal to the widest of audiences. That audience is comprised by all those included in the phrase "we liberal democratic souls." And though the bookish among this group will have an easier time with Rorty's thinking, it is clear that Rorty has something to say to individuals in all precincts of the intellectual community.

As a result of his change of audience, Rorty has altered his style. It is much less dialectical than before, more explicitly narrativist. He argues now by telling a story, replete with "good guys" and "bad guys." His appeals are less to arcane philosophical problematics and more to such existential themes as loneliness and the consequent need for solidarity, the presence of pain and the sense of humiliation as "forced redescription." These are the issues about which Rorty's constructive apologetics revolves. And these themes are relevant to us all.

A final cautionary word. One of the primary characteristics of this work is its employment of irony to illumine and critique Rorty's thought. Readers who fail to appreciate the constitutive employment of irony and humor in philosophic exposition will doubtless be troubled by my mode of exposition. (One reader of this work has, in fact, complained about the "archness" of my style.) As I indicate in the chapter on irony, philosophy has been thought a very serious enterprise by most of its practitioners and, as a consequence, resorts to irony often frustrate and madden the serious-minded, leading them finally to urge that all ironists celebrate Socrates' Last Supper.

To the charge of archness I shall plead guilty—but with these extenuating circumstances: Much of the antagonism toward Rorty is a response to his tongue-clucking ironism and the smugness of his Cheshire smile. I believe that Rorty ought be met on his own terms. These terms require the (seeming) condescension of irony. Further, *argumentum ad hominem*, and occasional attempts to hoist him on his own petard, are the means whereby Rorty's lightminded resort to the Cheshire smile are best highlighted.

On a more substantive note, since the methods of analysis and dialectic are extraneous to the sort of thinking Rorty expresses and defends, he is often wildly misunderstood, and as often severely excoriated, by those who insist upon playing by more traditional rules. There is no way to transform Rorty into a serious-minded dialectician, or a language analyst. Deductive and dialectical logics are irrelevant to his thought. And merely to extract his conclusions from their narrative context would yield little more than a digestive, reductive, précis. Such would be nothing but a rough and ready manual of philosophical dictation, a compendium of sorites, a sort of down-scaled travelogue meant to guide those who would tour only the inter-states of Rorty's mind. Such an exposition would make him look didactic, dogmatic, and foolish—precisely the way he has been made to look by those serious-minded caretakers of the philosophic enterprise who would scorn any who forsake the methodologically straight and the doctrinally narrow.

In sum, though I have some sympathy with the fear of a reader who complained that my "Rortyan interpretation of Rorty leaves us with Rorty *squared*," I believe that such an attempt to write Rorty large is the best means of magnifying both the important defects and the many virtues of his thought.

1

HOLDING ONE'S TIME IN THOUGHT

Rorty characterizes his thinking by recourse to a wide variety of self-descriptive terms. Thus he calls himself at various times, a "nominalist," a "historicist," a "nonreductive physicalist." In more colorful language, he claims to be a "postmodern bourgeois liberal," a "lonely provincial," a "new fuzzie." The first two of these self-descriptions are definitely the most significant. In this chapter we will discuss the manner in which Rorty's style of thinking and his mode of argumentation are shaped by his claim to be a "nominalist historicist." What we shall find is that a nominalist historicist doesn't argue by recourse to dialectical or analytical tools. What he does, rather, is to tell a story, to construct a narrative in order to contextualize his claims about the way things are and the direction they ought to take. A responsible exposition and critique of Rorty's thinking requires that we, first, ask after the character and implications of his narratives and then suggest alternative narratives as a means of providing a context for the critical assessment of his views.

RORTY'S GRAND NARRATIVE

Rorty claims that everyone has the right to hold forth on his own peculiar justification for the "spirit of the age." This exercise of "holding your time in thought" (Hegel's advice) means "finding a description of all the things characteristic of your time of which you most approve and with which you unflinchingly identify . . . a description of the end toward which the historical developments which led up to (your) time were means."[1] This activity involves the production of narratives (*geis-*

11

tesgeschichten) which help to shape the official canons that define intellectual culture. The philosopher, working within a historically volatile field, is actually engaged in the attempt to say who does and does not count as a philosopher or, at the very least, which problems count as *philosophical* problems.[2]

Rorty's point is that, with respect to any putatively autonomous discipline, there must be answers to questions about who legitimately belongs to the profession or discipline. The criteria employed in addressing these questions have to do with how one might characterize the right problems or how appropriate methods for solving those problems might be developed.

Geistesgeschichte may be compared with four other historiographical genres: doxography, rational reconstructions, historical reconstructions, and intellectual history. Rational reconstructions bring philosophers into the present as conversation partners, thus engaging the arguments of past thinkers with the issues of the present. The procedure is hypothetical, of course, and involves consideration of topics and questions of interest to the present philosopher which his ancestors might never have explicitly formulated. Nonetheless, such reconstructions permit at least the perception of an important continuity with one's intellectual ancestors.

Historical, as opposed to rational, reconstructions attempt to preserve thought within its historical context, seeking to capture the sense of conversations a past philosopher might have had with his own contemporaries. These reconstructions keep rational reconstructions honest by recalling the original sense of the philosopher's program. More importantly, they remind us that there have been ways of thinking markedly at variance with our own. Together, historical and rational reconstructions can maintain a sense of both the continuity and difference essential to any productive relationship with one's cultural past.

Both rational and historical reconstructions depend upon *geistesgeschichte*, since one really wants to be able to deal with the ideas of individuals whose work has been legitimated by consensus. In turn, *geistesgeschichte* depends upon historical and rational reconstructions to provide the data from which one culls and refurbishes those thinkers and issues which, from the perspective of the present, really *count*.

Intellectual history contextualizes *geistesgeschichte*, the self-justifying narrative which construes the past in terms of a privileged present, by appealing beyond the present canon to a variety of alternative thinkers and conditions that shaped the character of the times. In this manner, self-justifying *geistesgeschichten* may be brought to judgment before the plethora of data of the intellectual historian, who need not employ the term "philosophy" as descriptive of a specialized discipline, but only as an honorific denoting "people who made splendid but largely unsuccessful attempts to ask the questions which we ought to be asking."[3] The narratives of the intellectual historian are drawn from the broadest matrix of available evidences.

Rorty has little use for *doxography*, his final type of historiography. Philosophy cannot legitimately be doxography, since writing a *History of Philosophy* which presupposes either a final list of great philosophers or of common subject matters, problems, and themes is nothing less than the effort to literalize *geistesgeschichte*. The doxographical approach can lead to taxonomic or metaphilosophical efforts which presume a logical or semantic given from out of which one might construct the methods, principles, and subject matters of the history of philosophy. Doxography presupposes a belief that philosophy is an autonomous disciplinary matrix defined by an essentially unchanging set of questions, problems, and methods. Doxographers construe the history of philosophy after the model of a traditional science. Rorty would reject any such attempt to envision philosophy as a "natural kind."

Rorty doesn't think we ought to give up canons. We need only feel free to enlarge and revise them whenever necessary. And there is thus no need to give up the honorific sense of "philosopher," only the need to cancel any strictly disciplinary criteria for membership by appeal to a continually revised and enlarged list of canonical figures discovered through interaction with the intellectual historian.

Rorty toys with the idea that perhaps intellectual history would be sufficient for the historian of intellectual culture. His reason for finally claiming *geistesgeschichte* essential is a telling one. He believes that "we cannot get along without heroes. . . . We need to tell ourselves detailed stories of the mighty dead in order to make our hopes of surpassing them concrete."[4] The construction of such narratives involves manipulating a cast of historical characters in such a manner as to demonstrate how we have come to ask those philosophical questions we believe to be not only profound, but inescapable.

We might note at the outset that some of Rorty's critics believe there to be a problem with regard to his continual use of the term "we." If every individual has the *right* to hold his time in thought by isolating those things of which he approves, rather than the *duty* to get the story straight by appealing to some objective norms or consensual principles, then everyone has the right to characterize precisely who "we" are. Rorty seems to be engaged in doing just that. Thus Richard

Bernstein's accusation that Rorty employs the term "we" as little more than "a label for a projected 'me'"[5] is certainly justified. But this would be a telling criticism only if it could be shown that there is an alternative to beginning with "me" on the way to a construction of "we." One theme of Rorty's New Pragmatism will hinge on the question of the relationship between "me" and "we." Later, when we discuss this issue we will want to pay attention to whether Rorty uses "we" in such a manner as to presuppose consensus, or merely to invite it.

There are a number of important implications of Rorty's historiographical views just rehearsed. First, Rorty claims to be a nominalist and a historicist. As such, one would expect that he would be fundamentally satisfied with assembling the data of the past in the broadest and least coordinated fashion. Thus he well might take intellectual history as his historiographical model. The fact that he wavers with respect to this commitment suggests the sort of nominalism he espouses. For, though Rorty is willing to refer to himself as a "materialist," he is avowedly nonreductionist. Thus, though his nominalism might be physicalist with respect to the theories of the sciences, his historicist explanations need not follow from materialist assumptions. In fact, his is a romantic vision of history, and his historicism is decidedly *heroic*. Rorty is a *heroic* nominalist historicist.

Second, Rorty's historicism, unlike idealist or materialist varieties, entails the consequence that there are no necessary, only *contingent* questions, issues, or problems facing us. We should look for no historical themes or trends or continuities other than those established by the narratives we construct.

Third, holding our particular historical and cultural present in thought will require that we wield the sword not only to dub the noblest knights of intellectual culture, Sir Philosopher, but, as well, to cut down the villains who do not yet, no longer, nor ever shall deserve that honorific. This negative task is fully as important as the positive and, given the nature of the times, it is the one in which Rorty is perhaps most actively involved.

Finally, along with the strictures against necessity, Rorty recognizes that the decentered selves of postmodern culture will have an indefinite number of interests in accordance with which to construe the historical past. There will be many "we's." The aim cannot be that of coherence or consistency guaranteed by some grand conceptual scheme. We can only seek to be persuasive. Nor are we really to expect, as was often the case in the past, any full consensus. Thus Rorty can be both daring and idiosyncratic in the construction of his vision.

Rorty has provided several versions of his *geistesgeschichte*. His various accounts are overlapping narratives which highlight elements that suit the particular rhetorical context with which he is concerned. In the following pages I will rehearse a selection of these narratives, concluding with a construction of the Grand Narrative that serves as the broadest context of Rorty's views.

In order to hold his time in thought Rorty believes that he must tell a story of the origin and destiny of the modern age.[6] The modern age begins with the French Revolutionaries and the Romantics: The former showed that the vocabulary of social relations was contingent and open to transformation; the latter demonstrated that language, as an expression of imagination, was a self-creative tool. Romanticism helped to enforce a split between the traditional science-oriented Enlightenment thinkers and those who allied themselves with the poet and the revolutionary. The former sought reference to the real world, the latter thought of language and theories as tools whose descriptions and redescriptions change self and circumstances.

This same split gave rise to the modern sense of a philosophical discipline as distinct from the nascent scientific and humanistic disciplines. The sense of philosophy as *scientia scientiarum*—the determiner of the normative relationships of the alternative cultural interests—was cause and consequence of the Kantian organization of the value spheres into the scientific, moral, and aesthetic, and the Hegelian attempt to preserve and defend that organization. The Romantic separation of the activities of the poets and those of the scientists perpetuated the sense that scientific truth was thought to be *made*, while the spiritual truths of the poets still existed "out there."

The heirs of the Romantic movement and the French Revolution are the "strong poets"[7] and the utopian revolutionaries. The strong poet is the creator of "de-divinized poetry." This kind of poetry is occasioned not by the inspiration of the muses, but molded from the inner resources of the individual "genius." The utopian revolutionary is the activist with a de-divinized conscience. Such revolutionaries are no longer prophets acting in obedience to the will of God, but reformers who take responsibility for their decisions and actions. The *strong* poet and the revolutionary both maintain a critical stance toward the values of the past.

Rorty's celebration of the ideals of the French Revolution and the Romantic movement takes on a peculiar cast by virtue of his agonal interpretation of history. Readers of Harold Bloom's *Anxiety of Influence*,[8] in many ways a crucial work for Rorty's entire historiographical project, will recall that the power of the poet comes from his "strong misreading" of his predecessors. Such a reading reconstitutes the past as appropriated by the would-be genius of the present. Bloom's notion of strong misreading is rooted in the classically Oedipal dynamic in which creativity is born of patricide.

The Oedipal situation is certainly relevant to rationalistic cultures characterized by agonal interactions of programs and principles.[9] But there is always continuity. The "strong poet" and "revolutionary," each of them in turn, takes his place in the poetic and revolutionary traditions. It is this which allows the combination of patricide and apotheosis which Freud celebrated as a primary dialectic of our culture.

The present has no viable reality except as a perspective on the past which leads either to acquiescence, or to the revolts of the strong poet and revolutionary. Each of these latter individuals holds a conjured, appropriated past in thought. Each must lay claim to both originality and superiority with respect to the past. This condescension towards one's heritage makes of one's history a "white-man's burden" each generation of liberal *Geisteshistorikers* shoulders with a deepening sigh.

The aim of an enlightened, secular society is one not only without God and the institutions of the Church, or absolute political authority, but equally without a divine self or world. Thus, it is incorrect to believe that "finite, mortal, contingently existing human beings might derive the meanings of their lives from anything except other finite, mortal, contingently existing human beings."[10]

Such a society, even if it is a child of the Enlightenment in the sense that it has carried out with a ruthless consistency the desire for enlightened secularity, needs an improved self-description which avoids the old vocabulary of rational/irrational, absolute/relative, and so forth. For there is no foundation or goal shaping society. Just as language per se is contingent, the vocabularies permitting the descriptions and redescriptions of a society are contingent. There is no neutral standpoint, no ultimately *rational* perspective. In fact, the contrast rational/irrational is applicable only within a given language game and therefore cannot be used to explain movements among language games or the more radical changes in linguistic behavior associated with paradigm shifts.

The real triumph of the Enlightenment is, ironically, its transmogrification into a pragmatic vocabulary which best expresses a de-theologized, but also de-scientized and de-philosophized secularity. Thus, the end of enlightenment would not be a scientized but a poetized culture, one in which we "substitute the hope that chances for fulfillment of idiosyncratic fantasies will be equalized for the hope that everyone will replace 'passion' or fantasy with 'reason.'"[11]

Talk of equal opportunity for fantasy fulfillment might be thought bizarre unless one realizes that, on Rorty's terms, there are no privileged fantasies because there is no standardized reality by which to assess them. This can only mean that progress in the cultural interests of poetry, science, philosophy, or politics results from "the accidental coincidence of a private obsession with a public need."[12]

In this narrative, Rorty applauds the manner in which the Romantic poets and the political revolutionaries conspire to slay God the Father, and thence to weed out the vestiges of the divine in political life. The revolution is, of course, unfinished. "Reason" and "poetic genius," the standards used by the rationalists and Romantics, respectively, must themselves be de-divinized. When this is done, we shall have completed what was started at the beginning of the modern age.

We must be careful not to interpret this narrative as praise for the poet in the traditional sense. In his discussions of the strong poet Rorty is invoking the sense of *poieisthai*, "to make something into," "to hold something to be." This places, say, Francis Bacon on a par with John Milton. Bacon, as strong poet, is a significant proponent of "self-assertion."

Rorty agrees with Hans Blumenberg that "self-assertion" ought be distinguished from "self-foundation." The former involves the creation and/or expression of one's beliefs and desires. The latter is concerned with grounding the sense of one's self upon a transcendent principle or vision such as God, the Absolute, the Transcendental Ego. Essential to Rorty's Grand Narrative is his agreement with Blumenberg's claim in his *The Legitimacy of the Modern Age*[13] that historicist criticisms of Enlightenment optimism count against self-foundation but not against self-assertion.[14]

Rorty provides an interesting variant of this first narrative in his "From Logic to Language to Play."[15] Here he moves forward in time and begins his account with the interplay of science and philosophy in the twentieth century. The character of scientific and literary cultures at the beginnings of the twentieth century was in large measure a result of the alliance of philosophy with the scientific enterprise. Russell and Husserl turned to logic and mathematics as appropriate models for philosophical emulation. But Husserl's broadening of his project into that of the phenomenology of conscious experience made the axiomatic model of the mathematical sciences less relevant and opened philosophy to critiques such as that contained in Heidegger's

Being and Time,[16] which challenged its status as a science.

The move from substantialist to functional treatments of science, advertised best by Ernst Cassirer's interpretations of Einstein's relativity theories,[17] along with Carnap's employment of the logic of relations in place of predicate logic, provided the context within which a new pluralistic pragmatism developed. The anti-substantialist, anti-Aristotelian, and anti-essentialist temper of such a movement led away from scientistic and positivistic explanations in terms of atoms and substances and toward the increased use of the languages of processes and relationships.[18]

The recognition of intuitive descriptions of non-Euclidean systems, and the relativizing and historicizing of Kantian world-construction associated with C. I. Lewis and others, finally led to an instrumental, anti-realist view of physical science. The belief in the axiomatic certainty of geometry and in unchanging categories of the understanding gave way to the cultural and historical relativity of even our most substantial beliefs. Quine's attack on analytic truth (that which is true by definition) and Davidson's replacement of "the meaning of x" with "the place of x within a language game," shifted the interpretation of language from something which provides access to an objective reality into that of a mode of behavior, a tool for coping. Now, "there is no way to reach outside our language-game to an account of the relations between the language-game as scheme and 'the world' as 'content'."[19]

In this narrative Rorty continues the story of the first by indicating how philosophers and scientists came to call the rationality of their disciplines into question. The conclusion of the narrative is that we should reject both scientist and anti-scientist and understand philosophy as "no closer to science than to art, and no farther from either than it is from any other sphere of human self-creation."[20] Such an interpretation allows for an understanding of scientific, moral, or political theories in the same manner that we understand works of art—that is, as essentially metaphorical descriptions and redescriptions.

Again we see the emergence of "self-assertion" as a major theme characterizing the modern age. Metaphorical redescriptions result in the reconstitution of human experience. This may be accomplished idiosyncratically, as is the case with every novel act of self-description, or, perhaps globally, as is done in those rarer instances in which the creation of one's self serves as a model for other acts of self-creation.

A third variant of Rorty's history of modernity begins even more recently. Here he employs the vocabulary of isolation and professionalization. Recognizing the transition from the literary, "genteel tradition" of American philosophy to that of Dewey's social engineering that took place between the Wars, and thence to the increasing isolation of philosophy from highbrow culture criticism, Rorty notes the emergence of culture criticism as the abode of small "p" philosophical activity.[21]

Dewey was on the right track, but after the Second World War, there was a turn away from the social scientific orientation of philosophy and toward the notion that philosophy ought attain to the rigor of the natural sciences. Philosophy was as isolated now from the broader social scientific concerns as from the genteel literary tradition. The professionalization of philosophy isolated it both from the humanistic traditions within the academy and the wider concerns of the highbrow culture critic.

It is with regard to the professionalization of philosophy that Rorty associates Kant's most pernicious influence in America. Though he well appreciates that such a phenomenon has its roots as much in Britain as the Continent, it is the Kantian turn that Rorty finds most reprehensible.

> [T]he wrong turn was taken when Kant's split between science, morals and art was accepted as a donnée, as *die massgebliche Selbstauslegung der Moderne*. Once that split is taken seriously, then the *Selbstvergewisserung der Moderne*, which Hegel and Habermas both take to be the "fundamental philosophical problem," will indeed seem urgent. For once the philosophers swallow Kant's "stubborn differentiation," then they are condemned to an endless series of reductionist and antireductionist moves. . . . To be a philosopher of the "modern" sort is precisely to be unwilling either to let these spheres simply co-exist uncompetitively, or reduce the other two to the remaining one. Modern philosophy has consisted in forever realigning them, squeezing them together, and forcing them apart again. But it is not clear that these efforts have done the modern age much good (or, for that matter, harm).[22]

Professionalized philosophy insures both the perpetuation of its own disciplinary concerns, in large measure through its claim to be the adjudicator of value conflicts among the various cultural interests and the professionalized status of the areas of cultural interest which it purports to classify and organize.

In "Nineteenth Century Idealism and Twentieth Century Textualism,"[23] Rorty reverts to the Enlightenment beginnings and takes yet another run at the question of how we arrived at the present. The

Enlightenment contrast between science and superstition based upon the claim that Newtonian science provided the ground of knowledge was effectively a shift from religion to science as the guiding and grounding discipline of culture. The effect of this claim was to exclude questions of God, freedom, and immortality from the realm of responsible discussion.

This shift toward scientific rationality presented a problem which Kant finally resolved by offering philosophy in the place of science as the presiding cultural discipline. Philosophy now is employed to establish the legitimacy of scientific knowledge and to provide a place for moral, aesthetic, and (in a somewhat Pickwickian sense) religious interests within intellectual culture. This occurred in three stages: First, Kant claimed that the validity of scientific knowledge presumed that the subject matter of science was a world transcendentally construed. Second, this belief presupposed a distinction between the world as "made" and as "found." This distinction parallels the one between "science" and "morality." Our knowledge is of a world that is antecedently construed; we act in a world directly encountered. Third, Kant forwarded philosophy as that discipline which transcends both science and morality, and as the only discipline capable of telling us of the nature of things. This move leads us in the direction of contemporary foundationalist philosophy.

"The Kantian system . . . began by borrowing the prestige of science . . . then proceeded to demote science to the second rank of cultural activities."[24] Moreover, the Kantian system was a *system* in which the disciplines of science, morality, and art were institutionalized and organized in a manner that played one against the other in such a way as to set up "the contest of the faculties" which has since plagued modern culture.

For Rorty, the upshot of Hegel's characterization of how thought works is the celebration of the discovery or invention of new vocabularies, the presumption of their finality, and the recognition of their transitoriness, which leads each in turn to succumb to yet another contender. Hegel ushered in literary culture shaped by a Romanticism which replaces the pursuit of truth with the search for the appropriate vocabulary. According to Rorty, this emergent culture promised something like the substitution of literature for philosophy as the guiding cultural discipline. In this sort of culture science is placed in an ancillary role with respect to the most vital of human interests.

The final step away from the Enlightenment ideal of scientific rationality is taken by pragmatism. It was the thinking of Friedrich Nietzsche and William James that finally led to the replacement of Romanticism with pragmatism. "Instead of saying that the discovery of vocabularies could bring hidden secrets to light, [the pragmatists] said that new ways of speaking could help us get what we want."[25] They gave up the notion of truth as correspondence to reality, thus rendering philosophy on a par with science as a discipline capable of creating useful interpretations or construals of the world.

A literary culture does not need a presiding discipline in the sense of a ground or foundation. All it requires is a recognition of the contingency of the vocabularies which constitute our beliefs and desires along with a sense that the purpose of these vocabularies is the practical one of effecting our desires rather than the theoretical one of discovering something final or absolute about the way things are.

The refrain of each of these *geistesgeschichten* is: *In the Kantian Fall we sinnéd all.* The net effect of construing the modern age in terms of Kant's construction of the presumably autonomous value spheres and Hegel's defense of what he thought to be their threatened autonomy is to see modernity primarily through German eyes. But whether we take the German interpretation or broaden our perspective to include consideration of the British, French, and American contexts, there is one constant: The destiny of philosophy in the modern period has involved an erratic vacillation between the literary and the scientific enterprises as models of philosophic discourse. Rorty's preference is clearly for the literary, poetic model.

We may now isolate some of the themes constituting Rorty's Grand Narrative: First, modernity is characterized by a movement from religion to science to philosophy to literature. Second, that movement involved the development of idealist philosophy as an attempt to ground culture. Third, the effect of idealism has been to initiate a competition between science and philosophy, science and literature, and, finally, literature and philosophy, as cultural dominants. This conflict of the value spheres is a result of the two-sidedness of the idealist model of philosophy. In the late modern period, philosophers continue to vacillate between the literary and the scientific models as they attempt to resolve the question of their true function.

Fourth, the true heritage of idealism is its Romanticist impulse, deriving from the early Hegel. This Romanticism has constituted the primary dynamic in the transition from philosophy and science to literature as the constituting element of culture. Fifth, this literary culture is best articulated in terms of the pragmatist's concern for the utility of vocabularies. Pragmatism has reflected the ambivalence of philosophy per se. But even on its naturalistic, scientistic side it has concerned itself with functionalist, anti-essentialist, interpretations which led it away from rationalism and objectivism toward an operationalist, practice-oriented understanding. Meanwhile, its distinctively literary, Jamesian, side has stressed the issue of the utility of languages in achieving human desires. Importantly, it is pragmatism that combines the legitimate aims of both consensual and idiosyncratic vocabularies. Pragmatists promote the use of both vocabularies of private self-creation and vocabularies of public praxis. The latter vocabularies are concerned with the alleviation of cruelty. Sixth, a pragmatic culture, the heroes of which are the strong poet and the utopian revolutionary, needs no grounding since the aim of literary culture is the production of a variety of novel vocabularies of self-enrichment and the enrichment of public life.

Finally, the conflict of the value spheres is best resolved not through reduction or the introduction of a supererogatory adjudicating discipline, but through the recognition of the autonomy of languages. Every discipline can have something important to say without any having the last word. Thus, the languages of science, and of literature, and the discourse of common sense as well, can grow together without fear of reduction or sublation.

Rorty's Grand Narrative provides an explanation of why many presume that modernity is defined in accordance with the divided self, the soul at war. In his Grand Narrative he provides some suggestions as to how modernity could be conceived as requiring an account of the conflicts and mutual reinforcements of art and morality, science and art, morality and science, etc. The depression of art through technique, the reduction of science to technologies of purposive rationality (Weber's *zweckrationalität*), the insipidity of moralized or politicized art, the horror and distastefulness of art won free from the constraints of the moral sense, are all expressions of the value conflicts that define one aspect of modernity.

A more positive implication of Rorty's narrative is that science and technology may enlarge, enrich, and secure life. Ethical and political institutions secure and protect rights and freedoms of individuals; art sensitizes and ennobles the human being and underwrites quality leisure pursuits. This is possible if we arrange social and individual life around the aims of justice in the public sphere and the freedom of self-creation in private.

There are at least three important issues raised by Rorty's Grand Narrative. First, we should note that he begins with the so-called modern period. Why should he believe that the modern epoch, as opposed to the entire sweep of intellectual culture from the Greeks to the present, constitutes the epoch he needs to hold in thought? Rorty is taking his stand with those who hold that the modern age begins a distinctive epoch in human history. This raises the question of "the legitimacy of the modern age." In contemporary discussions, this question is normally divided into two parts: (a) Is the modern period the appropriate beginning point for historicist explanations of the origin and development of contemporary culture?, and (b) Is modernity still viable, or ought we be accounting for a transition to "postmodernity"?

Second, we recognize that in telling a story of the sort that Rorty tells, it is as important to distinguish what has been left out from what has been included. Thus, in order to contextualize Rorty's narrative we need to assess other plausible narratives of the origin and fate of the modern period, and then to ask whether narrative can legitimately take the place of theory.

Finally, Rorty's Grand Narrative is just that—a narrative. Does it count as "history" in any viable sense? More specifically, is Rorty's manner of thinking "historicist" in any of the more familiar senses of that word? At the very least, if we are going to accede to Rorty's claim that he is a historicist, we ought to understand the sense in which he is using that term.

THE LEGITIMACY QUESTION

By beginning with the Enlightenment and telling the story of the movement from the Age of Reason, in which science was the guiding discipline, to the present "literary culture," Rorty effectively claims legitimacy for the modern period as that in which the story relevant to himself and his times might be told. I want to briefly examine Rorty's reasons for this claim.

The traditional division of the Western cultural tradition into ancient, medieval, and modern may appear rather facile. After all, the mere act of giving a name is a form of legitimation. "The rhetorical function of names . . . is to lay claim to the legitimating weight of genealogy."[26] Reinforcing the weak legitimating effect of naming, there is the fact that mere persistence tends to legitimate. If we continue telling the same old story we will presume the importance of the tale even if we ourselves are not engaged in it. Inertia is a law of life. What hangs about has authority.

Presumably, however, there is more than just the name "moder-

nity" and the persistence of accountings of it to argue for the significance of the epoch. The core of the legitimation of Modernity lies in the
justification of the Enlightenment on its own terms, divorced from past
epochs. Rorty's Grand Narrative provides a description of the distinctiveness of the modern period in terms of the themes summarized
above.

It is important to realize, however, that the rhetorical function of
narratives can be most insidious. All narratives, particularly a metanarrative of the type that Rorty provides, avoid explicit argumentation.
And in the absence of analytical and dialectical arguments we tend to
suspend our critical sense. Dramatic narratives which assure us of the
importance of the struggle being recounted and provide some hope of
victory over the darker forces celebrated in the tale, tempt us to yield
our skepticism and disbelief in much the same way as we do when listening to bedtime stories which begin, "Once upon a time . . .".

There is another concern when considering critical accounts of
modernity. Some accounts seek to undermine the notion of modernity
by challenging its distinctiveness or the viability of the turning that
took place with the Enlightenment sensibility.[27] But we mustn't forget
that an epoch may be challenged at both ends. That is, we may ask,
however legitimate a period has been considered to be, whether it is any
longer viable. Proponents of "postmodernism" may claim that modernity was a legitimate epoch, but that it no longer has any real integrity
as a historical context. Rorty, having recently backed away from his
former association with what he termed "postmodern bourgeois liberalism," means to stay within the boundaries of the modern world.

Jean-François Lyotard has made a helpful distinction between
forms of legitimation. Metanarratives may be of two sorts—projective
and originary. Projective legitimation may attempt to argue for the
authority of an epoch on the grounds that certain trends that characterize the processes of the epoch ought to continue. Originary narratives
account for the meaning and significance of an epoch by appeal to its
origins. Originary narratives are concerned with the legitimation of the
present in terms of the past. Projective narratives are concerned with
accounts of presumed trends leading to an idealized future.

Arguments that promote the belief in the positive value of the
progress of knowledge or the growth of human freedom are examples
of projective narratives legitimating the modern age. Originary narratives often involve resort to mythical accounts. The grand myth that
founded our culture is one of the transition from chaos to cosmos.
Versions of this myth, whether in the form we find in *Genesis*, or in

Hesiodic and Orphic cosmogonies, may be used to legitimate Western culture in its entirety. Variants of this originary narrative have been employed, for example, by members of the Frankfurt school to demonstrate the origins of reason as an ordering, construing agency aimed at the shaping of an antecedent chaos.

Rorty begins with the origins of the modern period, thus advertising the relevance of the movement from the Enlightenment to the present as a means of indicating how we got to be the way we are. He doesn't find it necessary to go back to Plato and beyond as Heidegger does in recounting the History of Being, nor does he follow Alasdair MacIntyre, who returns to Aristotle for the sense of tradition that he feels has been lost in the modern age. These antimodern thinkers have no wish to legitimate the modern age. They hope to show that if we are to get back on the right track we must return to the origins and uncover the appropriate resources for a revitalization of our individual and social lives.

There are two criticisms which will help us contextualize Rorty's narrative. The first is that in offering a projective narrative which would legitimate trends in the modern period leading to increased autonomy and the value of "self-assertion," Rorty has depended upon the determinative significance of the Kantian turning. In fact, one may argue that the Kantian turn was less significant than Rorty suggests and that the "value spheres" and the contest of the faculties they entail, have their origins at the beginnings of Western culture.

A second, for our purposes more interesting, criticism is that Rorty's narrative of modernity leaves out altogether too much of what we mean by the modern age, and that his failure to engage significant alternative views amounts to an unproductively dismissive attitude toward some contemporary self-understandings. We shall be able to dispense with the first criticism in rather short order. The second, far more serious, objection will be dealt with in the following section.

The problem of legitimation can be restated in this fashion: Is the origin of what is modern about us the origin of what is most distinctive about us? One manner of answering this question negatively is by providing a plausible account of the history of our culture which finds the origin of the conflict associated with the value spheres in ancient times in the construction of Plato's tripartite structure of the psyche.[28]

One might argue that you could get more mileage out of an originary legitimation that finds the origins of the value spheres of science, morality, and art at the very beginnings of the articulation of the concepts of the person. In Homer, *psyche, noos,* and *thymos* adumbrate the elements of the Platonic version of the soul articulated in terms of *noesis* (reason), *thymos* (spirit), and *epithymia* (appetite). The same functions surface as value spheres in Aristotle's organization of the disciplines grounded in thought, action, passion. These activities ground the theoretical, practical, and productive disciplines. There is some basis for arguing that associating the origin of the conflict of the value spheres with the modern period is wrong-headed.

Rorty would likely reply that he is not so much concerned with this issue as he is with what is effectively a reinterpretation of one of the elements or functions which underlie the value spheres. The medieval period is distinguishable from the ancient by virtue of the introduction of Hebraic-Christian traditions into the Hellenic, Hellenistic, and Roman cultural streams. What is distinctive turns out to be the notion of *volition* which, if not "invented" by Augustine, was certainly spelled out most profoundly in his *De Trinitate, De Civitate Dei*, and *Confessiones*. This is the point that Hans Blumenberg ultimately makes by singling out the notion of self-assertion as the primary characteristic of the modern period. And there is certainly some reason to believe that volition, *arbitrium*, the power of the will, is the defining characteristic of modernity, since once self-consciousness demonstrates the arbitrariness of the foundations, there is no reason not to employ the will in the exercise of redefining or restructuring cultural significances. But the discovery of the human will awaited the recognition of an extramundane source of volition. In this sense, Nietzsche's cultural diagnosis was quite correct: Consciousness of will finally leads to consciousness of the unacceptability of competing wills—particularly that associated with the Will of God.[29]

With regard to the "legitimacy question," Rorty effectively sides with Blumenberg who finds the resort to "self-assertion" to be the distinctive quality of modern individuals. After encountering Blumenberg Rorty added Francis Bacon to his list of heroes. Rorty's Grand Narrative is, of course, not inconsistent with this recognition of the importance of Bacon. Rorty agrees with Blumenberg that "self-assertion" rather than the "realization of subjective freedom" is the driving force of modernity.[30]

Blumenberg finds the modern age legitimate in the following ways: First, the *querelle* is decisive for the sense of a transition from tradition to the belief in *de modo*. The break between tradition and modernity is achieved at the psychological level by the *sense of being modern*. Second, the modern age is characterized by a novel response to changes that led to the experience of radical contingency. This response depended on the dialectic of Christianity and Gnosticism and its role in shaping the Augustinian synthesis. The Gnostic Marcion expressed a vision of a world patterned by evil, having been created by a lesser god, which could be destroyed by the pure god as a means of redeeming the world. Augustine responded to this vision by making the fallenness of the world a consequence of the prideful self-assertion of man, the cause of which lay in the will itself and not in God.[31] When the nominalism of the later medieval period established the arbitrariness of God, however, the synthesis of Augustinian and Aristotelian theology of the High Middle Ages was dissolved into contingency and irrationality. Self-assertion replaced submission as the most legitimate human response to one's environs.

Augustinian Platonism and Thomistic Aristotelianism kept voluntarism from entering the mainstream from Christianity, but Nietzsche's introduction of radical contingency into secular culture had more immediate consequences. Nietzsche's recognition of the arbitrariness of the world creates the same two possibilities—either submission to the nihilism of Plato and Christianity, or self-assertion. Without traditional constraints, the self-assertive mode is raised to the level of consciousness and modern individuals begin to recognize the volitional foundation of rationality.

Individual self-assertion, then, is a legitimate response to this situation, and modern science is a primary agent of the need to face the contingency of reality and the arbitrariness of the divine agency. "Deprived by God's hiddenness of the metaphysical guaranties for the world, man constructs for himself a counterworld of elementary rationality and manipulability. . . . The exigency of self-assertion became the sovereignty of self-foundation."[32]

There is little for Rorty to disagree with in this analysis since it underwrites his nominalism and volitionalism and his sense of the arbitrariness of cultural artifacts. He gladly accepts the importance of Francis Bacon as a legitimate corrective to many accounts of the rise of modernity. Science is Baconian science, the science of manipulation and control. This opens Blumenberg, and pari passu Rorty himself, to criticism from those such as Heideggerians and the Frankfurt school who would claim that seeking to legitimate modernity in terms of self-assertion, the primary expression of which is that ubiquitous technology which threatens the earth, is highly questionable.

The concept of legitimation implicit in Rorty's Grand Narrative differs somewhat from that of Blumenberg. Rorty requires that "self-assertion" be able to function in such a manner as to avoid the problems of "demarcation" and "the contest of the faculties" characteristic of the post-Kantian age. But it is most difficult to believe that Rorty has altogether avoided these difficulties himself. When he says that philosophy has been construed as science, metaphor, or politics,[33] he is recapitulating the science, art, morality dispute begun with Kant. Rorty would, of course, reply that he is not endorsing this conflict only reporting it. But his resolution of the contest, awarding victory to the poetic and political models, may certainly be read as a resolution *on Kant's terms*.

Rorty wishes "self-assertion" to be characterized in such a way that we are able to view the construction of theories in the same way as we see the creation of works of art. But his claim that what modern thought does is to play the historical forms of modernity off against one another in the same way, for example, that "Blumenberg plays 'self-assertion' off against 'self-grounding'"[34] suggests that he too is stuck in this impasse. For Rorty's introduction of "self-assertion" can plausibly be read as little more than a referencing of culture in terms of one of the possible value modalities. He may claim that he has bypassed Kant, and that "self-assertion" is a reasonably neutral, historically grounded category, but, as I have indicated, one could easily argue that he has only appealed to the same intransigent value spheres in their quasi-Platonic or Augustinian forms.[35]

Rorty's appeal to "self-assertion" involves one of the reductions played out in our culture since Kant, or since Bacon, or since, for that matter, the ruminations of Protagoras and Callicles, Antiphon and Critias. Self-assertion may have a longer and more effective history than Rorty acknowledges. Nevertheless, I would say that even if one were to make a case for the existence of the conflict of the value spheres at the very beginnings of our culture, Rorty's focus upon self-assertion provides a distinctive enough legitimating criterion for his Grand Narrative. For we moderns are perhaps the first to name our own age through a self-conscious attempt to ask what sort of beings we are. And it is in large measure our consciousness of the degree to which our individual and cultural lives are defined by the relations of the principal value modalities that defines our sense of the modern period.

There seem to be plausible grounds for Rorty beginning his narrative with the modern period as defined by the notion of self-assertion. Moreover, he has at least as plausible grounds for holding that the modern period so defined is a continuing project. That is to say: self-assertion, expressing itself in terms of a transition from objectivist to historicist, from scientific to literary, modes of discourse still has work to do in bringing about a poetized culture.

Thus, on his terms, the most important competing narratives must be neither originary criticisms of modernity of the sort provided by Heidegger, the early Frankfurt school, or even Alasdair MacIntyre—all of which problematize the notion of modernity by promoting a return to the origins of our culture—nor projective narratives such as are illustrated by postmodern critics, who see us as having moved beyond the modern age. There is sufficient contrast between Rorty's view and these antimodern understandings as to render them effectively unengageable from Rorty's perspective.

Having established Rorty's reasons for claiming the modern age to be the distinctive epoch in terms of which our self-understanding might be contextualized, I will now begin to consider the implications of Rorty's Grand Narrative against the background of alternative narratives of the origins of the modern age.

STRANDS OF MODERNITY

The chief rivals of Rorty's *geistesgeschichte* are the family of accounts which seek to legitimate modernity. I intend in the following pages to outline some alternative plot-lines which constitute different accounts of how we got to where we are. I should reiterate here what I said at the very beginning of this work: A responsible evaluation of Rorty's thinking best proceeds, not by recourse to analytical or dialectical argumentation, but by the method of recontextualization. The point of the following rather lengthy detour from the direct exposition of Rorty's thinking will not be to undermine his Grand Narrative, but merely to highlight the consequences of following the route of narrative explanation Rorty has constructed.

In one sense of the term my account may be deemed more historicist than Rorty's. A narrative is different from history in that the former tends to have the unity of characters and plot while the latter may be, as Henry Ford noted, "just one damned thing after another." Narratives are the manner we shape those damned things into meaningful patterns. But if we don't hold these things as separately as we can, we will be left with theory-laden narratives instead of meaningfully historicist explanations.

The vast number and variety of published responses to the question of the meaning of the modern age attest to the difficulty of giving a coherent response to that concern. Matei Calinescu describes "five faces" of modernity classified under two general headings: the "bourgeois" and the "aesthetic,"[36] while David Frisby is content to assay "fragments" of its interpretation.[37] Each of these authors recognizes that the search for a univocal definition of "modernity" would be vain. Others who address this issue are often less modest—though their treatments have in general shown they have more reason to be.[38]

Modernity has been associated with secularization of the sort celebrated and scorned by Max Weber, which led to the development of formal rationality. Such rationality allows the modern self to exist in society as an empty, merely formal, decision-maker without the presence of any normative content by which to guide its decisions.[39] Renato Poggioli distinguishes a "humanistic" and a "romantic" version of modernity, the former dedicated to a restoration of the classical and the ancient, the latter to "a construction of the present and future not on the foundations of the past but on the ruins of time."[40]

Even granting the maximum amount of overlap among these visions, it is clear that we are in a desperate situation with respect to the idea of "the modern age," if it is a definition or coherent characterization that we seek. The fitful incoherence of our conceptions of modernity resists synthesis. Attempts at comprehensiveness will yield little more than the blurred eccentricity of a gnat's eye view. On the other hand, it is quite clear that any one of these characterizations of modernity could appeal to a particular audience whose members will resonate with the interpretation espoused. "The modern age" is, on this account, no more or less problematic than the meaning of "freedom" or "love."

Still, we sense that there is a difference here that needs accommodation. Some of those who discuss the term "modernity" are operating with a crisis mentality resulting from pitting modernity against the notion of "postmodernity," which serves to call into question at least its legitimacy, if not its very existence. A number of others take the defensive stance, attempting to vindicate the Enlightenment project. The controversial character of these discussions determines that we must attempt to look at the phenomenon in as inclusive a manner possible if we are to serve the interests of broad cultural self-understanding.

Until the arguments were refined over the last several years, many philosophers were at least certain when the modern age *began*. It was with Descartes, he who made the significant double move that defines the modern epoch: the internal move toward the grounding of the self in consciousness of itself, in the securing repose of self-reflection, and the outward move from the self to the material world armed with the coordinates of analytic geometry.

What is modern about the Cartesian stratagem is not merely the provision of an unsullied vantage point from which reason could inventory the extended world. The modern impulse is found as well in Descartes' use of the corpuscularian theory rediscovered by his contemporary, Pierre Gassendi.[41] Atomic theory, which characterizes the cosmos in materialist, mechanistic terms, is a principal motor of modernity, for it is the basis upon which the otherness of the world is both posited and overcome.

Objective knowledge is possible as knowledge of objects. Whether it be in classical physics and chemistry, or in the biology of Charles Darwin (and his sociobiological kinsmen), or in the psychology of Freud (and that of his cousin, B. F. Skinner), or in the sociopolitical thinking of Marx and Engels—the knower becomes an object among other objects.

After Descartes, the materialistic and idealistic versions of modernity bifurcated. The continuation of the idealist strain rendered the Descartes-Kant-Hegel axis decisive for developing the notion of modernity into the idea of subjective autonomy. Partly, this bifurcation came about because the Newtonian version of physical cosmology took precedence over the Cartesian. And Newton and his British epigoni, with the exception of Berkeley, of course, were not burdened by idealist dispositions.

Another fatal characteristic of Cartesian thought was the fact that it promoted a far stronger argument for the existence of self than for God and the external world. Though God might be claimed primary in the order of being and causality, the existence of the self turns out to be the only real certitude. It is not too much to say that the nineteenth-century "death of God" was foreshadowed in Descartes' failure to promote as epistemologically sound a status for God and the material world as he had provided for the self.

Descartes' project connects with the "German" reading of modernity in the sense that his subjectivism was carried through and rendered more consistent by Immanuel Kant, who attempted to recognize the autonomous relationships between the self and its cultural articulations and among these articulations themselves.

Readings of modernity which stress Descartes' influence have the advantage of providing some sense of the two origins of "individualism"—the autonomous *mind* associated with the *cogito* and the intransigent objectivity of atomic bodies swirling in the social space of the materialist nominalist.

Rorty would not find narratives which argue for the central importance of Descartes all that helpful. In the first place, this sort of account is sufficiently hackneyed as to lack much persuasive power. More importantly, interpretations of modernity which make Descartes the central figure are the prime targets of the proponents of postmodernism. It is too easy to show the failure of the Enlightenment project if one takes that project as primarily an extension of the Cartesian problematic.

Many of the postmodernists are concerned to show that the modern period begins with the *unreflective* reflexivity of Descartes—that is to say, the grounding of our awareness of the contents of the world, derived from the contents of consciousness, upon a distinctive awareness of the self without moving to the level of metacritique which would render *reflexivity* itself the object of further analysis. On this view the distinction between modernity and postmodernity lies in the latter's move to the meta-level which leads to the thematization of reflexivity.

For Rorty's purposes, which, as we have seen, involve the celebration of Hegel's Romanticism and historicism, Descartes is broadly irrelevant. Of course, the Rortyan reading of Hegel is quite different than the standard interpretations. A more familiar reading has it that, for Hegel, Kant was *the* philosopher of modernity precisely because he articulated the autonomy of the ways of knowing involved in the aesthetic, moral, and scientific impulses. But Hegel thought Kant altogether too sanguine about the continued harmony of the value spheres for whose autonomy he argued. Hegel sought, therefore, to provide some guarantee for the unity and harmony of these spheres of cultural interest.

Kant argued for the autonomy of thinking against the background of an explicit organization of cultural interests which contained the grounds for such rational autonomy. Newtonian science was rendered secure by Kant's first critique. A place for moral integrity freed from any bondage to religious sanctions was constructed by the second critique, and the *Critique of Aesthetic Judgment* vindicated, for the first time in systematic terms, the notion of an "aesthetic idea" as a freeplay of the imagination, unbounded by concepts.

Kant may be said to provide the schema through which we willy-nilly must set out to bring coherence into our discussions of modernity. Religion is the principal victim of the articulation, because it received no real status as object of critique in Kant and because it is sublated into the project of philosophy as the final avatar of the Hegelian system.

Art, religion, science, morality are the cultural interests with respect to which our modern sensibility has been expressed. Kant's three critiques assessed the construction of and response to the scientific, ethical, and artistic spheres of cultural life. *Religion within the Limits of Reason Alone* provided a more limited status for religion. In good

Enlightenment fashion, Kant advertised the distinctive sense of the holy while denying it autonomy.[42]

Hegel's reading of modernity highlights the separation of these value spheres and the reshaping of our cultural sensibility in terms of the shift of priorities in the direction of mutual critique which demands system. Thus, it is quite plausible to see Hegel, not as the system monger who tried to say it all, once and for all, but as the true champion of modernity who recognized that system was necessary to preserve the autonomy of the value spheres.[43]

But in whatever light one views Hegel's demand for system, it is the *systematic* Hegel that is the hero of such narratives. This is not Rorty's Hegel, but the Hegel of Jürgen Habermas, among others, who sees the "wrong turning" to be precisely Hegel's attempt to find in the resources of a kind of reason elaborated in terms of "the philosophy of the subject" the means of defending the autonomy of the value spheres. Habermas takes as seriously as did Hegel the need to defend that autonomy, but seeks to do so by appeal to a concept of reason as embedded in an intersubjective community.[44]

Rorty's view is that we have taken this German reading of modernity too seriously. "Had Bacon—the prophet of self-assertion, as opposed to self-grounding—been taken more seriously, we might not have been struck with a canon of 'great modern philosophers' who took 'subjectivity' as their theme."[45] Then we should see modernity as the story of "successive attempts to shake off the sort of ahistorical structure exemplified by Kant's division of culture into three 'value spheres'"[46] rather as successive attempts to articulate them, adjudicate among them, and defend their autonomy.

Rorty attempts to avoid taking the German reading of modernity too seriously by giving a historicist reading of Hegel. Is this a legitimate reading? In one sense it certainly is. It is, of course, the young Hegel of *The Phenomenology of Spirit* that Rorty lionizes. Marx turned Hegel on his head; Rorty has turned him on his side. His historicist reading merely provides a horizontal rather than a vertical interpretation of the march of Reason through history. "Hegel made unforgettably clear the deep self-certainty given by each achievement of a new vocabulary. . . . He also made unforgettably clear why such certainty lasts but a moment."[47] Clearly, if Rorty wishes to "adapt (Hegel's) thinking to a changed intellectual environment," this is one way to proceed. And as we shall see later on in this essay, Rorty's manner of reading philosophical and literary texts permits this sort of leeway.

In addition to the rather extreme difference of Rorty's account of the relations of Hegel to Kant from the more standard readings, there are a number of themes opened up by Rorty's narrative which need to be elaborated if we are properly to contextualize his understanding of modernity. I will, first, consider Rorty's treatment of "self-assertion." Next I will discuss his pragmatic rendering of Romanticism, and, finally, I will comment upon the rather striking fact of his neglect of the economic strand of modernity shaped by the capitalist/Marxist dialectic.

I should stress that, in elaborating these themes, narrative unity will necessarily be lost. The following attempt to hold my time in thought will necessarily revert to the taxonomic and morphological rather than the narrativist method. My purpose is not so much to suggest an alternative to Rorty's narrative, but, primarily, to assess the data from which other narratives might be constructed and, more importantly, to ask whether, in the light of the plethora of interpretations of modernity, any single narrative may be adequate to the task of holding one's time in thought.

With respect to the theme of self-assertion Rorty picks up from Blumenberg, and which he treats largely by rather general appeals to the figure of Francis Bacon, there is a wealth of resources which Rorty does not include in his narrative. Variants of this volitional interpretation of modernity can be found in the existentialists such as Kierkegaard, Nietzsche, and Max Weber.

Søren Kierkegaard's paradigm of the forced choice between the ethical and the aesthetic lives has the precise decisionist[48] character associated with Nietzsche and Weber. If, between the ethical and the aesthetic, one chooses the ethical, that choice presupposes preference for the consequences of the ethical. This, upon analysis, demonstrates that one has already made a choice before one pretends to reason through to the decision. Likewise, with the aesthetic. The incommensurability of the discontinuous, episodical life of transient pleasure and the unified life of duty and responsibility suggests that one should take a blind leap into the ethical or the aesthetic life. Likewise, with Nietzsche's decisionism. Value choices are arbitrary. The presumption that one set of choices is superior to another has its origin in the *ressentiment* of the weak who wish to disempower the strong through the shackles of moral discipline.

The existentialism of Kierkegaard and Nietzsche characterizes a thrust of the modern impulse which contributes a powerful dynamic to the field of forces establishing the context of modernity. This dynamic has its most articulated expression in the work of Max Weber. The process of secularization, a principal theme of Max Weber's account of the movement from traditional to rational societies, tells the story:[49] The values of morality, art, science, and religion are *implicit* in the culture as long as tradition reigns. They become *explicit* with the need to incorporate a diversity of beliefs and customs, as in fact occurred in the sixteenth century and beyond. Secularization is another name for urbanization—the collection into a concentrated sphere of diversities which tradition could no longer balance.

In this manner the content of social and cultural life is raised to the level of consciousness and the ensuing recognition of conflict and relativity leads to a process of abstraction, formalization, and generalization which eschews differences by suppressing content. Formal rationality is the result. Thus emerges the formal consciousness of the self as articulated into reason, appetite, and will, or thought, action, passion, or scientific, moral, and aesthetic interests. In becoming conscious of itself the modern self recognizes not only the internal contradictions associated with competing cultural spheres, but the contradictions of the self as the chaotic interspersal of rational, affective, and volitional impulses.

The very crisis which Kant sought to prevent by articulating the autonomy of the value spheres, and which Hegel wished to avoid through the aegis of The System, infected the modern age through the process of secularization which insured the volitional autonomy of the moral agent. This autonomy is assumed as the ground of rationality since, for Weber, decisions are the only activities guaranteed *content*. That is to say: formal rationality, the process of enacting formal procedures for implementing instrumental actions, is, in a technological society, indifferent to ends or values. And the particular values underlying moral actions are the results of irrational choice.

Weber's understanding of modernity is that with it comes the autonomy of the subjective will. Thus the creation of meanings lies in the choices and actions of individuals. At the same time, the downside of moral autonomy is the fact that tradition, which provides values as givens (and, therefore, as unquestioned principles for thought and action), gives way to the formal decisionism of the autonomous will whose freedom lies in choice, but whose choices, in the absence of traditional resources, lack any guaranteed meaningful content.

One way of expressing this is to say that modernity realizes a split between economics and politics. The political science of ends which focuses upon the mediation of individual will and actions in order to bring harmony and the good life is separated from the economic sphere motivated by "needs" and "desires." As a consequence (in Weberian

language) the victory of *zweckrationalität* (formal, instrumental, purposive rationality) over *wertrationalität* (value-saturated thinking) is well
nigh guaranteed by the failure to uphold a substantive meaning for the
notion of rational needs.

Weber's understanding of the freedom and autonomy of the individual makes of him a creator of meaning but his concept of the
increased tendency toward formal rationality, bureaucracy, dull routine,
and social roles as empty categories ("the executive," "the
entrepreneur," "the scientist") means that strait is the gate and narrow
the way. That is, Weber's ethics are elitist to the core. Only a few will
rise above the routinization of life.

There is a confusion in most treatments of Weber's concept of
modernity between the descriptive and normative dimensions. Weber's
pessimism is such that it is difficult to separate his diagnosis of the illness of the modern age from his characterization of the "modern spirit"
of individual autonomy. Indeed, the heroic or exemplary character of
his ethical views are such that we are faced with something like an
Augustinian split between the City of God and the City of Man.

The supererogatory character of the Weberian ethical vision is such
that there is little hope that we shall use our freedom aright.
Nonetheless, it would be a mistake to hold Weber's views to be pessimistic per se. The autonomy of the will permits a freeing from tradition and an acceptance of the fact that, in principle, decisions lie at the
basis of all value commitments. To be free, and to recognize that freedom, is the culmination of self-actualization, which is the essential quality of modernity. But the likelihood that we shall abuse that freedom
and yield ultimately to the "iron cage" of bureaucratization does not
cancel the greatness of modernity. Better freedom to risk and fail—better the "iron cage"—than the unselfconscious immersion in "the treacle
of tradition." Weber's analysis can be compared pari passu to the more
speculative and dramatic visions of Kierkegaard and Nietzsche, with
both of whom Weber shares a decisionist and heroic ethic. None of the
three may be said to hold out much hope for the ruck of mankind.

Rorty's pragmatism employs the fact of self-assertion in a significantly different manner. He essentially agrees with the existential side of
Weber when he contends that the fundamental challenge confronting
the reflective individual involves the acceptance or rejection of the contingencies from which thinking and action begin. Rortyan pragmatism
is somewhat less individualistic than existentialism, though its problematic is the same: Whether alone or in the comforting presence of
gesprächspartneren, we face a chaos of contingencies.

Rorty believes that the disenchantment of the world through secularization and the consequent rise of instrumental reason is an acceptable price to pay for the increased freedom and autonomy of modern democracies. In this regard, Rorty believes he is siding with John Dewey, whom he claims was as aware as Weber of the price that modernization exacts. But he insists, along with Dewey, that "no good achieved by earlier societies would be worth recapturing if the price were a diminution of our ability to leave people alone, to let them try out their private visions of perfection in peace."[50]

The pessimism of Kierkegaard, Nietzsche, and Weber is largely absent in Rorty because of the reversal of priorities associated with the spheres of public and private life. Rorty does not need a sense that the public world is anything other than a rationalized, technologized sphere of a relatively bland sort. With regard to the public enterprise, Rorty is most sanguine about the improvements in social existence, the growth of freedom and autonomy associated with North Atlantic democracies. "Enchantment" is reserved for private life, for the sphere in which one may try out his "private vision of perfection."

Much of the downside rhetoric of critics of modernization depends upon the theses implicit in Weber's analysis of the growth of *zweckrationalität*. Rorty's narrative of modernity omits any such rhetoric and its consequences, because it is in fact a narrative which has as a central theme a detailing of those conditions permitting the growth of the private sphere. Since Aristotle, there is a strong theme in the Western tradition that associates meaningful life with participation in the activities of the *polis*. Rorty's account of the rise of modern democracies tells of a transvaluation of the private and public spheres. A truly meaningful life must allow, above all, for the pursuit of private perfection.

There is an elitism expressed in Rorty's account. Only a few will be able to pursue the project of self-perfection. The vast majority of individuals in a democratic society will, at best, lead rather insipid lives. At worst they will be victims of economic and spiritual poverty. Rorty's democratic sentiments (or, at least, his democratic expectations) are seriously qualified. Democracy is the vehicle for the rise in the minimum standards of life—increased freedom and autonomy. But the freedom is a formal freedom, empty in the sense that only a very few will be able to exercise it in a meaning creating and, therefore, meaningful manner. And the autonomy is, for most, a blind autonomy, unguided by a sense of relevance.

The elitist consequences of Rorty's appeal to self-assertion are further ramified by his understanding of the rise of Romanticism. Rorty treats the historicist Hegel as the paradigm Romantic. Defining Romanticism as "the thesis that the one thing needful was to discover not which propositions are true but rather what vocabulary we should use,"[51] Rorty claims that Hegel's chief contribution to the nineteenth century was to effectively liberate it from science by forwarding just this thesis. Metaphysical Idealism becomes a brief interlude on the way to a Romanticist, literary culture.

Traditional readings treat Romanticism as a reaction to the excesses of the Age of Reason. The so-called Romantic reaction provided a means of self-articulation in which, through the alliance of *assertion* and *affect*, the emotional life was protected from the strictures of rationality. Or, as a rather more accurate interpretation would have it: the removal of the locus of rationality and volition from the Mind and Will of God to the individual thinker and actor carried with it the implicit translation of *affect* as well.

Through this transvaluation, a novel, more immediate mode of access to the reality of things was uncovered. "Not just the concept of the whole, but the whole in its concrete immediacy or nature; not just accurate knowledge about nature, but sensuous intuition of it and active involvement within it as a process—that is the earmark of the Romantic."[52]

The Romantic contribution to the sense of modernity includes, therefore, the uncovering of both the creative and demonic potencies of the human being. Or, as both William Blake and Freud would suggest, the intimate connection between creativity and the irrational forces in the human being is intrinsic to his character. The distinctly aesthetic component of modern subjectivity emerged, and exists still, as a much prized but nonetheless ancillary element functioning in a visionary and critical capacity with respect to the general cultural milieu.

We can't discuss the aesthetic interpretation of modernity by singling out the great poets and painters of the modern period. For the thematic of art from the seventeenth to the middle of the nineteenth century was a *moral* not an aesthetic one. Milton stands as the greatest representative of that thematic. His vision of Satan, ramified by Blake's on-target interpretation, was a watershed in the development of the modern sensibility. There are many names for this development—the positivity of evil, the internalization of the moral sense, the acceptance of the inner resource of moral decisions, responsibility, and heroism.

Life in submission to *Eros* is akin to the aesthetic life of transient enjoyments since both involve a continuing process. But life in service to an Ideal is without momentary satisfactions, nor is it ever complete.

Such a life provides the ultimate experience of delayed gratification. The Ideal is the only reality. An ideal lures one on, but never satisfies. Noble actions, aesthetic objects, historical events are means to an unrealizable end. As such they are little more than irrelevant consequences, by-products, detritus. Goethe, with a rather cloying bathos, named his Ideal . . . The Eternal Feminine.

The moral problematic is continued in other of the Romantic heroes. Byron's *Manfred*, inspired by Goethe's *Faust*, takes the step beyond Milton and Goethe. Manfred seeks no contest with extramundane forces. Instead he struggles with the powers of darkness within himself and controls them, even at the cost of his own life.

Art and literature take up the aesthetic interpretation of the modern individual only after the final step is taken. In Poe and Kafka we will find the denial of extramundane powers. Evil is resourced in the human being and the powers that stand over against the individual are themselves to be located, finally, in other individuals. Only when good and evil no longer may be referenced beyond the actions and intentions, however vaguely defined, however amorphously realized, of individual human beings can art have anything other than a morally propitiating impulse.

Baudelaire, though seldom ranked among the Romantics, is the best representative of the poet who finds in art the basis for an aestheticized culture. His is not, as is often thought, simply *l'art pour l'art*, but art which reveals the meaning of modern life and nurtures and sustains individuals thrown into the modern age.

Baudelaire's classic definition of modernity as "the ephemeral, the transitory, the contingent, the half of art the other half of which is the eternal and immutable"[53] concentrates upon the aesthetic experiencing associated with the modern age. At the same time, Baudelaire's description of the artist as a pioneer of modernity hints at the essential connection between the economic and the aesthetic versions of the modern self. Both economic and aesthetic interests are rooted in the passions. The former is concerned with production and acquisition, the latter with creative expression.

For Baudelaire, the origin of modernity lies embedded in the nineteenth century as "the immediately actual existence of immediately actual time." We are not, as moderns, to experience "Eternity in an hour" nor "Heaven in a wild flower." Baudelaire's *Fleurs du Mal*, presents episodes in which the experiences of "immediately actual time" are invoked to present the thickness and sinuosity of urban life. In fact, "almost all our originality comes from the stamp that *time* imprints upon our feelings."[54]

This experience of time is an experience of the artificial and con-
trived. Time is expressed in urbanized, citified rhythms of life cut off
from the organic and the natural. "Evil is done without effort, natu-
rally, inevitably; good is always the product of an art."[55] The artist is
involved in celebrating the artificial.

The difference between Rorty's view of Romanticism and alternative views lies in the historicist reading he gives the movement. The
ultimate import of the Romantics is not to be found in any concern for
discovering something fundamental about "nature" or about the "self."
Rorty is not looking at those aspects of the Romantic movement which
are seeking an alternative access to the real, but rather to those elements of Romanticism which, filtered through the pragmatic concern
for the expedient, support the generation of novel vocabularies.

Rorty shares with the Romantics a vision of the artist as creator of
meaning and as moral exemplar. His shift away from the question of
truth to the pragmatic concern with achieving one's desires, demystifies
the Romantic impulse, rendering it into another form of "self-assertion." It is this which allows Rorty to discipline the Romantic in such a
manner as to keep him within the sphere of the modern. The aesthetic
impulse, freed from such an anchoring in morality, is the motor of *post-*
modernity.

For Rorty, the strong poet serves two functions: As a model of the
pursuit of private perfection, he stands forth as one who has created
himself and who allows each of us to hope that we may shape our own
beliefs and desires in a manner which, "if only marginally,"[56] belongs to
us. As moral exemplar, the poet and novelist sensitize us to the pain and
suffering of others.

Rorty doesn't wish to perpetuate any formal distinction between
the moral and the aesthetic. His aim, rather, is to distinguish between
sorts of works which are aimed at private perfection and the sorts that
are directed toward the recognition of public insensitivities. This is the
core of Rorty's pragmatized Romanticism. Art does not reach for the
ineffable or the sublime; art lets us get what we want. What we want,
above all, is the freedom and imagination to create ourselves in private. A second aim is to avoid behaving cruelly to other people. There
are no hard and fast rules to guide us in our attempt responsibly to
balance these two aims.

The Grand Narrative Rorty provides has, as one might expect,
idiosyncratic and controversial elements in abundance. The story offers
us an account of Hegel as historicist, a privileging of the private over the
public sphere which effectively yokes the activity of self-assertion to

the private sphere, and a dirempted and pragmatized Romanticism.

As revealing as these factious elements are, they do not tell us as much about Rorty's distinctive vision as does a strand of modernity he effectively omits from his Grand Narrative. I refer to the account of the interweaving of the capitalist/Marxist dialectic in the origin and development of the modern age. In the following pages I will offer a brief account of an economic interpretation of modernity as a means of highlighting the consequences of Rorty's omission of that strand from his Grand Narrative.

Locke, Hume, Smith, and Marx constitute the main sources for a discussion of the economic interpretation of the rise of the modern age. These sources provide the conceptual tools for the discussion of the dependence of the modern conception of self upon the redefinition of, and increased emphasis upon, the phenomenon of *property*.

Locke discovers the basis of property interest in the fact of self-ownership. One owns one's person. One's person includes the "labour of his body and the work of his hands." "Whatsoever, then, he removes out of the state that nature hath provided and left it in, he hath mixed his labour with, and joined to it something that is his own, and thereby makes it his property."[57]

In David Hume's consideration of the ground and consequence of human passions,[58] property plays the central role since the acquisition and maintenance of property insures the presence of pride, self-love, and the love by others of the propertied self. The absence of property and the means to acquire it guarantee that one shall be an object of the hatred of others and of one's self as well. The doubling effective in this gambit is one highlighted in advanced capitalist societies: property grounds both world and self. One comes into one's own by *owning*.

Hume shares a difficulty with John Locke. Whereas the rationalists such as Descartes and Hegel begin with a self-reflective act which guarantees the existence of the self or of personal identity, and the volitionalists such as Kierkegaard, Nietzsche, and Weber find the self-deciding agent to be primary, Locke and Hume begin with "sensations" or "impressions" and must build the idea of self or personality from that primitive source. Hume's consideration of the passions in Book II of his *Treatise* is the *locus classicus* for this construction.

Passions, or emotions, are secondary impressions which may be either direct or indirect.[59] Direct passions derive immediately from pleasure and pain. Desire, aversion, hope, and fear are examples. Indirect passions are ramified by other qualities. The principal indirect passions are pride and humility and their social manifestations in love and hate.

Pride and humility have as object "that connected succession of perceptions, which we call self"[60]—one's own "self" or the "self" of others.

The social context of the self may be understood best by noting the relationship between property and selfhood. "The relation, which is esteemed the closest, and which of all others produces most commonly the passion of pride is that of *property*."[61] Property and "riches" (the means of acquiring property) make oneself an object of pride for oneself and of love for others. Poverty evokes humility and hatred.

The mechanism for the evocation of these passions lies in Hume's doctrine of *sympathy*.

> The pleasure, which a rich man receives from his possessions, being thrown upon the beholder causes a pleasure and esteem; which sentiments, again, being perceiv'd and sympathiz'd with, encrease the pleasure of the possessor; and being once more reflected, become a new foundation for pleasure and esteem in the beholder.[62]

Sympathy serves both to evoke and to reinforce those passions—pride and humility, love and hate—which constitute the self's basic inventory. But the creation of an object of esteem or of contempt, as is accomplished when the wealthy or the poor receive sympathetic attention, also serves to solidify the otherwise ill-defined self or personality.

A second element which serves to solidify the self is the convention of "justice." Justice is characterized in terms of property as that "convention entered into by all the members of a society to bestow stability on the possession of those external goods, and leave every one in the peaceable enjoyment of what he may acquire by his fortune and industry. By this means every one knows he may safely possess."[63] For Hume the self has the meanings of both a "bundle of perceptions" and an "object of the passions." The former meaning is construed in terms of thought and imagination; the latter in terms of passions or self-concern.[64] As object of the passions, the self has its most fixed and coherent identity.

Hume's dilemma is well known. There is no direct evidence nor rational argument for the existence of the self as person-through-time available to the introspective individual. The presumption of personal identity is grounded in the imputed selfhood associated with isolating self or other as an object of pride or envy, or love and hate, respectively. Indirectly, the self becomes even more solidified by the need to establish the stability of ownership through appeals to justice which requires, of course, the ascription of responsibility in a social context. In this latter sense, the self is a social fiction, albeit an essential one.

The Scottish school of "moral sentiments," to which belonged Hutcheson and Hume, looked for those resources permitting moral judgments with respect to self and others in the face of the drives for "self-preservation" and "self-interest." Smith, resonating with Hume in this regard, found sympathy to be such a source. In each of us there is an inner man, an impartial spectator capable of assessing the worth of our own and others' possessions, sentiments, and behaviors. Reason and sympathy discipline the egoistic passions which drive each of us.

Smith's *The Theory of Moral Sentiments* employs the notion of sympathy as a means of social harmonization. His *Wealth of Nations* emphasizes the alternative mechanism of "competition" to account for the stability of society. Underlying both the notions of sympathy and competition is the internal struggle between reason and the passions in each of us.

> The property which every man has in his own labour, as it is the original foundation of all other property, so it is the most sacred and inviolable. The patrimony of a poor man lies in the strength and dexterity of his hands; and to hinder him from employing this strength and dexterity in what manner he thinks proper without injury to his neighbor is a plain violation of this most sacred property.[65]

Smith's essentially Lockeian understanding of property as nature appropriated through human labor is ramified by the stress upon the division of labor as a means of increasing wealth. "The greatest improvement in the productive powers of labour, and the greater part of the skill, dexterity, and judgment with which it is anywhere directed, or applied, seem to have been the effects of the division of labour."[66]

The division of labor "is the necessary, though very slow and gradual consequence of . . . the propensity to truck, barter, and exchange one thing for another."[67] It is this division which radically increases the potentiality of the individual to be a consumer of luxuries. And these luxuries may soon become (in conformity with the infinite elasticity of desire) *needs*.

When applied to the subject of the development and evolution of societies, Hume's and Smith's moral psychology presents the perfect foil for the later Marxian critique. For Smith the motor of history is the inner struggle between self-interest and impartial sympathy and reason. The external struggle associated with "competition" is moderated by appeal to "the invisible hand," and so is not really seen as a struggle. The internal struggle proceeds historically within a series of social stages: hunters, nomads, feudal farming, and commercial independence. For Marx the struggle is outside the individual, *between* the classes characteristic of each evolutionary stage: primitive communism, slave, feudal and capitalist. Competition is seen as a disharmonizing factor in this development. "The only wheels which political economy sets in motion are *greed* and the war *amongst the greedy—competition.*"[68]

To the similarities and differences associated with the historical stages of development toward capitalism we must add a rather striking agreement between Marx and Hume/Smith on the relation of property to selfhood. As Hume indicated, property and riches lead to the objectification of the person in terms of pride and love. The absence of property and riches lead to objectification in terms of contempt and hatred.

According to Marx, "*private property* is only the perceptible expression of the fact that man becomes *objective* for himself and at the same time becomes to himself a strange and inhuman object."[69] Thus each sees labor and property in terms of objectification of the self. Hume and Smith assess this process positively, Marx assesses it negatively. Marx's rationale, of course, lies in his division of society into a propertied class of owners and unpropertied workers. A worker's products yield loss, not gain, since "labor produces not only commodities: it produces itself and the worker *as commodities.*"[70] Labor's realization is its objectification. In the sphere of political economy this realization of labor appears as "*a loss of realization* for the workers; objectification as *loss of the object* and *bondage to it*; appropriation as *estrangement*, as *alienation.*"[71]

The dialectic between the Locke-Hume-Smith model of selfhood and that arising out of Marxian critique sets the tone for the discussions of the economic self in modern times. Thus, to interpret modernity as "the realization of subjective autonomy" or, with Rorty and Blumenberg, as the consequence of "self-assertion," is to make a claim that needs adjustment by appeal to the economic interpretation of selfhood. The importance of economic considerations should be clear: Taking the Humean perspective, the self is created by self-objectification and objectification by others, through the passions of pride and humility, love and hate. These passions are elicited and gauged by the presence or absence of property and riches. Alternatively, according to Marx, the self is created through self-estrangement or alienation—an appropriation of nature through labor that leads to loss.[72]

Plato, perhaps, provided one of the first grounds for economic conceptions of the self when he said "Eros is the stepchild of abundance and need."[73] Hobbes echoed Plato when he claimed that desire signifies "the absence of the object." Much depends upon the type of objects one desires. This is the crucial point since the distinction between "legitimate" needs and merely undisciplined desires is a difficult one to make in any hard and fast manner. When we consider how the specialization of labor and the emergence of a commercial society based upon *money* can serve to liberate desire to express itself in an indefinite number of ways, we can see how important is the fact of desiring in the production of the self.

Karl Marx believed that there are authentic needs which serve to discipline the elasticity of desire which otherwise must rapidly transform yesterday's wants into tomorrow's necessities. Hume and Adam Smith, on the other hand, find in the multiplication of needs a mirror of that division of labor which both laud as a fundamentally positive element in society. The individual is enriched both internally with respect to those pleasurable passions of pride and self-esteem reflected from the directed sentiments of others, and in relation to his external goods, which are rendered more varied and refined, and which in turn articulate and discriminate new desires which promise soon to congeal into tomorrow's novel needs. For Hume and Adam Smith, the refined and articulated self is in large measure a creation of complex operations of production which stimulate new desires. Marx finds the effect of such artificially produced needs to be self-alienation.

In modern society, the capitalist celebrates the multiplication of desires and their transmogrification into needs. This is a process not unlike the manner in which metaphors, once their tropic status is forgotten, suddenly become the elements of literal discourse. But the counterdiscourse of Marx critiques the notion of needs defined by private property and the desire for self-gratification.

Marx has employed the *pecca fortiter* principle in his work, praising the bourgeoisie for laying bare the sins of its fathers. But there is more than just the dialectic working here; Marx is not simply praising "p" for serving as an excuse for "not-p," there is in Marx himself the same modernist dynamic which exists at the darkening heart of the developing capitalist. Nowhere is there a greater recognition that Marxian discourse is a *counter*discourse, an ideological co-dependent of capitalism, than in *The Communist Manifesto*, the work Marshall Berman names "the first great modernist work of art."[74] Here Marx celebrates

the theme of insatiable desires and drives, permanent revolution, infinite development, perpetual creation and renewal in every sphere of
life; and its radical antithesis, the theme of nihilism, insatiable destruction, the shattering and swallowing up of life, the heart of darkness,
the horror.[75]

The virtue of Berman's proclamatory treatment of Marx as the pro-
totypical modernist is that it shows clearly how modernism may spring
full blown from the sphere of economic modernization. Marx appreciates bourgeois culture for its hectic dynamism, its energy:

> Bourgeois society, through its insatiable drive for destruction and
> development and the need to satisfy the insatiable needs it creates,
> inevitably produces radical ideas and movements that aim to destroy
> it. But its very capacity for development enables it to negate its own
> negations: to nourish itself and thrive on opposition, to become
> stronger amid pressure and crisis than it could ever be in peace, to
> transform enmity into intimacy and attackers into inadvertent allies.[76]

There is little in Richard Rorty's writings to indicate that he is interested in providing an analysis of the economic strand of modernity.
Should he be? It seems to me that if, as Rorty contends, pragmatism
"helps us get what we want," then we should certainly be worried
about the manner in which a *capitalist* liberal democratic society helps to
shape the character of wants and needs.

Later on, when we discuss Rorty's characterization of the self as a
"centerless web of beliefs and desires," we shall be better prepared to
see how Hume's and Marx's analyses of the relation of personality and
property are clearly relevant to the consideration of the contingent, historical, conditions for self-creation obtaining in liberal democracies
shaped by the capitalist-socialist dialectic.

I insist that this point is not the least affected by the contemporary
demise of Marxism. All around the world Marxist societies have shown
themselves to be seedy, effete top-down bureaucracies which have as
little relation to the Marxian counterdiscourse considered above as contemporary capitalist societies have to the rather sanguine expectations
of Adam Smith. The point I am making concerns the *purely contingent*
effects of economic considerations upon the nature and character of
desiring, given the assumption that the self is shaped by its desires,
indeed is its desires, and the further presumption that these desires
may be externally manipulated by mechanisms which aim at satisfying
needs they themselves produce.

As we shall see when we consider the implications of Rorty's notion of self-creation, he is, on the most generous reading, much too sanguine about the freedom and autonomy individuals may have in liberal democratic societies. Given a more severe, and I believe even more plausible interpretation, the heroic character of his criteria for self-creation render him altogether elitist, forcing him to reserve the capacity for self-perfection for but a few "strong poets."

One of the reasons the way is so narrow and the gate so strait is that the conditioning factors associated with the manipulation of needs and desires through economic means produces a leveling effect upon contemporary societies. Rorty has met this basically Weberian point by asserting that, though there may indeed be trade-offs, we who live in wealthy democratic societies are much better off than are our nondemocratic (noncapitalist?) neighbors. But I believe it to be much easier to make this sort of assertion in the absence of any serious discussion of the economic determinants of contemporary society. Further, the persuasiveness of Rorty's narrative will be in direct proportion to his success in ignoring the troubling implications of economic interpretations of the relations of property and selfhood, of selfhood and desiring, and of desires and their determinants.

I must stress that such a discussion as I am calling for would not require that Rorty give up his nominalist and historicist stance in favor of the introduction of any totalizing principles of the sort associated with *Ideologiekritik*. I am not suggesting that we look at economic *theories* at all. My concern is with the broadly empirical question as to whether the sort of social goals Rorty recommends—namely, private freedom and public justice—are attainable in an economically motivated society given the assumption that desiring is so susceptible to economic manipulation, and that manipulation seems so successful in affecting what most of us hold to be the privatest areas of our lives.

THE NEED FOR NARRATIVES

Of the several contrasting themes in the discussion of modernity the professional philosopher may cite at least the following conventional starting points: The "rational" source associated with Hegel deriving ultimately from Descartes by way of Kant, defining the human being in terms of *theoria*. A second, the Baconian strand, is often associated with Max Weber and the explicit proponents of instrumental reason as the most prominent expositor of the self-assertive, purposive rationality. A third, the aesthetic strand includes the Romantics and Baudelaire. A fourth, the economic strand, is a variant of the third in which the "making" associated with economic consumption is substituted for the artistic varieties which aim at a more refined set of enjoyments.

Modernity has, thus, received what initially appear to be radically contrastive interpretations: Descartes, Kant, Hegel, and Habermas stress the notion of reason as critique. Bacon, Nietzsche, Weber, Heidegger, Blumenberg, and Rorty variously emphasize the concept of self-assertive action; and from Hume, Smith, Baudelaire, John Ruskin on to Walter Benjamin, Bataille, and Lyotard, modernity is associated with the peculiar exercise of the passions, in terms either of economic needs and desires or aesthetic actions and appreciations.

If nothing else, my discussion of the strands of interpretation of the modern age has demonstrated Rorty's claim, cited earlier, that modern philosophy has consisted in a continual realignment of the value spheres. For the interpretative strands I have highlighted are obviously based upon differing emphases upon the infamous modalities of value.

Having engaged Rorty's Grand Narrative with various alternative interpretative strands, we are in a position to make the following generalizations: Rorty's narrative weaves together elements of the second and third strands, employing the notion of self-assertion as his principal theme. In the process, he transmogrifies the rational strand into a form of the volitional by turning away from Hegel the rational system builder to the "Romantic" Hegel of *The Phenomenology of Spirit*. Finally, I believe it quite significant that Rorty has effectively ignored the economic interpretation of modernity.

In the remainder of this chapter I will address the following questions raised by this contextualization of Rorty's narrative: First, is Rorty's Grand Narrative grand *enough* to allow him to hold his time in thought? That is to say: Is he really justified in leaving out the alternative interpretative threads? A second question concerns whether or not Rorty's Grand Narrative may be productively discussed as an illustration of historicism at work.

Rorty's Hegelian suggestion that the philosopher should seek to hold his time in thought seems straightforward enough until we consider the dimensions of that task. What Hegel achieved in the early nineteenth century has become a much more daunting task in the late twentieth. A twentieth-century version of *The Phenomenology of Spirit* is highly unlikely unless, *per impossibile*, we could tell a single story that included all of the major thematics of contemporary cultural development. Granted, we are able to bring some coherence into the topic of modernity by demonstrating that the principal discussions of the notion are shaped in accordance with the model of self as a rational, volitional, and affective creature, this coherence is altogether abstract and formal. Furthermore, it cannot be sustained through formal theorizing.

Rational analyses of modernity associated with Descartes, Kant, and Hegel, and volitional analyses of the sort we may associate with the self-assertion of Bacon or Kierkegaard, Nietzsche or Max Weber, and aesthetic analyses of the kind found in the Romantics, and economic analyses deriving from Hume, Adam Smith, and Marx are incompatible expressions of the sense of modernity. Not only is there an incommensurability among theoretical expressions of these positionings, there are, as well, serious practical disagreements and conflicts among the proponents of these positionings.

There seems to be no coherent method of making an adequate report on the theories of modernity that would bring about a single consistent theory. Reductionism of some sort is inevitable. Weber, Baudelaire, and Hegel won't fit in a single theoretical scheme without damage being done to at least two of the three. Blumenberg, Habermas, and Heidegger perpetuate partial descriptions of modernity into the contemporary period.

Theoretical attempts at coherence are doomed to failure. The power of reason associated with the subjective autonomy of the human spirit forms an awkward alliance with the aggressive human desire to organize and control the natural environment, while the aesthetic impulse offers its embarrassed artifacts and advices aimed at moderating the excesses of reason threatened always by political assertion and economic desire. Self-reflection, self-assertion, self-gratification, and self-articulation are the contrasting, and conflicting, means of fabricating the modern self.

There have been several ad hoc consensual developments, of course, though they have never lasted long. For example, at approximately the same period in which Hume was articulating his theory of the collusion of property and the passions in the creation of the modern self, the union of mathematical and physical science with technology was finally achieved through the increasing complexity and power of machine technology that offered sufficient demands upon the intellect, and sufficient material rewards, so as to stimulate the scientific brain emerging pari passu with these changes.

It was a single, short step to the conspiracy of property interest and technological self-assertion in the rise of industrial capitalism that provided a framework in which the modern self's capacities for speculative rationality, active engagement with the natural world, and construction of economically productive enterprises were thought to be accommodated. But this accommodation is without intellectual articulation or justification, as is evidenced by the failure of any attempt to sum the total.

The futility of overarching theoretical aspirations is advertised by the rabid (cultural) self-consciousness that has forced us above first intentional considerations to the level of taxonomic endeavors. In the absence of any consensus as to a theoretical grounding of culture, those still inclined toward synthetic theories feel the need to become aware of all the alternative semantic analyses that may be given any particular subject.

There is a sense in which the exposition of the strands of modernity provided above better conforms to the aim of holding one's time in thought. For even though mine is a mosaicist approach which makes no claim to narrative unity, there is, in the service of candor, some justification for simply acceding to the chaotic character of "the times." On the other hand, it might be said that my accounts have reduced to absurdity the notion of holding one's time in thought in the sense of encompassing all of the important efficacious strands of modernity in a single vision.

The movement from *theoria*, the attitude of open-eyed wonder about the multifariousness of things, to *theory*, the product of the squint-eyed garnering and assemblage of conceptual surrogates for a selection of those things, seems to have dead-ended. The world is too much with us and we can see that our accountings are altogether too partial, or worse, they are taxonomically complete but are perforce rendered inert, "like a beautiful embalmed child."

There are two principal responses to this situation. In the first place, one can continue to abet the modernist impulse either through attempts to reconstruct the value spheres or, as Rorty has done, through the construction of a narrative which recounts the continuing story of the Enlightenment's secularizing and poetizing of culture at large. An alternative response is that of the postmodernist who accepts the condition of psychic fragmentation and its cultural implications as an improvement over the rationally ordered psyche, celebrating the divided self in its dirempted, deconstructed state. Postmodernism critiques the very idea of consensus, rejecting any theoretical grounding for culture.

The postmodern move takes Nietzsche's definition of truth as "the sum total of interpretations" and attempts to see the duck and the rabbit held in a single intuition. The postmodernist is the poignant figure of a rationalist in irrational times, a Don Quixote who hangs on to ideals long past their demise. In order to understand, to truly know the way of things in an age of multiple meanings, the senses of terms are not "arrived at" in the sense of weaning and honing until univocality is achieved. In postmodernity there is an absence of univocality and linearity. Postmodernists recognize the principal terms defining our cultural past as "cluster concepts" whose meanings can't be determined by logical or semantic analysis but by aesthetic juxtaposition and contrast. Derrida's deconstructive wordplay is but one of a number of illustrations of this recognition.

In spite of his some-time self-description as a "postmodernist bourgeois liberal," Rorty does not identify himself with the postmodern movement. The story he tells attempts to establish continuity with what he considers the legitimate aims of the Enlightenment. Rorty remains a modernist. As to the charge that he has failed to hold his time in thought in any adequate manner, Rorty may be said to be guilty—but with extenuating circumstances. No one, not Hegel himself, could hold this time of ours in thought. Ours is, largely due to the efforts of Hegel himself, too self-conscious an age. We live in a world of warring second intentions. Already in the sixteenth century, Montaigne complained that there were more "books on books than books on things." In our age there are more theories about theories than theories about things.

Rorty has at least made a virtue of necessity. His move from theory to narrative is perhaps the only manner of thinking efficaciously in an age of hyperconsciousness. One might disagree with the content of his narratives, but since the aim of the narrativist can only be persuasion, not logical refutation, real engagement can take place among alternative narratives strands. Our age of theoretical pluralism has little use for resorts to grand theories since, as closed conceptual schemes, theories perpetuate partiality while precluding meaningful intertheoretical engagement.

This still leaves us with the worry whether Rorty's narrative provides an adequate context within which to address the most important issues in contemporary culture. To provide at least a tentative response to this question we need to rehearse the major predicaments which define the "crisis of modernity."

Certainly, Rorty has identified an important strand of modernity in his discussion of the Kantian value spheres, and his later addition of the thematic of Baconian technology. But the crises in modernity extend beyond these issues. It is true, as Rorty suggests, that the Hegelian interpretation of the conflict of the value spheres has given rise to reductive and nonreductive counterdiscourses associated with the reconstructive efforts of recent modern thinking. But in addition to the crisis shaped by the conflict of the value spheres, there is that determined by our emergent "metamentality" occasioned by the raising to awareness of all the principal theoretical interpretations defining modernity. This is a form of the "excess of history" that Nietzsche diagnosed and for which he prescribed the technique of "active forgetting." Rorty's narrative explicitly attempts to bypass the crisis of the value spheres associated with Kant and Hegel. Further, simply by virtue of its narrative status, Rorty's thinking seeks to avoid being seduced by metamentality.

The third main crisis of modernity is associated with the recognition of the arbitrariness of our cultural artifacts. This recognition targets the power/knowledge conspiracy unmasked by Nietzsche and Foucault. This crisis is associated with the uncovering of the arbitrariness of cultural artifacts, including those artifactual constructs we term "theories." Michel Foucault's analysis of the conspiracy of knowledge and power[77] demonstrates the manner in which discourses are always determined by the power relations in a society. This sort of analysis has taken the heart out of all but the most obsessive of the modern reconstructionists.

Rorty responds to Foucault's unmasking of the true relations of knowledge and power by saying in effect, "Who could ever have thought otherwise?" Rorty's narrative attempts to render plausible the shift away from a search for objective knowledge to the creation of vocabularies for the purposes of getting what we want. Further, his association of the creation of these vocabularies with the activities of the strong poets, and his application of these vocabularies in the service of liberal democratic societies, provides some grounds for arguing that knowledge is not solely a function of institutionalized power. It should be said, however, that his failure to confront the broader issues central to the economic interpretation of modernity seriously weakens his case.

The pluralism of programs, ideologies, and theories faced by both intellectuals and social engineers in our present age is disastrous if it is taken as a conflict among values and beliefs, only one coherent set of which may be finally vindicated. Equally disastrous is the easygoing, sophomoric relativism which has it that any set of beliefs is as good as any other. Thinkers who seek a minimum of coherence have no choice but to be partial.

Miguel de Unamuno once said something to the effect that "the fact that the consequences of a proposition are disastrous says nothing against the truth of the proposition." I believe that the sentiment of this statement provides the best defense of Rorty's strategy. Rorty's narrative strategy is an appropriate response to the inevitable pluralism of society. The creation of narratives in the place of overarching theories does not preclude alternative narratives anymore than writing one novel prevents others from exercising their novelistic talents. Theories function reductively with respect to other theories; narratives are less totalitarian.

Rorty's measures, desperate as they may seem, are hardly out of place in our desperate times. One wonders how any reasonably sensitive, self-conscious, engaged thinker could believe that the perpetuation of the same tired strategies of logical analysis or dialectic which generate "truths" about the character of the world will improve our state. Rational appeals based upon stipulated meanings of evidence, argument, reason, and so forth, at variance with other theoretically stipulated senses, are broadly *irrational*.

There is reason to believe that Rorty's philosophic strategies constitute a plausible response to the major issues and crises defining the current cultural situation. For whatever criticisms one might have of the substance of Rorty's views, at least he cannot be accused of the scandalous irresponsibility and unearned arrogance of those Learned Doctors of Philosophy who continue on the long march to truth, each one of whom is capable of claiming emphatically, in the face of the equally imperious counterclaims of his colleagues, that he at last has gotten it right.

Far from closing down the philosophic enterprise through the creation of a comprehensive theory to end all theories, Rorty invites the construction of alternative narratives, not only as a means of enriching the intellectual activities of our cultural elites, but equally to sensitize us to the need for private self-actualization and the attainment of justice in the public sphere.

IS THIS HISTORICISM?

Our second question concerning Rorty's use of narrative to contextualize his philosophical arguments has to do with his claim that he is a historicist. I have suggested that Rorty is overly sanguine about his ability to free himself from Kant, that he remains bound to a quasi-Kantian form of the modernist problematic. On the other hand, I would claim that he may indeed have freed himself from an area of thinking to which he wishes to remain bound. That is, he may have stretched the word "historicism" beyond usable limits. In the following pages I will reflect upon the emergence of the historicist sensibility in the broadest of manners as a means of contextualizing Rorty's claim to be a historicist.

I should say again that my aim will be clarification, not refutation. I do grant, however, that this seemingly humble aim at clarifying Rorty's views may serve to enhance or diminish the readers' attachment to them.

Our cultural heritage from the Greeks has presented us with three models for the giving of accounts. Traditionally, these are termed *mythos*, *logos*, and *historia*. *Mythos* is the original model. Myths have come to be understood as etiological tales, stories of origins. We give an account of something when we tell how it came into being. Hesiod's *Theogony* provides accounts of the origins of the gods and of the structure of the cosmos. The myth of *Genesis* tells of the birth of the ordered world and of living things. The primary allies of myth are "meter" and "metaphor," which give *mythos* substance and form. Mythic themes, which gauge the profoundest dimensions of human life, ground our aesthetic sensibilities not unlike the manner in which principles ground our rational understandings. Meter provides mimetic resonances of the cyclical themes of myth. Metaphor protects us from the fatigue which otherwise might be occasioned by repetitions of form and content. Less profound themes, unmetered and without the comforts of metaphor, are trivialized and effectively lost to us. Art, literature, and music have their origins in the mythological mode of accounting.

A second kind of account is provided by *logos*. We have privileged this account in the scientific age, and it has largely determined the manner in which we understand both *mythos* and *historia*. In this mode, meter is replaced by logical structure. Metaphor is pressed into the service of reference. *Aitia* and *archai*—causes and principles—are discovered. Rational, causal discourse is born. The separation of *logos* from *mythos* is the heroic theme of rational culture.

Historia, "enquiry," is the third factor which constitutes us as self-conscious creatures. It is both in principle and in fact the most problematic of the three. The disciplines of history and of philosophy have their prominent origins among the Milesian Greeks. The first philosophers wished to provide an account of the *physis* of things. This term has come into our tradition through the Latin, *natura*, both terms being translated "the nature of things." Both *physis* and *natura* have roots suggesting "birth" and "growth," though these associations were lost with the dominance of substantialist and causal interpretations in later Greek philosophy.

Philosophy provides an account of the *physis* of things—the way things are. But the search for this *physis* involves *logos*. Thus it is a structured accounting that is sought. History provides an account of the important public events. Such events quickly come to be identified as those of war and the structure of states and empires.

Herodotus performed *historia*, enquiry. His work constituted *logoi*, accounts. He told stories of things seen and heard, as did Thucydides, who (because he was chronicling even more recent events) was able to promote a more stringent, and from the social scientists' point of view, more acceptable methodology. But because he dealt with concrete particularities and included ethnographical data, we might learn more from Herodotus than Thucydides about the concreteness of public experiences.

History was not in the beginning motivated by a love of the past or a sense of giving an account of the origins of things. This was initially the purview of philosophy, and of myth, its alien progenitor. Yet, it must not be thought that *historia* is easily dissociated from the philosophic search for *logos* and *physis*. Herodotus, as a Milesian, was shaped by the materialism of the early *physiologoi*. His *historia*, therefore, was informed by the material cosmology of the Milesian thinkers and of Heraclitus, as well.[78] On the other hand, Thucydides propounded historical interpretations heavily endowed with the power-oriented principles of the Sophists. Nor is philosophy to be thought independent of history. What later came to be called "philosophy," was itself enquiry, *historia*.[79] Indeed, Heraclitus speaks of Pythagorean philosophy as *historia*. And Pythagoras himself called his geometrical investigations *historia*.

The two most important classical interpretations of *historia* are those of Aristotle and of Augustine. We recall that Aristotle believed poetry to be more serious and philosophical than history since it considers universals, while history considers particular events. The poet is a maker of objects of imitation. He imitates actions primarily through the construction of narratives shaped by universal themes. By the time of Aristotle, history has taken on the familiar character of a recounting of things that actually took place in contrast to what might have been.

Augustine's *De Civitate Dei* incorporates the narrative structure of poetic art. The interweaving of *mythos* and *logos* in Augustine's tale of two cities demonstrates the problematic character of history as neatly as does Aristotle's hapless reduction of history to a meaningless congeries of events which lie inert and meaningless before our gaze, unless one introduces a meaning bestowing *mythos* in the form of narrative structure, or *logos* in the form of moral or political principles.

A further complexity arises when Augustine replaces the classical sense of *logos* as causal account with the Johanine notion of *Logos* as the Christ. Here both the blind *logos* of Herodotus borrowed from the Milesian cosmologists and the *realpolitik* of Thucydides are held to be inadequate for the interpretation of the development of the two cities. God's providence, mediated through the *Logos* as word made flesh, now constitutes the standard whereby the meaningfulness of events is to be assessed.

The need for the historian to implicate the universal themes of *mythos* and *logos* into his work in order to render it meaningful has brought history into competition with intellectual culture as alternative weavings of the rational and aesthetic thematics. Insofar as history comes to be construed merely in terms of the interpretative scheme employed to make sense of it, *historia* is reduced to culture. Alternatively, history and culture are held in tense relationship as alternative expressions of the same meanings—one a diachronic, the other a synchronic version. Culture is the presented matrix of meaning and interpretation constituting the communal resources of consciousness and activity. History is the narrative that concludes with this presented matrix.

The historical enterprise in fact attempts to defend itself against reduction to synchronicity by reverting to its status as shepherd of particularities. This positivist defense is paired with its alternative extreme which involves the claim that culture is merely the presented immediacy of "the known," "the felt," and "the achieved"—which is but the latest in a series of historical products.

We may recall here Nietzsche's twin strategies: Opposing the bloated awareness offered by a surfeit of historical consciousness, Nietzsche suggested the cultivation of "active forgetting." But we do well not to take this suggestion seriously. Nietzsche's irony aside, the cultivation of ignorance of the past is no more satisfying than is the metatheoretical activity of charting grand narratives that make sense of our cultural existence. In the first instance, history is deemed inimical to creativity and survives only at the cost of excessive repression of its contents. In the latter case, history is reduced to the repetition of interpretations deriving from the inventories of *mythos* and *logos*.

It is Nietzsche's second strategy that was prophetic. Claiming that "only interpretations exist," Nietzsche was able to find the truth of things in the accumulation of perspectives. The additive sum of all accountings of a thing constitutes the truth of the thing. Meaning is no longer a function of coherence or consistency. "God," as the name of the guarantor of such coherence, is dead.

History has thus become the blind gathering of mere accretion. We are trapped in our search for meaning between the resort to some thematic unity expressed by those tediously "old hat" justifying narratives or (and this is the direction of our immediate future) the experience of sheer massiveness as meaningfulness. Narratives seem the only resort if we are to make sense of our past. This was essentially our argument of the last section.

In the contemporary period of hyperconsciousness, history is a twice-told tale and more. History can be the story of forces of production, libidinal expressions and sublimations, adventures of ideas, Foucault's laundry lists, the celebration of intertextualities, a temporal chain of sorites (or, in the case of Derrida, of puns).

"Historicism" thus means a number of distinct through relatable things depending upon whose theory one is examining. Many critics of historicism agree that the historicist mentality requires that individual actions and events derive their meaning from "social wholes" whose laws of organization and development, once understood, permit significant predictions of future events. In this form historicism assumes an almost antihistoric sense to the degree that it undervalues the contributions of individuals to change and development.

The discernible laws of development of social complexes illustrated in Hegel, Comte, or Marx not only tend to provide a roadmap charting historical changes, but tend, as well, to be teleologically structured so as to define an end-state, be it the realization of absolute consciousness in the institutional state, the achievement of a classless society, or the realization of positive knowledge. The holistic interpretation of historicism is historicist in a rather Pickwickian sense, therefore, since it denies the fundamental status of change as well as the significance of the particularities of historical events.

Forms of historicist thinking which take time seriously and which assert the priority of individual agency over that of institutions and social complexes are much better illustrations of the interaction of history and culture in the meanings given these terms in our present discussions. The essential character of all historicist notions is to be found in metonymous principles of explanation—that is, in the notion that the event in history is a part of a developing whole to which reference must be made if an understanding of the character and consequences of the event is to be achieved. The various forms of historicism are distinguishable one from the other mainly in terms of the degree of dependence of the part upon the whole, and the generality and complexity of the wholes which provide the context for the events examined.

The holistic interpretation of historicism is hardly distinguishable from nonhistoricist discussions of transcendental conditions of reason as determining the principles of knowledge and action. If one affirms the constituting power of reason in its atemporal form, it matters very little whether this transcendental rationality is placed at the end of a historical period or above a set of events whose inner meaning renders the outer character of change and development illusory.

Historicism becomes interesting philosophically only if history is understood to be an open-ended enterprise the metonymous character of which permits the explanation of associated parts of conventional wholes in a relativistic manner. This means that there can be no transcendentally determined structures which define the wholes in accordance with which events are to be construed. This type of historicism recognizes the determining power of individual agency while at the same time finding the explanation of that agency in the social and temporal complexes from out of which it emerges as well as those complexes authored by the agency.

As things stand, there is no single history, there are *histories*. These are ad hoc manners of construing an effective past in terms of a selected present. The search for a single, exclusive, thread connecting past and present can only be motivated by objectivists holding to the certainty of a given *logos*. Such objectivists might be political ideologues committed to the rapidly disintegrating principle of consensus, or rationalists propounding the equally anemic story of scientific and technological progress.

History has, from the beginnings of our culture, been a comfort station servicing those who make the long journey from myth to reason and back again. It is impossible to give historical accountings without reversion to *mythos*, or *logos*, or both. In its most generic sense, historicism means something like this: to give an account of the temporal development of *x* is to say what is most interesting and important about *x*. But, as we have seen, that definition of historicism is general enough to cover a multitude of sins, not the least of which is the Rortyan vice of providing a morphology of historiographical tasks in advance of undertaking the genetic analysis of one's selected subject.

What Rorty has done by isolating *geistesgeschichte* from other modes of historiography is to employ a taxonomy in such a manner as to establish candidates for meaningful accounts. This is not in itself a historicist move, but a logical one. But his preference for *geistesgeschichte* moves historical narratives away from *logos* in the direction of *mythos*. Rorty's mode of historicism, like any which maintains structural coherence, is the result of an interplay of *mythos*, *logos*, and *historia*.

Because he wishes to align himself with poets rather than scientists, and because narrative is an isolatable literary category distinct from the dramatic and the lyric, perhaps we ought to clarify Rorty's argument by shifting away from the use of the word "historicism" to describe his stance. Otherwise, we shall allow Rorty to have it both ways. That is, when his historical narratives are challenged he might say that he is really only constructing a dramatic narrative. And when he is challenged as to the pedestrian character of his narratives, he might say: "Yes, but you see, I'm just a philosopher trying to perform the modest role of a (nominalist) historicist."

Rorty would defend himself against the perverse implications of this sort of criticism by claiming that anyone "who offers large generalizations about the history of philosophy has to flit back and forth between playing up the similarities and playing up the differences,"[80] and that the construction of narratives this requires is essentially a nonmethodological procedure. That is a rather banal claim to be sure, one with which few would disagree. The issue, however, is precisely where and how this flitting takes place. Rorty flits furiously once he sets up his narrative. But there is to my mind very little by way of playing up differences in abstraction from his peculiar historicist stance.

The so-called "crisis of historicism" is that of the apparently inevitable skepticism and relativism consequent upon the denial of transhistorical determinants of change. This crisis would appear to be avoidable if one recognizes that "self" and "circumstance" are abstractions from that which may indifferently be termed self or circumstance. The historical agent makes the circumstance which in turn makes him. And, of course, vice versa.

Rorty's heroic historicism is a sophistic or existential variety which by no means exhausts the sorts of historicisms, not even of the *geistesgeschichte* variety. Moreover, telling a story in which the heroes are really names for certain virtues (Bacon = "self-assertion") or vices (Kant = "self-grounding") is questionable as history. We usually call this sort of thing allegory.

Rorty's allegorization of history is reinforced by his constant resort to typologies as a means of introducing his narratives. A nominalist historicist cannot be comfortable with the discussion of themes and trends, of overarching ideas. He can only make lists. Thus, more often than not, before launching his principal argument Rorty provides us with a list of types of things which contextualize his remarks: In addition to there being four (legitimate) kinds of historiogaphical genres, there are two ways of giving meaning to one's life,[81] and two sorts of pragmatists.[82] There are three ways of characterizing pragmatism,[83] and three ways of acquiring new beliefs.[84] Philosophy may be construed as science, as metaphor, or as politics. And so on. These lists come neither from a philosopher undertaking the task of cutting reality at the joints, nor (at least not altogether) from a rhetorician attempting to pack the straw tightest at the most vulnerable spots. In the absence of principles, real essences and natural kinds, there is no choice but to list things, and offer examples.[85]

The real difference between lists containing thises and thats and full-blown taxonomies of the sort Rorty rightly wishes to avoid is that a metatheory is an a priori tool, while the items on a list ought to have been stumbled upon in the course of telling one's story. But Rorty's metaphilosophical lists almost always precede his narratives. Thus before we can tell a story of "how we got this way" we must distinguish the *sort* of story we tell from other principal sorts—historical or rational reconstructions, doxographies, intellectual history. Rorty's concern for *geistesgeschichte* focuses his avowed commitment to historicism. His sympathy for intellectual history further specifies the sort of historicist he finally turns out to be. He is a nominalist Hegelian equipped with no deposit/no return typologies.

Narratives generated from taxonomic features consciously entertained are the sorts of things most self-proclaimed historicists would decry. Hegel's narrative shaped by the form of the dialectic has more to do with compressions and rarefactions of pale triads than with the thises and thats of brute circumstance. It is only by grossly overvaluing the *details* of his *Phenomenology* that we feel at all comfortable calling Hegel a historicist.

By listing five historiographical genres, eschewing one (the doxographical), and describing the modes of interaction among the others, Rorty allows his topological consciousness to extrude into his historicist project such that the purity of his nominalism is seriously threatened. Moreover, his interest in intellectual history significantly qualifies his avowed enthusiasm for *geistesgeschichte*. For if, as often seems the case, his heroes are not encountered in the course of historical ruminations but selected in advance of them, they serve as little more than stereotypical metaconstructs about which narratives are erected. This mode of narrative construction, more clever than creative, may be all we have a right to expect of one educated first in the abstract arts of philosophy.

Rorty's taxonomies are so many instruments employed in his effort to reconstruct the countenance of our intellectual history. The method here may not be as formally grounded as is that of the professional taxonomists and "systematic pluralists," but it is equally central to Rorty's style of thinking. It doesn't really matter very much that the distinctions are ephemeral rather than final and foundational, nor that the content of the doctrines shaped by these distinctions is not permanently relevant. Ad hoc principles, as much as essentialist ones, shape one's evidence and arguments, thereby reading alternatives out of court.

Rorty's belief in the causal, rather than rational, understanding of the acquisition of beliefs and desires lies at the very heart of his philosophical enterprise. This view may be plausibly read as an attempt to escape the plenary awareness of the metaphilosophical know-it-all. Such a reading can only appear arbitrary and tendentious until we have been able to examine the character of Rorty's thinking in greater detail. The evidence that he is in fact still struggling with the demons of his past lies primarily in the conflict his thinking expresses between the hyperconscious metamentality of the taxonomist and the allusive vagueness of the poet. Rorty has not been able to integrate the logical and the metaphorical strains in this thinking, nor does he seem to think such integration possible.

I believe that Rorty is at his best when advocating social and cultural change by resort to "piecemeal nudges"[86] (something close to the *fin de siècle* Viennese notion of *fortwursteln*). His thought is weakest when (in the attempt to avoid "going transcendental"[87]) he offers lists and a narrative as a means of setting up his arguments. For narratives cannot stand alone. Intellectual endeavors interweave both morphological and genetic accountings. The conceptual and narrative strands of significance derived from these accountings form a diachronous web of interpretations. This is the web of culture itself. The privileging of a single narrative or conceptual element construes the whole as one of its parts. Thus, both morphological and genetic accountings involve the resort to synecdoche.

If we cannot achieve a single best theoretical context within which to understand rationality, neither can we depend upon historicist accounts to weed out currently irrelevant notions and provide us the understanding of reason best suited to our contemporary situation. This is not only due to the partiality of each sort of account; more importantly, it is because *there are no unmixed accounts*.

Synchronic or morphological interpretations bear the impress of their origins and histories. And diachronic interpretations, however specific and nominalistic they appear, are themselves shaped by an antecedently selected vocabulary (idealist, behaviorist, existential, and so on) which construes the movement of past to present in a tendentious manner. Historicisms of the philosophical variety, such as Rorty's, are metahistorical narratives. Thus all historicisms, however rhetorically robust, are conceptually wan and anemic since the coherence and narrative unity they require depends upon special pleadings generalized from a narrow selection of evidences.

With the aggressive candor hyperconsciousness enjoins, Rorty openly celebrates the *arbitrariness* of his enterprise. One of the consequences of this celebration is a masking of the theoretical commitments his views entail.[88] Rorty's historicism has not escaped the hyperconsciousness of contemporary intellectual culture. His narratives are but motorized versions of provincial theories. His affirmation of "self-assertion" is less a naive appeal to history than it is an implicit introduction of existential, volitional, sophistic thematics into his discourse.

I don't mean to suggest that the intransigent impurity of either genetic or morphological understandings presents any real difficulty. That is simply the way of the world. Nonetheless, problems arise when Rorty attempts to wash away the guilty stains of essentialist theories by plunging them in the polluted waters of a taxonomized historicism.

Though always interesting, Rorty's rather bloodless narratives would bear far greater weight if read as metaphilosophical picaresques. For the Rortyan type of historicist is forced consciously to confound history and narrative. Thus, the Hegel-inspired historicist, even of the nominalist variety, is always attempting to show how the events of the past conspired to create the present-as-culmination. We must expect, if not apocalypticism, then certainly apocatasticism.

In fairness to Rorty we ought recognize that he makes no claims for a metadiscourse beyond the moment of its rhetorical use. But when persuasion is the aim of the discourse, that is a crucial claim indeed. According to Anthony J. Cascardi,

> Lyotard's insistence on the place of language games in philosophy, and Rorty's insistence on the role of philosophy "in the conversation of mankind," although historicist insofar as they assert the contingency of all discourse, constitute further refusals of the attempt by history to mediate and thereby recuperate the differences among divergent accounts of human nature or the world. . . . "History" may thus assert itself in these and other contemporary projects not as the court of the world's judgment but rather as the *fabula* or story line in terms of which its own extinction can be retold.[89]

If we distinguish, in accordance with recent trends in narratology, the *fabula*, or story, the elements of which form the raw material for the plot of a given narrative, from the plot itself, then we can see that

Rorty's historicism is a poetized one which cannot provide a general accounting of the way things really happened. The plot of Rorty's Grand Narrative is constructed from a *fabula* which, when recontextualized by Rorty's readers in something like the fashion I have tried to do, cannot maintain its coherence.

Rorty could defend himself against the charge of incoherence in one of two ways, neither of which would seem to serve his interests: either by a postmodern celebration of incoherence and complexity, or by threatening a reversion to a narcissistic privatization of the narrative process which impoverishes the *fabula* of history by appeal to the idiosyncrasies of the plot.

I believe Rorty ought to reconsider his claim to be a historicist. For one of the consequences of allowing himself greater sympathy with the poet than the philosopher, is that his narratives are more like epics or novels than histories. It is far better, I believe, to take full responsibility for one's literary pretensions than to mask them by claims to historicist practice.

In his *The Art of the Novel*,[90] Milan Kundera speaks of the novelist as one whose characters illustrate "experimental selves" which we as readers might try out in our acts of self-articulation. Rorty's metahistoricism is populated with "great dead thinkers" who offer us possibilities for just such articulation. Indeed, his transvaluation of the role of the intellectual insures that this must be the case.

I think it best that Rorty abandon the term "historicism" as descriptive of his thinking. He should simply call himself a "narrativist," thereby celebrating both his elision of the distinction between philosophy and literature, and his preference for a poetized culture. But, recalling Aristotle's claim that "poetry is something more philosophic and of graver import than history since its statements are of the nature of universals, whereas those of history are singulars,"[91] we should locate Rorty's narrativism somewhere between traditional understandings of poetry and history. His statements, qualified by his ad hoc taxonomies, lack the singularity, specificity, and concreteness of the historian, but as his taxonomies are ad hoc and dispensable, neither do they express universal or necessary features.

If one sought to maintain some sort of distinction between philosophy, poetry, and history in the vague and clustered meanings these terms carry, Rorty would certainly remain a philosopher. For, though he is more a poet than a philosopher or historian, he is far more a philosopher than a historian. His historicism, therefore, is strongly shaped by literary and philosophic pretensions.

In deference to Rorty's wishes, however, I will allow him his use of "historicist" as a self-descriptive term. I should stress, however, that the sort of historicism Rorty represents is a nominalist, heroic, Romantic, existential, poetic, and narrativist historicism. As such, it is at least as close to epic poetry as are the more expansive narratives of Hegel's *Phenomenology*. For this reason, when the term "historicism" is used in the following pages I shall mean it to be tacitly preceded by qualifiers such as "narrativist," "poetized," and "epic" when this is not explicitly the case.

2

AN OLD NAME FOR SOME
NEW WAYS OF THINKING

Rorty's epic, poetized mode of thinking shapes his form of
historicism, which in turn provides an interesting character
to the relationship he seeks to maintain with the American
pragmatic tradition. The question of this chapter is whether
such a literary stance precludes Rorty from calling himself a
pragmatist. Though many deny him the right to claim alle-
giance to pragmatism in anything like a traditional sense of
that term, I believe that he has largely succeeded in his
efforts to adapt (one stream of) pragmatism to "a changed
intellectual environment." Indeed, there is a real question
as to how changed this environment is. For all the ways in
which Rorty might be said to move against the grain of the
American pragmatic tradition, his thinking nonetheless has
the *feel* of American thought, at least to this reader of our
intellectual history.

In the first section of this chapter I will discuss the "aesthetic pluralism" of traditional American thought as a means
of articulating the sort of relationship Rorty attempts to
maintain with the pragmatic tradition. The second section
will be concerned with the shift away from "experience" to
"language" as the central metaphor for the interpretation of
pragmatic theory. In the next section I shall try to show how
Rorty's peculiar sort of nominalism leads him to move away
from the naturalistic toward the "literary" strain of pragmatism. The fourth section concerns the relevance of the New
Pragmatism to issues in political theory. Finally, I will con-
clude this chapter with a discussion of the principal "heroes
and villains" of Rorty's Grand Narrative.

THE AESTHETIC AXIS OF AMERICAN PHILOSOPHY

I believe Rorty qualifies as a legitimate heir to the pragmatic tradition by virtue of his implicit focus upon a problematic deeply embedded in the American experience: the fact and consequences of *plurality* in its psychological, social, and political forms. It is this more than anything else that moves Rorty along the path of traditionally American thinking, aligning him with what we might call the "aesthetic axis" of American philosophy.[1]

A tradition of "aesthetic pluralism" is established at the very beginnings of American thought. Jonathan Edwards' reconstruction of Calvinism proceeded from a basic assumption of the primacy of beauty. Reading Edwards, one is constantly confronted by the word "beauty" in places one would expect to see "goodness" or "truth."

> God is the fountain and foundation of all being and beauty . . .[2]

> God is God, and distinguished from all other beings, and exalted above 'em [sic!] chiefly by his divine beauty, which is infinitely diverse from all other beauty.[3]

> It was more especially the Holy Spirit's work to bring the world to its beauty and perfection out of chaos; for the beauty of the world is the communication of God's beauty.[4]

Roland Delattre in his *Beauty and Sensibility in the Thought of Jonathan Edwards*,[5] provides a detailed and persuasive defense of the aesthetic basis of Edward's theology. Delattre notes that Edwards, contrary to the dominant interpretations of the Platonic tradition, makes Being prior to unity as a metaphysical principle. It is this that sustains the pluralistic interpretation permitting Edwards to deal with beauty as "consent to being." Since beauty serves as the principle of unity, whatever unity being has is a gift of beauty. Beauty, as consent to being, conforms to the conditions of consent set by the character of specific beings. The principal condition is diversity, plurality. Thus, if there is beauty in God, there must be diversity. "One alone cannot be excellent, inasmuch as, in such case, there can be no consent."[6] The unity of being is the ordering emergent from patterns of consent. The richer the diversity, the more complex the order, the greater is the beauty of the whole.

I have two reasons for considering the influence of a theologian upon the ostensibly nontheological Rorty: First, we are asking about the intellectual environment from out of which Rorty's New Pragmatism emerges. There is good reason to believe that Edwards' contribution to that environment is, mutatis mutandis, consistent with the sort of aesthetic pluralism that characterizes other, more traditional, pragmatists. But quite apart from the obvious interest in the aesthetic character of Edwards' thinking as a part of the aesthetic axis of American philosophy, I believe there is a commonality of tone between Edwards and Rorty. For all Rorty's apparent strictures against religion, theism, and theology, there seem to be strong, if suppressed, spiritual yearnings in his writing.[7] I will allude to these yearnings later with respect to thinkers such as Whitehead and Tillich.

The same sort of problematic to which Edwards appeals is celebrated by a thinker who otherwise would have had little sympathy with our most original theologian. I refer to Emerson. And though, as Perry Miller suggests, Edwards was "prepared to dissent in advance from the Emersonian transcendentalism that would . . . seek the good and the beautiful in sunsets and woodchucks,"[8] there is much less disagreement among these two thinkers than one might think. Each understands the relation between mind and its environs to be defined by the encounter with diverse particular elements.

Emerson answers the question, "What would we really know the meaning of?" in this way: "The meal in the firkin; the milk in the pan; the ballad in the street; the news of the boat; the glance of the eye. . . ."[9] Knowledge is not of patterns or principles, but of the various insistent particularities of our concretely experienced environs.

Like Edwards, Emerson presupposed the value of diversity. And though statements such as, "There is no trifle, there is no puzzle, but one design animates the farthest pinnacle and the lowest trench,"[10] are often read (by those who have "listened too long to the courtly muses of Europe"[11]) as if they were made by an Absolute Idealist, these words must be understood in the light of Emerson's most familiar apothegms: "Whoso would be a man must be a nonconformist,"[12] and "A foolish consistency is the hobgoblin of little minds. . . . Nothing is at last sacred but the integrity of *your* mind."[13]

The misinterpretations of Emerson that make of him a sentimentalist and a fool are drawn from construals overly influenced by stale idealistic models. Emerson, whom Dewey rightly called *the* philosopher of democracy, was an aesthetic pluralist, which simply means that he recognized that the aesthetic, not the logical, model must be employed to order diversity since aesthetic contrast thrives on diversity where logical consistency cannot.

Emerson's conception of beauty and the aesthetic sensibility was put forward as a response to the democratic pluralism of his society in a manner not unlike the way Edwards responded to the presumed ontological pluralism associated with a being's consent to being. Though Rorty has little directly to say about Emerson, he is clearly in sympathy with those aspects of his thought which promote the value of individual freedom, self-reliance, and autonomy. Moreover, he just as clearly holds Emerson to be one of the inspirations of John Dewey's brand of liberalism.[14]

Though more qualified in his pluralistic leanings, Charles Sanders Peirce continues the line of aesthetic pluralists. In his attempt to organize the ways of knowing, he held aesthetics to be the capstone science, adjudicating logic and ethics. Logic concerns itself with developing tools for realizing the ends of thinking. To construct these tools, the logician must know what the end of thought is. It is the task of ethics to define the end of thinking. One cannot be thoroughly logical without concerning herself with ethics.[15] Further, ethics depends upon a yet more fundamental question:

> Ethics asks to what end all effort shall be directed. That question obviously depends upon the question what it would be that, independently of the effort, we should like to experience. . . . The question of esthetics is, what is the one quality that is, in its immediate presence καλος? Upon that question ethics must depend.[16]

It is certainly true that Peirce found pluralism much less congenial than the other pragmatists, indeed he claimed that "life can have but one end." But that end was, effectively, Tennyson's "far off divine event," to be realized in mundane terms by the ideal convergence to truth consequent upon the efforts of a community of inquirers. That community was one constituted by competing hypotheses which must be allowed to grow together until the harvest. Short of that convergence which finally would lead us to Truth, psychological and social existence presupposes diversity and plurality.

Rorty claims to find Peirce's thinking uncongenial because he believes that Peirce "remained the most Kantian of thinkers," whose "contribution to pragmatism was merely to have given it a name, and to have stimulated James."[17] Though one can certainly understand Rorty's distaste for Peirce on other grounds, his claim that Peirce was strictly Kantian is a rather odd statement since, by reconstructing the dreaded "value spheres," Peirce was able to circumvent many of the problems of the Kantian inheritance which still plague Rorty.

Peirce applied his categories of Firstness, Secondness, and Thirdness to consciousness as a means of reinterpreting the Kantian faculties of feeling, knowing, and willing and the value spheres associated with them—namely, the aesthetic, scientific, and moral. Peirce's analysis returns the notion nearer to the original Platonic theory of *psyche* and in so doing bypasses the demarcation problem associated with the conflicting value spheres and their cultural instantiations.

> The true categories of consciousness are: first, feeling, the consciousness which can be included with an instant of time, passive consciousness . . . ; second, consciousness of an interruption in the field of consciousness, sense of resistance . . . ; third, synthetic consciousness, binding time together, sense of learning, thought.[18]

For Peirce the categories of consciousness may be analyzed in terms of quality, relation, and synthesis where "relation" involves any sort of activity (including, but by no means exhausted by, the volitional or purposive activity) and "synthesis" is interpreted in terms of "learning" or the "acquisition of knowledge" rather than the substantive sense of "cognition." Finally, the qualitative dimension of consciousness, associated with the aesthetic sense, is provided a normative status.

By replacing Kant's category of willing with the sense of action and reaction, the "polar sense,"[19] Peirce was able to relativize the Hebraic-Christian concept of "volition" (inherited from Augustine), which had narrowed the Platonic notion of "spirit" and contributed, at least as much as Descartes' *cogito*, to the increased subjective bias of modern thinking. Also, Peirce's replacement of the "cognitive faculty" by the notion of "learning" or "acquisition" brings process notions to bear upon the enterprise of thinking and coopts Platonic "Eros" for process philosophers in a manner supplementary to that in which A. N. Whitehead achieved the same result. Peirce's revision of the Kantian categories provides an alternative characterization of the problematic Kant sought to address with his value spheres.

Peirce's revision of the Kantian categories offers a resource for the development of a much richer notion of the value modalities than does that deriving from Kant. Since Peirce's categories are not caught in the web of modernity, Peirceian naturalism is less anthropocentric (subjectivist) than that of either Hegel or Whitehead.

But Rorty's agonal, existential, narrativist stance, dependent as it is upon the notion of "self-assertion," cannot accommodate itself to

Peirce's more diffuse category of Secondness expressed as "the polar sense." Apparently, Peirce has taken the aesthetic category much more seriously than Rorty. In fact, one might suggest that it is Rorty who has remained Kantian in a manner that Peirce has not. Rorty's continual allemande with Kant's doctrine of the value spheres binds him to the Kantian problematic. It is against the ghost of that Kant Peirce himself has slain that Rorty protests in abjuring Peirce.

The strictures expressed against Peirce, along with his preference for a poetized culture, would suggest that Rorty would find in William James the most sympathetic figure for use in revamping pragmatism. Indeed, Rorty confesses that, as a student, he had a greater admiration for James than Dewey.[20] Moreover, Rorty seems dispositionally more attuned to James than Dewey. Not simply his literary predilections, but his tender-minded approach to intellectual problems, and his concern for self-perfection, give Rorty something of a James-like presence.

It is quite likely his closeness to James that precludes Rorty appealing to his thought. The situation here, at least as regards personal taste, is not altogether unlike that of the relation of Freud and Nietzsche. Freud claimed that he avoided reading Nietzsche because of the sense of too great a proximity. Rorty requires a collaborator who will also serve as a foil. It is likely that Rorty would be unable to give a productively strong misreading of James since James' psychological and literary interests, along with his private, introspective stance, simply do not offer sufficient tension with Rorty's own views to create the proper dialectic. It is precisely Dewey's (qualified) leanings toward metaphysical explanation, scientific naturalism, and the method of inquiry which, as we shall see, Rorty is able to employ as a bridge between those aspects of analytic and Continental thinking he wishes to emend.

For James, the universe is one in which "things are 'with' one another in many ways, but nothing includes everything, or dominates over everything. The word 'and' trails long after every sentence."[21] Both monism and pluralism are grounded in aesthetic intuitions. Beliefs such as "nature is simple and invariable; makes no leaps or makes nothing but leaps . . . express our sense of how pleasantly our intellect would feel if it had a nature of that sort to deal with."[22] As with Peirce, James believes the effort of thinking presupposes some response to the question as to "what, independently of the effort, we should like to experience."

We should pause here to recognize that Rorty's dismissal of Peirce leads him to part ways with one of the two principal strains of

American pragmatism. The Peirceian strain maintains a (critical) relationship with the scientific enterprise. The use of the methods of science and the search for consensus characterize this strain. The Jamesian strain, on the other hand, is more literary than scientific. It celebrates the affective and volitional dimensions of human experience and insists upon the proper recognition of the plurality of beliefs and actions prior to the search for any consensus.

John Dewey combines in his thinking both the Jamesian and Peirceian modalities of pragmatism. Rorty's ultimate choice to take his stand with Dewey actually means that he stands with the Jamesian against the Peirceian Dewey. Thus, many of the criticisms of Rorty's pragmatism come either from followers of Peirce or from those who believe that true pragmatism cannot exist without something like Dewey's adjudication of Peirce and James. I will be discussing the relationship of Rorty to John Dewey in some detail in the following section, and so shall omit any consideration of Dewey's thought here.

We may continue developing the line of aesthetic pluralists by mentioning the name of a contemporary of Dewey who in many ways sums up the speculative strain of aesthetic pragmatism. An adopted American, A. N. Whitehead was both influenced by, and significantly influenced, the character of aesthetic pluralism in America. His avowed metaphysical interests must exclude him from Rorty's list of heroes, but it is difficult to avoid the belief that Rorty, who early in his career spent a great deal of time on Whitehead's texts,[23] could have remained insensitive to the breadth of historical vision Whitehead offers to those who would hold their times in thought.

Rorty approached Whitehead with what many hold to be *the* question of modern philosophy: How one might account for the experience of unrepeatable particulars without undue resort to abstract, repeatable, categories and principles. Whitehead addressed this question by appeal to the processive, transitory, character of "actual occasions," contextualizing the concept of "logical order" with reference to the broader notion of "aesthetic order."

Whitehead's "actual occasions" are the final things of which the world is made. They constitute types of order through the mutual adjustments of their aims and actualizations. The chief aim is balanced complexity of experience, and it is aesthetic not logical order which best manifests such complexity. Logical order is that which is realized through the instantiation of an abstract pattern, while aesthetic order involves the mutual adjustment of concrete particulars which aim at the inclusion of the maximum of intensities of immediate experience.[24]

Whitehead employs the contrast of logical and aesthetic order in such a manner as to ontologize the repeatable/unrepeatable distinction. The constitution of a triangle by mathematical points exemplifies logical order; the particular composition, colors, and brushstrokes constituting the original creation of a painter illustrates aesthetic order.

In a perceptive essay written in 1963, Rorty claims that Whitehead's thinking shares with the analytic philosophers working after the "linguistic turn" the realization that "the subjectivist bias of modern philosophy can only be reconciled with realism if we can find a way of reconciling the fact that all knowledge is *perspectival* with the fact that such knowledge is about objects distinct from and independent of the experiencing subject."[25]

When he wrote this essay, Rorty was becoming convinced that, after the linguistic turn, new and better methods were made available for showing that "our knowledge may be about an independent reality without its being the case that it is even logically possible that this reality should be described independently of the observer's perspective."[26] These methods permitted the movement away from the speculative, systematic use of a language of "experiencing subjects" toward the employment of "the language of language."

We shall see as we proceed in the discussions of the following chapters that Rorty has maintained the essentials of his former position but has radicalized the notion of perspectival knowledge in two ways: (1) He has begun to emphasize the creative power of poets to introduce new metaphorical extensions of language, and (2) he has accepted the "closed shop" status of individual language games, denying the rationality of intertheoretical conversations. There still may be an external world, even though we may not agree with one another concerning its status and character. These emendations of his former position move Rorty back in the direction of the speculative philosopher, albeit without the questionable comforts of theory and system.

There is a second manner in which Whitehead's thinking may be said to influence Rorty. Rorty's attempt to hold his time in thought shares with both Hegel and Whitehead a desire to accommodate as broad a range of ideas as possible within his vision. He shares with Whitehead, and Hegel before him, the belief that "the chief danger to philosophy is narrowness in the selection of evidence."[27] Thus, though he sees the necessity of narrowing one's evidences in the creation of single narratives, he celebrates the creation of many alternative narratives.

Though it might seem surprising to find elements in Whitehead that would appeal to the nominalist Rorty, I will argue in chapter 3 that the aesthetic grounding of Rorty's thought, along with his broad vision of the history of contemporary intellectual culture, requires him to resort to irony in much the same manner as Whitehead is required to do. Moreover, I shall indicate in the closing chapter of this work that Rorty's strictures against speculative philosophy are qualified by the constitutive irony of his thinking. This means that, though Rorty has eschewed resort to speculation in the modes of *ontologia generalis* and *scientia universalis*, he has provided us with a novel model of speculation, the method of an aesthetic pluralist, which is a nominalized version of the analogical method Whitehead and others have employed in their writings.

The point of highlighting elements of the thought of American philosophers from Edwards to Whitehead is to indicate that these thinkers presupposed the same problematic. Each of them at least implicitly asked, given the plurality and complexity of experiencing, how one might realize order without the undue exclusion of particularity at the ontological, epistemological, and practical levels.

American philosophy is pluralistic. Thinking remains legitimately pluralistic only if it discovers some means other than logical or rational organization to realize the appropriate ordering of the insistent particulars which comprise our psychological, social, and natural environs. This is the basis of the aesthetic orientation of American philosophy.

There is another movement in American thought which, though it seems to lie outside the mainstream pragmatic tradition, shares the positive appraisal of pluralism represented by the pragmatists. I refer to the tradition associated with metatheoretical pluralists such as Richard McKeon and Stephen Pepper. The philosophic pluralism of American thought includes the resort not only to the mutual adjustment of values, opinions, or beliefs, but of self-consciously articulated systems of thought as well. American philosophers have been more concerned than have their European colleagues with the metatheoretical tasks of organizing and classifying types of philosophic theory.

Stephen Pepper's *World Hypotheses*[28] provided a taxonomy of ways of thinking in terms of a selection of hypothetical constructs each of which is thought to ground a coherent characterization of the world. These hypotheses ("formism," "mechanism," "contextualism," "organicism") are grounded in "root metaphors" ("similarity," "machines," "historic events," "organism"). The hypotheses, together with their root metaphors, underlie general directions in thinking, as well as more formal systems of thought.

Each of these visions was derived, according to Pepper, from an assessment of actual ways of thinking. Each served as relatively complete means of operating with and interpreting the data of intellectual culture. Any attempt to organize two or more of them into a more general theory would be doomed due to the fact that they function as closed systems, autonomous languages.

The second major metatheorist in twentieth-century American thought is Richard McKeon, who developed a semantics of philosophic views by appeal to logical and rhetorical categories.[29] Through the analysis of the categories of "things," "thoughts," "words," and "terms," or "selections," "methods," "principles," and "interpretations," (notions analogized from the Aristotelian doctrine of the four causes), McKeon was able to formulate what he held to be exhaustive categories permitting him to classify systematic philosophers and to assay the lineaments of potential controversies engendered by the co-presence of mutually incompatible forms of thinking.

Pluralists of this sort ground their taxonomic interests on the intransigent diversity of ways of thinking. The aim of the metatheoretical pluralist is not dialectical refutation nor the resort to dismissive reductionism; his purpose is to account for the variety and diversity of viewpoints. The effect of work such as that of McKeon and Pepper has been to render more rigorous and self-conscious a type of thinking that has gone on in philosophy from the beginning. Plato's Divided Line was implicitly employed as a means of classifying types of thinking in terms of levels of clarity of knowledge. Aristotle begins his *Metaphysics,* as many of his other works, with an examination of previous opinions which employs his "four causes" as a classificatory device.[30]

Pepper and McKeon have provided tools for the consideration of types of thinking which had been accepted under more informal classifications ("Platonism," "Naturalism," "Idealism," "Pragmatism," etc.). The effect of raising to the level of consciousness the variety of ways of thinking, and then of demonstrating not only the relative adequacy of schemes of thought, but their closed status as semantic systems invulnerable to the logical, dialectical, or semantic arguments emergent from alternative points of view, is to cancel a principal motive for intertheoretical engagement. The more aware we become of the variety of autonomous visions, the greater is our indifference to the questions of the merely theoretical adequacy or inadequacy of the selected alternatives comprising the elements of their taxonomic schemes. Thus, the proponents of single theories become increasingly aloof and unresponsive to any engagement with alternative views.

No one really consults a dictionary to discover *the* meaning of a word. Dictionaries provide us a plethora of meanings of any given word. Moreover, the academic intellectual has usually encountered the alternative theoretical contexts within which a given locution takes on its various meanings. The demand that one stipulate or define a concept, therefore, advertises both the narrowness of any particular univocal sense and the plurality of alternative significances.

The belief in subjective connotation as constitutive of the meaning of a word or term is creeping back into our professional philosophic discourse. One of the distinctive aspects of the pun-ishing idiosyncratics of the later Derrida[31] is the manner in which he manipulates the "emotional baggage" of words. Likewise, Rorty's praise for Harold Bloom's strong poet as the creator of new metaphors presses philosophic thinking away from the scientific and toward the literary mode of reflection.

There is, I believe, a real question as to the degree to which stipulations aiming at either intra- or intertheoretical clarity serve the ends of communication. Often the greater the clarity of opposing views, the greater is our assurance that we have not communicated anything other than the extent of our disagreements. Even if we find that we agree by virtue of sharing the same theory, a next level of clarification may lead to a further theoretical split.

The first consequence of clarification is either to set up opposing semantic contexts or to create a context in which agreement is (temporarily) achieved. If the former is the result, our ships will either pass in the night, or collide in a storm. Neither alternative leads to effective communication. If the latter is the consequence, increased levels of clarification lead to differences in the understanding of the meaning and the import of the explicated notions or propositions and we find ourselves back to indifference or unproductive conflict.

In any given intellectual discipline, sophisticated theoretical activity could lead to the generation of a large number of closed systems. In principle, we could strive for a situation in intellectual culture in which no unambiguous uses of language remain. Vagueness would be lost. If there is no viable realm of unprofessionalized or demotic discourse, intertheoretical engagement is impossible since the constitutive rules of alternative discourses frustrate communication across ruled-defined boundaries. We see this phenomenon with the contrast of alternative axiomatic systems within a given scientific discipline. Such systems have as their aim the exclusion of anything like intertheoretical vagueness. The extremes of clarity would lead to a situation in which there are as many languages as language users.

Axiomatized language may be the paradigm of clarity, but communication succeeds at this level of clarity only if, *per impossibile*, the communicants employing the language agree on the stipulations. This agreement is harder to realize than one might think. One may instance the creation and subsequent interpretation of Whitehead and Russell's *Principia Mathematica*. The general philosophical dispositions of the two men were, of course, vastly distinct. Their interpretations of the axioms housing their views on the relations of mathematics to logic were subsequently just as diverse.

The consequence of clarification is the generation of opposition and closed systems. The final result is a move toward opposing idiolects with increasingly fewer communicants employing the same language. The ignominious activities of the taxonomist seeking to classify alternative semantic contexts leads finally to the promotion of a solipsism by default.

In spite of the tendency of taxonomists to promote the classification of forms of thought rather than their engagement, there is a distinctly pragmatic implication of the taxonomic art. This implication is illustrated by the recent split in the pluralist ranks between the right-wing "systematic" pluralists, who favor a closed taxonomic approach which argues for a few relatively adequate views, and left-wing "interpretative" pluralists, who eschew exhaustive typologies and in general place no limits on the number of interpretative perspectives philosophic thinking might generate.[32] The latter are more involved in the use of perspectives as interpretative devices; the former are concerned with the meta- metaproject of organizing ways of organizing interpretative theories.

The difficulties faced by both parties to this predictable ideological split are themselves predictable: the conservatives will likely spin off an ever more complex set of taxonomies in which not only shall we arrange philosophic views but the manner of arranging philosophic views will itself be arranged. For a well-planned flight from first intentions cannot stop at second and third intentional considerations. Indeed, the movement from a system to a system of systems to a system of systems of systems is in principle without terminus. The self-conscious pluralism of late modernist culture thrives on schemata, taxonomies which attempt to provide us with an exhaustive list of the ways of making lists.[33]

Interpretative pluralists, on the other hand, since they lack antecedent grounds for determining what an adequate orientation or hypothesis might be,[34] must struggle against degenerating into relativists. Their primary purpose will be to develop conceptual instruments which may be used to examine textual meanings, recognizing the value of alternative tools for different interpretative projects. The more conservative systematic pluralists articulate what they take to be exhaustive schemes which purport to adequately characterize the number and variety of theoretic perspectives. Interpretative pluralists identify tools; the systematic pluralists construct toolboxes.

There are quite plausible grounds for claiming that Rorty has been influenced by the metaphilosophical interest of contemporary American pluralism. This claim is even more plausible by virtue of his early exposure to the thought of Richard McKeon.[35] Rorty's approach to the problem of intertheoretical communication and relativism may be seen as his particular means of escape from McKeon's "boxes."[36] The first step is evident as early as 1961[37] when Rorty, after himself distinguishing approaches to metaphilosophy into three principal types, with a variety of subcategories, discusses metaphilosophical pragmatism as a view which sees "philosophy as the greatest game of all precisely because it is the game of 'changing the rules.'"[38]

Pragmatic metaphilosophers are meta- metaphilosophers. "Metametaphilosophy makes possible communication among metaphilosophers [and] since communication is the goal, rather than truth (or even agreement), the prospective infinite series is a progress rather than a regress: it becomes a moral duty to keep the series going, lest communication cease."[39]

If one treats "truth" pragmatically in terms of the "satisfaction of needs," and if one claims that the need philosophy best satisfies is that of communication, then, in our age of hyperconsciousness, the pragmatist trained in the philosophic art has no moral choice other than to be a metaphilosopher. This outlook, Rorty contends, "is fairly close to the attitude Dewey adopted toward the history of philosophy."[40] In his metaphilosophical pragmatism Rorty differs very little from the thrust of Pepper and McKeon.

Rorty's second response to the metaphilosophical character of our contemporary period involves his treatment of philosophical relativism. Rorty believes relativism to be the most odiferous of red herrings. Sophomoric formulations of relativist positions such as "Everybody has a right to his opinion" and "Any belief is as a good as any another" are too crude to count for very much. No one, upon interrogation, would hold to such a view. On the other hand, nuanced formulations of relativism in terms of the incommensurability of semantic contexts leading to the irrefutability of one theory by another, err in the other direction. Such convictions are sound enough, but irrelevant to the actual circumstances which define the sphere of praxis to which theories are meant to be applicable.

Rorty wants to distinguish between *philosophical* theories and *real* theories. The former constitute schemes which serve to ground special theories; the latter are detailed and specific formulations pertinent to concrete issues in physics or politics.[41] Relativism with respect to philosophical theories does not entail relativism of real theories. We might easily accede to the relativity of Pepper's world hypotheses or McKeon's types of semantic systems, but that is a rather empty and unproductive assent. When it comes to the specific ways in which Platonic or Aristotelian or Kantian or Heideggerian language is employed to address issues of technical or practical concern, we are no longer relativists. In these circumstances, we reflect upon, discuss, and debate the alternatives with the realization of specific desires in mind.

I confess that I am not as optimistic as Rorty seems to be about our ability to avoid all of the relativizing effects of pluralism by distinguishing *merely philosophical* theories from real ones. The philosopher (or any other theory-monger), having raised to the level of consciousness the plurality of systems and narratives within which important terminologies are developed, is hard pressed to background at will all but the single one relevant to his particular concerns.

What is perhaps most novel among the defining characteristics of late modern intellectual culture is the degree of our theoretical awareness. This awareness forces all but the most dogmatic of intellectuals into a mode of hyperconsciousness which encompasses a variety of diverse, mutually incompatible, ways of thinking. Responsible intellectuals then become (if only tacitly) pluralists who, formally or informally, employ conceptual and metaphorical classifications to sort and organize their interlocutors prior to assessing their views. The purpose of such activity cannot be the search for truth or the realization of consensus, only the promotion of a context within which communication is made possible. The effect of such bloated consciousness is that stipulations which aim at selecting a single, univocal meaning for a concept from among a variety of possible meanings are often simply unsuccessful. When they are successful they lead to the alienation and idiosyncrasy of the closed shop mentality, a mentality which leads to the abdication of the intellectual's duty to engage his peers.

I believe Rorty is a good illustration of a thinker who has taken very seriously a very serious problem. Theoretical pluralism (if not the relativism that threatens to come along with it) is a fundamental, intransigent aspect of our intellectual culture. Most philosophers (along with other assorted academics and intellectuals) attempt to ignore the phenomenon, maintaining a rather closed-minded preference for their own particular theories, believing (it seems) that wan hope coupled with bold rhetoric can eventually carry the day.

I do agree with Rorty that philosophy is pretty much done for if we continue to expend the major portion of our energies pumping out newer, subtler, versions of the same-old same-old. As one of the few outside the ranks of the meta-theoretical movement to engage the issues of theoretical pluralism at a sophisticated level, Rorty well understands that the metatheorist's views are relevant to both the theoretical and practical spheres. There are serious problems attending not only our acts of defining our terms at the request of others, but also our attempts to rationalize our practices, and to employ actions to illustrate the meaning of an idea or belief. The clarity and articulation often required in order to respond to questions such as, "What do you mean by that?" or "Why did you do that?" or "Would you show me what you mean?" will more likely mitigate than promote communication.

Rorty's approach to the question of relativism is an attempt to render the efforts of the systematic pluralists, the makers of toolboxes, broadly irrelevant and mildly comical. But it may be otherwise with the interpretative pluralists. These are true pragmatists in the Rortyan sense. Moreover, even the systematic pluralists can serve to remind us of the complexity and variety of tools employed by thinkers, both formally and informally, in the rationalization or defense of their beliefs.

As a *pragmatist*, Rorty's metaphilosophical interests are directed toward the aim of communication rather than truth or agreement. And it is this which leads him away from a concern with the virtuosic manipulation of formal theories in the direction of more informal categorizations and ultimately toward the development of ad hoc narratives and the appreciation of metaphorical language as the source of real communication.

I have been stressing the continuity of Rorty's thinking with a strain of aesthetic pluralism characteristic of American thought from its beginnings. Rorty is an "aesthetic pluralist" who continues the tradition of American thought which runs from Edwards to Dewey, Whitehead, and McKeon (and ultimately, as we shall see later, to W. V. O. Quine, Wilfrid Sellars, Nelson Goodman, John Rawls, and Donald Davidson), a tradition which approaches the issue of the plurality of belief and action by promoting the order and harmony of beliefs and actions through aesthetic and inclusory, rather than logical and exclusory, means.

An implication of my tracing of the aesthetic axis of American thought is that one might expect that any reconstruction in American philosophy which draws upon its roots will stress the aesthetic dimension deriving from the concrete, social character of American experience as rooted in the problem and promise of pluralism.

Rorty might wish to challenge my categorizing his efforts in the manner I have just done. But any attempt to contextualize his thinking within the broadest of construals of the American tradition perforce must lead to such nominalizations. Otherwise, there can be no productive engagement with that tradition. The point of Rorty's objection, were he to have one, could only be that he himself has not set the terms of the engagement.

We shall see that, with respect to his own constructive activities, Rorty wishes to operate at the metaphorical level, the level at which novel language may be developed. Moreover, in eschewing the logical mode of analysis with respect to theories and texts, and by illustrating how holding one's time in thought often requires a strong misreading of the influential figures who helped to shape one's present, he manages to avoid having to engage his friends and foes at the level of logic or dialectic and offers *conversation* and *debate* as models of interaction among different sorts of beliefs and desires. Further, by constructing narratives, Rorty transmogrifies his conversation partners into the heroes and villains of his narrative constructions.

FROM EXPERIENCE TO LANGUAGE

Having rejected Peirce, and bypassed James, Rorty turns to the remaining member of the trio of classical pragmatists, John Dewey. Still, it is the Jamesian Dewey that he wishes to coopt for his new pragmatism. And the effort of co-optation is to be performed by one who is himself strongly influenced by the metatheoretical pragmatism of Richard McKeon and the linguistic pragmatisms of Quine, Sellars, Goodman, Putnam, and Davidson.[42] This has created some problems, not the least of which is that many of his critics see Rorty's Dewey as little more than an empty sack into which his would-be disciple has packed handfuls of straw until, Lo! is risen the anti-foundationalist scarecrow Rorty wishes us to appreciate. Contrary to these critics, however, I believe Rorty's reading of Dewey—admittedly a *strong misreading*—allows many who might otherwise have continued to ignore Dewey's thinking to find in his works a valuable contemporary intellectual resource.

Rorty agrees with Emerson that we have listened too long to the courtly muses of Europe, but when he sets out to listen to American thought he cannot simply be reductive (that is scientistic), nor can he be merely synoptic (a systematic pluralist). Again following Emerson, he chooses to "leave . . . theory, as Joseph his coat in the hand of the harlot, and flee."[43] In the construction of his philosophical narrative, he develops his own particular version of pragmatism, which is one that promotes the broad intellectual tolerance that insists upon leaving room for alternative narratives. Rorty is prevented from falling into relativism by his further insistence that the freedom to develop alternative views doesn't guarantee that all views will be equally viable as tools for the resolution of particular problems.

In America, reconstruction has become associated with the name of John Dewey, but in one sense of the term reconstruction names a perennial task of the philosopher. One attempts to meet changed cultural conditions brought on by developments or revolutionary transformations in art, science, politics, or religion by constructing new priorities, new questions, new vocabularies better able to describe, explain, or interpret the changed circumstances.

Twenty-five years after Dewey first published his *Reconstruction in Philosophy*, he claimed that a more appropriate title for the work would be "Reconstruction *of* Philosophy."[44] Of course, anyone familiar with the spirit of Dewey's work would recognize that he would have liked to contribute to a situation in which a work such as his could responsibly be entitled, "Reconstruction *by* Philosophy." Dewey's conception of philosophic inquiry was formed during a period which marked the practical instantiation of many of the conceptual changes associated with the modern period. Major philosophic statements still reflect a prescientific (including pre-Darwinian and pre-Freudian), pretechnological, predemocratic, and precapitalistic world. Dewey sought to reconstruct the aims and instruments of the philosopher in such manner as to meet the needs of the new world.

In addition to his vaunted antipathy toward the theory/practice dichotomy, Dewey was particularly sensitive to two other alterations in the postclassical, scientific culture.

Theory in formal statement is as yet far behind theory in scientific practice. Theory in fact—that is, the conduct of scientific inquiry—has lost its ultimacy. Theories have passed into hypotheses. It remains for philosophy to point out the untold significance of this fact for morals.

For in what is now taken to be morals the fixed, the immutable, still
reign, even though moral theorists and moral institutional dogmatists
are at complete odds with one another as to *what* ends, standards and
principles are the ones which are immutable, eternal and universally
applicable. In science the order of fixities has already passed irretriev-
ably into an order of connections *in process*. One of the most immediate
duties of philosophical reconstruction with respect to the development of viable instruments for inquiry into human or moral facts is to
deal systematically with human processes.[45]

The tensions in our practical and intellectual life continue to be shaped
by the distinction between the theoretical and practical, the visions of
theories as practical instruments (hypotheses) rather than characterizations of that which is, and the increased dominance of change or process over the fixed, the substantial, the immutable.

As opposed to those who chart the history of speculation and
inquiry as a continuous development from the pre-Socratics to the present, Dewey saw a rupture in that history associated with the development of scientific modes of inquiry and their application to the
human social world. Reading Dewey, one cannot avoid the idea that
this rupture has something to do with the peculiar character of the
American philosophic tradition.

What characterizes Dewey's philosophy is the centrality of noncog-
nitive experience, of a pluralistic, nonholistic conception of experience
and world, and of the significance of the aesthetic as promoting the
sorts of penultimate unities that punctuate experience. The resort to
spontaneous feeling within the context of a normative pluralism is central to American philosophy from its inception.

Rorty wants to contrast the Bad Dewey of *Experience and Nature*
with the Good Dewey of *The Quest for Certainty* and *Art as Experience*.
Here are some vintage words from the latter book:

Experience is the result, the sign and the reward of that interaction
between organism and environment which, when it is carried to the
full, is a transformation of interaction into participation and communication. Since sense organs with their connected motor apparatus are
the means of this participation, any and every derogation of them,
whether practical or theoretical, is at once effect and cause of a narrowed and dulled life-experience. . . . Full recognition, therefore, of
the continuity of the organs, needs and basic impulses of the human
creature with his animal forbears . . . makes it possible for him to carry
to new and unprecedented heights that unity of sense and impulse, of

brain and eye and ear, that is exemplified in animal life, saturating it with the conscious meanings derived from communication and deliberate expression.[46]

For Rorty, Dewey's "experience," is replaced by "language"—that is to say, "communication and deliberate expression."

Rorty suggests that "'language' is a more suitable notion than 'experience' for saying the holistic and anti-foundationalist things which Dewey and James wanted to say."[47] (Whether it is as useful in supporting the scientistic and foundational things Dewey at least sometimes wanted to say is another matter.) But it seems clear that the shift from "experience" to "language" may be easily justified on Dewey's own terms. For Dewey would certainly agree that language is the principal form experience takes when the environment of a human organism is dominated by other human organisms.

Along with his naturalism, Rorty rejects the Peirceian elements in Dewey's thought. These include his "logic," his "method," and his claims that philosophy and science are distinctive disciplines. Also, in order to make of him a historicist philosopher of the sort he would commend, Rorty must truncate Dewey's notion of experience by ignoring "the continuity of the organs, needs and basic impulses of the human creature with his animal forbears."

Rorty calls this revised Dewey his "hypothetical Dewey." The clearest description of this figure is found in Rorty's essay, "Dewey between Hegel and Darwin."[48] By stressing Hegel's historicism, rather than his idealism, and Darwin's positivism, rather than vitalism, Rorty produces a Dewey who navigates now between the extremes of "historicism" and "scientism" rather than those of idealism and empiricism.

In order for Rorty to read Dewey as a historicist in the sense of one who holds "that . . . no image of the world projected by language is more or less representative of the world than any other,"[49] he must get rid of any hint of Dewey's scientistic belief that "natural science is privileged over other areas of culture."[50] This requires that one find a way of attributing to the "hypothetical Dewey" a belief that, for example, relativizes Darwin's view as one among numerous images of the world.

Though Dewey might well wish to hold out for some naturalistic grounding for linguistic behavior, Rorty's belief in the contemporary importance of Kuhn's and Feyerabend's historicizing of science would lead him to think that there is little reason to uphold Deweyan naturalism. In fact, one might say that the relations between democracy and science ought involve a democratization of science which leads to its historicization as well. This revision may seem severe. But Rorty might well reply to the criticism that he "has abandoned Dewey's science and therewith Dewey's naive faith in the mutual support of science and democracy,"[51] that so might Dewey *redivivus* were he writing today.

What makes this hypothetical Dewey an effective thinker is the manner in which Rorty has drawn out the implications of the shift from a metaphorics of "experience" to one of "language." For, as long as Dewey was worrying about the character of experience and its relationship to "nature," he was tempted to spend his energies seeking a metaphysical grounding for his thought. Translating Dewey's thinking into linguistic terminology from the language of experience subverts that temptation and directs fellow pragmatists toward the concrete problems Dewey wished to address.

Rorty's Dewey is a surgically revised specimen to be sure. But this reading of Dewey, though radical, is certainly consistent with Rorty's wish to make pragmatism relevant to a new intellectual environment. Further, I don't see that we have any more reason to complain about Rorty's revised Dewey than to complain about James' strong misreading of Peirce. James' revision of Peirce led the latter to recoil in horror and adopt a new name for the movement he originated. This paroxysm effectively produced the two viable streams of pragmatism which have come to define the movement for most of us.

Rorty is not seeking a new theory of pragmatism. He believes theorizing to be passé. There are no new *ideas* per se. Culture is always stagnating at the upper end. There are, however, novel metaphors and practices possible. We do not need metaphysical or epistemological theories; we need sensitivity to novel possibilities of a practical social or institutional nature.

How do we come by these new possibilities? Though it is not for the philosopher to create them necessarily, she may well be called upon to "broker" them.[52] Often coming late to the conversation, the philosopher must mediate, evaluate, facilitate, in such manner as to promote the acceptance of novel possibilities. This is the motivation for Rorty's strong misreading of Dewey. To win the mantle of the Prince of Pragmatists he must shift the ground. We may argue whether Rorty is standing on Dewey's shoulders or stepping on his toes, but we should see that he is perfectly consistent in his giving Dewey a principal role to play in the self-justifying narrative he claims each of us has a right to create.

It is Rorty's vision of the use, the cash value, of intellectual history that allows him to escape the strictures alluded to above. For only if we view him from the perspective of the doxographer or the historical reconstructionist would such criticisms count. But that is the wrong way to look at Rorty. We should in fact view him as a poetic narrativist . . . who has taken Harold Bloom's *Anxiety of Influence* to heart.

Most of Rorty's critics have stressed the idiosyncrasy of his thought at the expense of its very real continuity with the pragmatic tradition. I think this is a mistake. Insofar as Rorty is a strong poet and (verbal) revolutionary, he is part of a continuing American revolution the nature of which has more often than not been seriously misunderstood. The most obvious reasons for this misunderstanding are, first, that many of our more insightful thinkers of the last two generations abandoned American thought and began whoring after the false gods of England, France and Germany and, second, that even those who stayed down on the farm were urged to accept European problematics as the pivots around which to spin their interpretations of indigenous American thinkers. By virtue of having avoided, for the most part, both of these mistakes, Rorty may be far closer to the mainstream American tradition than his critics have allowed.

Consider, for example, Rorty's "postphilosophical" attitude. He believes that "philosophy is not a natural kind"[53] and thus cannot be one of the transcendental interests that define a Kantian or a Whiteheadian or a Habermasian "cultural milieu." Rorty wants to give up the *geisteswissenschaften* approach to philosophical history and interpretation for a more free-wheeling mode of culture criticism. This desire is a perfectly feasible reflection of his own enculturation into the thinking of Jonathan Edwards, Ralph Emerson, William James, John Dewey. *These* great dead thinkers have an ambiguous association with that professionalized discipline of philosophy which thrived in the German context.

Edwards, perhaps the greatest native intellect of our country, was a preacher; Emerson an essayist; James a psychologist from a literary family; Peirce a philosopher, yes, but without portfolio. Dewey (on his nonsystematic, Jamesian side) was a sociocultural handyman, a *bricoleur*, ready with practical and technical advices on education, politics, and art. Why shouldn't Rorty think of philosophy as he does? Most of the other American greats have done so! Rorty is looking at philosophy and seeing the post-Kantian *Fach* on the one hand, and condemning it in favor of the thinker-at-large.[54] Surely there can't be anything un-American about this.

Viewed in this context, Rorty seems far less a prophet crying in the wilderness than a lead-tenor backed by an (often involuntary) chorus of reasonably harmonious voices. Rorty's is, indeed, a *new* pragmatism, as we shall see. But, as Rorty himself continues to insist, this pragmatism is a plausible consequence of its parent tradition.

Rorty's New Pragmatism draws upon the so-called linguistic turn, the first phase of which was the substitution of language for mind or consciousness as the tertium quid between self and world. Its second phase involved the dismissal of language as a *medium* between self and world by virtue of the recognition that both are lacking in essential core characteristics and are rather products of strings of sentences focused by desires and beliefs, which Rorty terms "vocabularies."

Language is analogous to a set of tools rather than a jigsaw puzzle and the contrast between the tool model and the puzzle model compares with the distinction between "the will to power" and "the will to truth." This is the distinction between "creation" and "representation." The tool metaphor stresses the transitive character of linguistic behavior, denying that language could be somehow sufficient apart from its transformative uses. Thus language is rendered contingent in the following way: Truth is a property of sentences; sentences depend upon vocabularies; vocabularies are drawn from languages; languages are human creations. Therefore, truth is a human creation.

Denying that the mind intervenes between self and world, as did Ryle, or that language intervenes between self and world, as does Davidson, moves us away from both representational and expressivist theories of mind and language. According to Davidson, "we should give up the attempt to illuminate how we communicate by appeal to conventions."[55] To ask about the relation of language to the rest of things is to ask a strictly causal question. But a causal question which presumes that language is without intrinsic purpose cannot but lead to a charting of contingencies much as Mendelian evolutionary theory charts in a mechanistic manner the consequences of accidental mutations.

> For all we know, or should care, Aristotle's metaphorical use of *ousia*, Saint Paul's metaphorical use of *agapē*, and Newton's metaphorical use of *gravitas*, were the results of cosmic rays scrambling the fine structure of some crucial neurons in their respective brains. Or, more plausibly, they were the result of some odd episodes in infancy—some obsessional kinks left in these brains by idiosyncratic traumata. It hardly matters how the trick was done. The results were marvelous. There had never been such things before.[56]

Rorty does not deny that "the world" is out there in the sense that "most things in space and time are effects of causes which do not include human mental states."[57] But truth is not "out there" (including, of course, the truth of the sentence, "Most things in space and time . . .") because truth is a quality of our descriptions, our sentences. These sentences are strictly ours and cannot, therefore, be external to us. For "to say that truth is not out there is simply to say that where there are no sentences there is no truth, that sentences are elements of human languages, and that human languages are human creations."[58]

Again we see the Kantian residue that plagues Rorty. The "world" as an extralinguistic datum is nothing more or less than the Kantian *ding an sich*. Rorty is willing to use Dewey's notion of "funded experience" to refer to the cash value of the notion of the world, but "as soon as we start thinking of 'the world' as atoms and the void, or sense data and awareness of them . . . we are . . . well within some particular theory about how the world is."[59]

In this nonrepresentational, nonexpressivist theory of language the distinction between literal and metaphorical is now characterized as one between "familiar and unfamiliar uses of noises and marks."[60] Metaphors are new ways of speaking which produce an effect without in the strict sense having a meaning. If accepted, these new ways of speaking can become candidates for literal terms. Dead metaphors are allowed to serve in truth functional sentences.

The reductionist view of metaphors disciplines them by recourse to the literal. The expansionist view holds them to be mysterious sources of inner meaning. Rorty's basically Davidsonian view of language[61] is neither reductionist (there are no reductive definitions of "truth" or "reference") nor expansionist (there is no Heideggerian "language speaks man"). The instrumentalist, causal view of Davidson and Rorty has different consequences: The poet offers metaphorical redescriptions which depend upon the desire to escape being merely a replica of other selves. The strong poet is more than the passive channel through which the muse extrudes novel metaphors. The poet, as well as the revolutionary, depends upon the activity of self-assertion. Philosophy begins in poetry which itself is born of self-assertion. In the beginning was . . . *die Tat*. This is the essence of Rorty's romanticized pragmatism.

"The claim that the world splits itself up, on its own initiative, into sentence-shaped chunks called 'facts'"[62] has no basis. It is contextualized by a vocabulary which permits the formulation of that sentence. And, as "the world does not tell us what language-games to play,"[63] we have no grounds for claiming this sentence about the world to be "true" or "false."

Clearly, there are difficulties here. The distinction between sentences and vocabularies, like all Rortyan distinctions, is not backed up by claims to essential characteristics about language or the world. One can only distinguish between sentences and vocabularies within a vocabulary that permits that distinction. Further, since Rorty's vocabulary only allows that dichotomy on heuristic, pragmatic grounds, the distinction is a difficult one to maintain. At one extreme we have isolated sentences such as "The butler did it," the truth of which the world can help us decide. At the other extreme lie axiomatic systems (Euclidean and non-Euclidean geometries, for example) which, as criteria-governed systems, are neither isolated sentences nor, strictly speaking, vocabularies, and so must be assessed on different grounds.

Most theories, including almost all scientific theories, are vocabularies in Rorty's sense and are subject to stylistic shifts and changes associated with the nonrational vagaries of cultural change. Axiomatic systems, on the other hand, may be a different case. The development of non-Euclidean systems, and the subsequent employment of at least one of these within physical theories, seems to suggest a different sort of development than merely a vocabulary shift. The movement from Aristotle to Newton to Einstein may jibe with Rorty's ideas about changing vocabularies,[64] but the actual resort to Riemannian geometry to shore up one aspect of Einstein's interpretation of the curvature of space may be a different matter.

This issue concerns the distinction between "reasons" and "causes."

> Within a language game, within a set of agreements about what is possible and important, we can usefully distinguish reasons for belief from causes for belief which are not reasons. . . . There is, to be sure, no neat way to draw the line between persuasion and force, and therefore no neat way to draw a line between a cause of changed belief which was also a reason and one which was a "mere" cause. But the distinction is no fuzzier than most.[65]

The realm outside a language game, however, is a realm of causes, not reasons. Thus the shift from one vocabulary to another is irrational and the new metaphors that replace the old "are causes, but not reasons, for changes of belief."[66]

The contingency of language entails and encourages the contingency of self. This claim is supported by Rorty's Bad Kant *mythos*. Kant raised the aesthetic to the level of disciplinary consciousness, setting limits to aesthetic genius in order to make greater room for the categorical imperative and moral consensus. But he unwittingly gave support to the Romantic attempt to divinize the inwardness of the creative self.

In an odd, oblique manner Sigmund Freud supports efforts to rescue the aesthetic sensibility. By de-universalizing the moral sense, "making it as idiosyncratic as the poet's inventions,"[67] he places it on a par with the aesthetic sensibility. Thus Rorty's "contingent self" is the self-as-poet recognizing, in the wake of Freud's democratizing of genius through the recognition of a creative unconscious in all human beings, the need to redescribe himself "in terms which are, if only marginally, his own."[68]

Rorty's New Pragmatism is a function of his opting for the literary, Jamesian Dewey over the scientific, Peirceian Dewey. That choice leads him further to denature Dewey by appeal to "language" over "experience" as the central focus of philosophical reflection. The final step toward his version of pragmatism is taken by distinguishing language as a medium of expression from language as a "tool," and favoring the latter. I believe that the resultant causal theory of language, refined in the furnaces of Donald Davidson, still has James and Dewey as its inspiration, and still addresses the pluralism of principles and practices in the problem-oriented manner which has defined American philosophy from its beginnings.

KEEPING PRAGMATISM PURE

In an essay entitled "Keeping Philosophy Pure,"[69] Rorty argues against the need to maintain the "purity" of philosophy in any of its principal senses, either as a synoptic vision, as an academic discipline, or as an enterprise which studies "definite and permanent problems." Denying the necessity to keep philosophy pure is a function of Rorty's nominalistic rejection of its disciplinary status as a natural kind.

By denying to philosophy its traditional forms of purity, Rorty has in effect suggested the means of providing pragmatism a purity it has never really owned. It is Rorty's nominalism that serves as the purifying agent. A proper understanding of that nominalism will move us a long way in the direction of understanding his purified pragmatism.

Just as it was necessary to poetize Rorty's historicism, so we shall have to understand his nominalism as a tropic rather than a metaphysical device.[70] For in saying that he is a nominalist he is not presupposing any philosophical arguments, he is only trying to prevent his attempts at generalizations from being taken as essentialist. Thus he insists not only upon the freedom to "flit back and forth between playing up the similarities and playing up the differences,"[71] but wishes to be able to highlight similarities and differences in alternative manners in different contexts.

Rorty's nominalism is not based on a conviction that universals do not exist, or that there are no abstract entities, or that there are no such things as nonindividuals. Though he may implicitly believe all these things, his is essentially a linguistic nominalism which makes at least the following important claims: (1) There are no nonlinguistic entities (save pain and causality); (2) language, as the repository of all descriptions, is contingent upon use; and (3) "meaning" is what is produced by using words in familiar manners. Thus an implication of Rorty's nominalism is that the metaphorical/literal distinction is (à la Davidson) a distinction between familiar and unfamiliar noises. One simply employs languages to describe. Where argument is unsuccessful, one provides narratives.

It is easy enough to believe that, since Rorty is both a nominalist and a materialist, it is his materialist sentiments that lead to his nominalist stance. But, I take it, the two have little to do with one another. Indeed, one is tempted to say that it is Rorty's interest in the strong poet and prophetic revolutionary as models for philosophical change that is the real motor of his nominalist convictions. For it is difficult, apart from biases derived from an overconcern with the origins of the nominalist-realist disputes, to say whether materialist science or existential poetics has been the most fruitful sphere of nominalist activity in recent times. It will be interesting, then, and most productive, to investigate the strange alliance of nominalism, materialism, and poetic sentiment in Rorty's thinking.

Rorty, ever considerate of any potential expositor, and ever responsive to his strongest critics, has clarified this important alliance in an essay entitled "Texts and Lumps."[72] Here he attacks the problem of the relations of science and poetry (the endeavors which contest for the soul of the pragmatist) by distinguishing between "texts" and "lumps." This is "a division which corresponds roughly to things made and things found."[73] The distinction between things made and things found is itself roughly equivalent to that between interpretations and facts. Thus the fact/interpretation spectrum may be overlaid on the distinction between science and literary criticism in such a way as to elide any real division. Science concerns itself with lumps and literary criticism with texts. Borderline cases include nonlinguistic artifacts such as an arrowhead or stone axe, on the one hand, and discarded or useless waste products such as flattened tin cans or wadded-up plastic bags, on the other.

The character of texts may be encountered at the lowest level in terms of the mere graphic or phonetic features or, at the most general level, in terms of the role of the text in the larger contexts of one's personal or political existence. Thus a copy of the Bill of Rights may be construed typologically, or as a document that has rendered the search of my house by the police an illegal act. At one end of the scale, lumps are encountered as mere sense data and, at the other, as the larger interpretative contexts beyond the science which investigates and theorizes about lumps of that sort. Thus, I may move from sensing the color, texture, or temperature of sand, to the study of the analysis of the structure of a silicon crystal, and finally to a consideration of the consequences of the fact that silicon constitutes more than one fourth of the earth's crust. Given the distinction between texts and lumps, one can say that "the *only* interesting difference between (them) is that we know how to form and defend hypotheses about the author's intentions in the one case but not in the other."[74]

This reverses one common interpretation of the relations of science and poetry since, on this view, we can come to know texts in a way that we shall never know lumps. Rorty accuses realist scientists of a "primitive animism" which leads them to try to have the same knowledge of scientific objects as is available to the *Geisteswissenschaften*. It is as if a ghost of the notion of the Will of God served to undergird the "intentionality" of natural objects. The scientist seeks the God's-eye view which envisions things as they are in themselves.

One might say, of course, that the distinction between texts and lumps is enough to make for more of a division between science and literary criticism than Rorty admits. For, on the one hand, only human beings, as authors of texts, have *insides*. That is pretty significant, and would seem to privilege the human over the rest of nature. On the other hand, the status of this insidedness often seems to be called into question by Rorty's appeal to physical determinism.

Rorty's pragmatism has a nominal ontology. We begin with a fundamental dualism: what there is divides into the linguistic and the nonlinguistic. The nonlinguistic is privileged with respect to the linguistic in the sense that it serves as the transcendental condition of receptivity stimulating the spontaneity of beliefs, theories, and so forth. This spontaneity is characterized as so many "ways of putting the causal forces of the universe to work for us."[75]

Rorty wishes to follow Davidson in claiming that, while explanation is always under a description, causation is not. But if Rorty really does (as he says that he does) agree "that there is such a thing as brute physical resistance—the pressure of light rays on Galileo's eyeball, or of the stone on Dr. Johnson's boot,"[76] what is the exact status of the propositions characterizing this belief? Do they not constitute an interpretation? Are they not conventional "facts" in Rorty's sense?

This would seem to follow from the assumption that "the only way to get a noninstitutional [that is, nonconventional] fact would be to find a language for describing an object which was as little ours, and as much the object's own, as the object's causal powers."[77] But Rorty terms this a "fantasy," and concludes that the inability to discover a noninstitutional fact will throw us back on the character of the conventions that contextualize facts. The real distinction, then, is between those institutions in which diversity and controversy reigns and those in which there is, now and again, a relative stability of interpretation.

But if the notion of getting a noninstitutional fact is a fantasy, what about the mere claim that such exists? Are we to say that in the locution, "the object's causal powers," it is the word "object" which is under a description (alternative descriptions = "event," "actual occasion") and not the locution "causal powers"? Rorty obviously believes we have more interpretative leeway with regard to objects than we do when dealing with causation.

> To say that we must have respect for facts is just to say that we must, if we are to play a certain language game, play by the rules. To say that we must have respect for unmediated causal forces is pointless. It is like saying the blank must have respect for the impressed die. The blank has no choice, nor do we.[78]

Does the attempt to collapse the distinction between facts and interpretations while allowing for extralinguistic desiderata leave us with an "I know not what" or *Ding an Sich*? One must believe so since Rorty includes among the nonlinguistic desiderata more than merely loaded terms such as "unmediated causal forces"; he also allows an *over*loaded locution—namely, "the ability to feel pain." This ability "is what is important . . . differences in vocabulary are much less important."[79]

Is there no continuity between causal powers and the possible painful effects as extralinguistic desiderata and notions such as "cru-

elty" and "humiliation" which are under a description? Rorty characterizes humiliation as "that special sort of pain which the brutes do not
share with the humans."[80] He is certainly free to say that his use of the
word "humiliation" to describe a sort of pain is a way of putting the
causal forces of the universe to work for him. But in so doing he seems
to have provided "nonlinguistic brutality" the status of a fact.

If causality is not under a description, but "cruelty" is and if, as we
must assume, the nonlinguistic ability to feel pain is not under a
description but the ability to be humiliated is, then what has one done
by moving between pain and a special sort of pain (humiliation) and
between causality and that special sort of causal action covered by the
term "cruelty"?

Rorty would reply that speaking of causality as he does is a mere
acknowledgment of the fact that causal language cuts across any number of nomological (criterion-governed) modes of discourse. In any
case, one doesn't assault the doctrine of cause. Rorty holds fast to this
bedrock physicalism even as he yields himself up to model of the poet.
And it is as *strong* poet that Rorty speaks. But when the strong poet
and revolutionary, armed against the authority of the past, set out to
destroy the Father and bring about a new age, the language of physical
causation (but not the necessity of causation) takes a back seat. We own
no univocal means of characterizing in causal terms the successes or
failures of those who determine the shape of our future. Indeed, for
Rorty "it hardly matters how the trick was done."

Rorty's distinction between lumps and texts may be clarified by
recourse to the arguments of his essay entitled "Non-Reductive
Physicalism."[81] There, Rorty espouses the Davidsonian view that physicalist and psychological (nonintentional and intentional) descriptions of
the same event may be equally satisfying. The value of this essay lies in
the patient and rigorous manner Rorty (with the aid of his sometimes
reluctant compadre, Donald Davidson) attempts to rid the relationship
of self and environs of the ghosts of representationalism.

Nonreductive physicalism is an implication of three theses implicit
in Davidson's work: (1) reasons can be causes, (2) nonsentences and
nonbeliefs have no "making true" relationship to sentences and beliefs,
and (3) metaphors are without "meaning."

To say that reasons can be causes is to say that beliefs and desires
may lead to actions. The physicalist would want to find some causal
explanation involving brain-states and nerve-muscle activities; the
"folk-psychologist" might be content with an explanation involving
beliefs and bodily activity. What goes on in the brain, involving electri-

cal activity, and what goes on in the mind, involving perception and the formulation of a belief, are two descriptions of the same process. On the view of the nonreductive physicalist, "the difference between mind and body—between reasons and causes—is, thus, no more mysterious than, e.g., the relation between a macro-structural and a micro-structural description of a table."[82]

Now if the physicalist is one who claims that every event can be described in microphysical terms, a *reductive* physicalist in the strong sense is one who wants to claim that "X's are nothing but Y's." The problem is that language intervenes and the relation between X's and Y's turns out to be a relation between two descriptions. And, if "to be an X is, roughly, to be signified by the set of true sentences which contain the term 'X' essentially,"[83] then to demonstrate that there are no X's and thus that X's are nothing but Y's, the reductive physicalist would have to show that there are no such sentences or that there is no longer any need to talk about X's now that we have begun to talk about Y's.

Rorty believes that there may be a fading away of X-talk, not directly by virtue of discovery, theory, or invention, but by a kind of natural attrition. After centuries of using the language of secular culture we may give up God-talk, just as we have given up Aristotelian language centuries after the Newtonian revolution.

This first thesis continues the argument whose *locus classicus* is to be found in *Philosophy and the Mirror of Nature*. In an oft-quoted section of that work we find Rorty claiming that, once the distinction between normal and abnormal discourse is separated from the distinction between science and nonscience, a good humanist can comfortably assert that

> every speech, thought, theory, poem, composition, and philosophy will turn out to be completely predictable in purely naturalistic terms. Some atoms-and-the-void account of micro-processes within individual human beings will permit the prediction of every sound or inscription which will ever be uttered. There are no ghosts.
>
> Nobody will be able to predict his own actions, thoughts, theories, poems, etc., before deciding upon them or inventing them. (This is not an interesting remark about the odd nature of human beings, but rather a trivial consequence of what it means to "decide" or "invent.") So no hope (or danger) exists that cognition of oneself as *en-soi* will cause one to cease to exist *pour-soi*.[84]

The nonreductive view is guaranteed by the incommensurability of discourses. But though there is incommensurability among discourses, there is not incompatibility. The main point, however, lies not in the issue of the compatibility of discourses, but in the meanings of "decide" and "invent."

I think I understand Rorty's point here. He is saying that, properly understood, atoms-and-the-void descriptions of deciding or inventing are not perniciously reductive. Still, two descriptions (an intentional and a nonintentional) may be compatible without both of them being deemed *relevant* or *interesting*. Given the proximity of the physicalist to questions of material and efficient causation, what is to prevent us, once physiology is able to predict utterances on the basis of brain-states, from no longer being interested in the folk-psychology or the language of intentionality associated with deciding and inventing? What if we no longer want to use the language of creativity? Or, what if, motivated by moral abhorrence at the robotic mentality of scientists, we wish to be obscurantists who hide out within the interstices of poetic or theological discourses? This question raises the issue of what we might hope for the future of a pragmatic society which begins to "worry less about having general principles which justify our procedures."[85]

At the very least this raises the question of the status of science in a way that Rorty seldom discusses it. Surely, at least part of Peirce's and Dewey's approval of scientific methods of inquiry lay in the recognition of pragmatic successes accorded science that seem not to obtain with respect to other areas of inquiry.

An easy argument for science consists in the fact that it has as its putative subject matter, "causality." For even if it deals with that subject always under some sort of description, causal accounts often do have cash-value in terms of prediction and control. By virtue of its focus upon causality, science gains in pragmatic import.

The argument for nonscientific, humanistic genres such as literature and literary criticism is that they too have a special nonlinguistic subject matter—namely, "pain." As we shall see, it is the poet and novelist who can sensitize us to the existence of pain and humiliation. The pragmatic import of literary and poetic discourses is guaranteed by that fact.

It is an open question, of course, as to whether one could say that science is more or less successful with respect to its selected subject matter than is literature. Thus, both the Peircean and the Jamesian, the scientific and literary, strands of pragmatism may have valuable contributions to make to human welfare. I see no reason why one should prefer one strand above the other and it seems, therefore, that we should hope that scientific and literary pragmatisms will progress pari passu without the need for mutual reductions.

The question whether, for example, excessive scientism is a serious threat is a political question which deals with the issue of the social and political context within which healthy relationships between science and nonscience can be maintained. The question whether excessive aestheticism might distort our understanding of, and sensitivity to, pain is also a political question.

The second Davidsonian thesis undergirding nonreductive physicalism is the belief that sentences or beliefs cannot be made true by things in the world. The attempt to reduce X's to Y's involves the employment of discourses which, in the specific sense which reduction would require, are incommensurable. So there can be no demonstration that X's are nothing but Y's without an appeal to some extralinguistic entities.

But the world and its inventory cannot be articulated extralinguistically, so there is nothing "out there" that could serve to make sentences or beliefs true. The world is already a sentence- and/or belief-set. As Rorty indicates in his essay "The World Well Lost," what philosophers, scientists, and the common person alike call "the world" must be "either the purely vacuous notion of the ineffable cause of sense and goal of intellect, or else a name for the objects that inquiry at the moment is leaving alone: those planks in the boat that at the moment are not being moved about."[86] Since the world can't make sentences or beliefs true, truth is an intralinguistic issue. And we are free to use languages for a variety of purposes—theological, scientific, ethical, poetic, philosophic.

Davidson's third thesis concerns the meaninglessness of metaphors. Metaphors are "unfamiliar noises." They are the revolutionaries which motor the shifts from an old to a new language game. In the truest sense, a metaphor is a rule-breaking utterance which, by failing to conform to the language game within which it is putatively functioning, brings about the movement to a novel game. Wit and genius are functions of the ability to utter unfamiliar noises in such a way as to lead to a reweaving of beliefs and desires.

The striking aspect of this view of metaphors is, on the one hand, how simple and direct it is, and on the other, how it manages to give fundamental support to the pragmatists' desire to recognize the plurality of languages. This understanding of metaphors not only allows for rich varieties of language, it also undercuts any reductionist tendencies by making metaphor the root of language and the literal. The reductive physicalist is a victim of "the myth of the literal." The belief that literal language is something intimately associated with the world rather than merely a set of dead metaphors is, according to Davidson and Rorty, unproductive.

The implications of these three theses together are rather dramatic. First, the existence of a variety of languages irreducible to one another entails the consequence that there is no privileged vision of the world from which one can define elements causally related to sentences and beliefs. There may be no disciplining of beliefs based on extralinguistic, physical stimuli. This implication applies not only to the world, but to the self as well. For Rorty it is not only the world, but the self, also, that is "well lost."

The consequences of Rorty's nominalist understanding of the self are most clearly seen in his discussion of the changed relationship of self and world presumed by the new pragmatism. As we discussed above, Dewey's organic naturalism had supposed the self to be an organism in transactional relations with its environment which, at its most sophisticated level, would be constituted principally by its own bodily states and other high-level organisms. Rorty's shift from experience to language changes the self from an experiencing organism to a being defined by sentential attitudes. Further, as we shall see, Rorty's nominalism requires that this self not be a "thing" with attitudes, but simply the set of attitudes themselves.

It does not necessarily follow that because the self is a set of sentential attitudes it is thereby centerless. All one needs for a focus or center is a set of relatively intransigent core beliefs. But Rorty's nominalism will not allow even that, for he wishes to elide the distinction between necessary and contingent beliefs. With Quine, Rorty claims that there is no argument establishing a real difference between dispensable and indispensable beliefs. Some beliefs are less easily given up than others, but all are finally contingent.

The beliefs forming the self are, of course, not representations but rules for action. The relationship of self and world is not a picturing relation, but an interactive one in which language is a set of tools for making one's way in the world. The inventory of sentential attitudes, along with their present priorities, may change with alterations in the character of the world one encounters. The self is a centerless web of beliefs and desires which are continually changing through a process of reweaving. This reweaving process takes place through *perception, inference*, and *metaphor*.[87]

First impressions are perceptions and we may be led by subsequent perceptions to alter our initial beliefs. If I see an enemy performing a truly charitable act, I might be led to alter my opinion of him. Juxtaposing two beliefs may lead to an inference that forces a reweaving of one's sentential attitudes. For example, to paraphrase Josiah Royce's familiar example, a statement made by one party ("The first person Father Stevens ever confessed was a murderer") conjoined with an assertion made independently by a second party ("John was the first person Father ever confessed") can lead, via inference, to a rapid reweaving of one's beliefs about John.

The most dramatic and revolutionary manner which enables one to reweave the pattern of beliefs and desires constituting the self is through the use of metaphors. Certain uses of metaphor are paradoxical statements for which one might wish to give arguments. Consider Russell's "The author of *Waverly* is Scott." It would be initially paradoxical to turn the sentence around and say "The author of Scott is *Waverly*." One might argue, however, that much of our understanding of Walter Scott as author (the Scott at issue in the first sentence) comes from reading the Waverly novels. His status, his fame, his overall historical presence, are functions of his works as read and appreciated, or perhaps, now and again, deplored. In the same manner, "The Special Theory of Relativity discovered Einstein," and "War declared England in 1939."

The shock of metaphors calls for us to reweave the patterns of our beliefs in order to take account of them, to cope with them, and to use them to cope with things about us. Successful metaphors are those kenotic locutions that pour themselves into the world, losing their unfamiliar character in the process—dying that the world might live.

Philosophy professors love to trace the history of the concept of "matter" backward to *materia* and thence to *hyle*, celebrating the scandalous fact that the root of "matter" is to be found in a word which literally means "lumber." They are equally fond of discussing the origins of the concept "cause" in the Latin "*causa*," (which is primarily a legal term) and in the Greek *aition* which has the sense of source or origin. The purpose of such discussions is to show how distant are the modern meanings of terms from their original senses. But the important point is the illustration of the manner in which so-called "literal" terms are rooted in informal metaphoric language.

There are two responses to such a discovery. The first, the Enlightenment response, is to applaud the movement from vague metaphor to the literal, technical vocabulary of philosophy and science. This response has given us the familiar "mythos to logos," "religion to philosophy" interpretations of our cultural history. A second response is to accede to the metaphorical grounding of language and either seek to refurbish old metaphors, or to create completely new ones. Heidegger's translation of Aristotle's four causes as "four occasions of indebtedness" is a perfect illustration of the strategy of refurbishment. Contrary to those, such as Heidegger, who wish to enrich language by recycling dead metaphors, it is probably better to search for novel redescriptions that do not serve the purpose of philosophic reconstruction of the past. For it is as difficult to breathe new life into a dead metaphor as to enjoy a joke whose punchline has just been explained.

Rorty's appropriation of Davidson's sense of metaphor permits a closer understanding of the role of causes and reasons in the fixation of beliefs. An unfamiliar noise can function as a *cause* for a belief. Only after the metaphor has lost its unfamiliarity and begins to be self-consciously contextualized within one's web of beliefs and desires can it be a reason. Locutions such as "unpricked ball of my breath" and "emperor of ice cream" will (we should hope) maintain their allusive status and their utterance will involve a "mentioning." Other metaphorical locutions, such as those expressed by paradoxical sentences such as "No evil can befall a good man," can be *used* as the grounds for justifying beliefs. The first sort of locution will maintain a causal character; the second achieves the status of a reason.

This nominalist, pragmatist, historicist, poetic, nonreductive physicalist view of the self receives striking elaboration in Rorty's revaluation of the Freudian notion of personality. Again following Davidson,[88] Rorty develops a vision of the upshot of Freud's influence by giving an account of Freud as New Pragmatist.

Noting that Freud saw his work as allied to the decentering projects undertaken by Copernicus and Darwin, Rorty attempts to articulate the sense of decentering that would ally Freud's work with that of those individuals who thought the earth an eccentric member of a vast system of planets and stars and its inhabitants merely one of a number of contingently developing species of animal life.

Rorty argues that Freud's act of decentering was distinct from that of Hume, who mechanized and nominalized the self and claimed that "reason is, and always ought be, a slave of the passions." In his most central utterances, Freud did not contrast the "conscious" and "unconscious" in Humean terms as "reason" and "passion"; his contribution was to note that there was as much (or as little) rationality in the unconscious as the conscious. The unconscious has a coherence permitting it to serve as a source of alternative networks of beliefs and desires which actually compete with the conscious self.

Rorty elaborates what he takes to be Davidson's arguments as follows: A self is best described as "a coherent and plausible set of beliefs and desires."[89] Irrational behavior indicates that an individual sometimes acts in ways that cannot be referenced to a single such set. The interpretation of the unconscious then is that it "can be viewed as an alternative set, inconsistent with the familiar set that we identify with consciousness, yet sufficiently coherent internally to count as a person."[90]

Normally, one would not have conversational relations with the alternative person or persons resident in one's unconscious, so the relations among the various selves are usually unrecognized. Further, unconscious beliefs may cause changes in conscious beliefs as well as determine movements or actions of the body.

The war of reason against the passions, which was celebrated as a major theme of Platonic philosophy, becomes the complex set of interactions between relatively coherent sets of beliefs and desires, more or less conscious or unconscious, competing for causal dominance. The imperative "Know thyself" now is interpreted as coming to a knowledge of that which is private, idiosyncratic. The object of self-knowledge is whatever divides the public from the private self, and the private self from all other public and private selves.

This quasi-Freudian description of the human being is far more challenging than those associated with mechanical or physical reductions of the person to mere machines or neural networks. The pragmatist can always appeal to nonreductive physicalism to show how one might continue to have compatible alternative descriptions of the person at the micro and macro levels. It is much more difficult to see how one might develop a means of accommodating alternative descriptions which account for the presence of different selves in the "same" mind-body complex.

Freud's legacy is to be found in the humanizing of both the seething forces of the id and the quasi-divine "conscience" expressed as moral preachments of the superego. Id, ego, superego are now simply means whereby Freud identifies the authors of three distinct accounts of the wealth of experiences from the past. Interpreting Freud along nominalistic lines allows us to see these competing vocabularies as "instruments for change, rather than as candidates for a correct depiction of how things are in themselves."[91]

Rorty's New Pragmatism has now been sketched in the barest outline. Baldly stated, Rorty's pragmatism is characterized by an attempt to project a nominalist bias in terms which do not privilege any ontological perspective. This means that Rorty's denial of "natural kinds," either with respect to the objects that might be said to populate the world, or the disciplinary interests that attend to such objects, is meant to offer no priority to any sort of thing, or to any perspective on things.

Nonetheless, there does appear to be some privileging with respect to our knowledge of the world. On the one hand, that we can know texts in a manner that we can never expect to know lumps does seem to suggest the priority of the humanistic over scientific ways of knowing. But Rorty's "nonreductive physicalism" promotes insofar as possible the belief in the parity of discourses. Moreover, Rorty's nominal ontology suggests that pain and causality, as the two nonlinguistic data, constitute (what shall we say?) "quasi-natural kinds." Further, the scientific and literary treatments of these subject matters constitute *Fach*-like interests.

A final characteristic of Rorty's New Pragmatism concerns the understanding of the self as a "centerless web of beliefs and desires." As we shall see in the discussions of Rorty's "methodology" in chapter 5, selves, as much as the objects perceived and understood by them, constitute "vague clusters" which any attempt to render in a univocal manner cannot but falsify or trivialize.

The senses in which the New Pragmatism differs from the old are, first, with regard to the shift from experience to language and, second, with regard to an acquired suspicion of "scientific method" deriving from the historicizing of science in the works of thinkers such as Thomas Kuhn and P. K. Feyerabend.[92] The first difference is of interest primarily to philosophers seeking an *au courant* means of engaging other philosophical views. The second, however, has some implications for politics and law. For it provides reasons for acceding to a thoroughgoing historicism not only in science but in political theory as well.

PRAGMATISM AND POLITICS

Rorty distinguishes two fundamental types of political theorist.[93] The first is the Kantian absolutist. She is the sort of theorist who speaks of "absolute rights," "essential human dignity," "human nature," "conscience," and so forth. The second is the Hegelian historicist. There are two sorts of such Hegelians. First, there are those such as Dewey and Rorty himself, who wish to dispense with any foundation for the principles defining liberal democratic society and revert solely to contingent arguments and deliberations which defend and extend these principles while critiquing the inadequacies of their application. A second group, which Rorty identifies as "communitarians," are those who accept the historicist implications of a naturalized Hegel, but who feel that the proponents of a liberal society, themselves heirs to Enlightenment absolutism, are discredited along with the foundationalist dispositions of the Enlightenment. Alasdair MacIntyre is a principal illustration of this latter position.[94]

Rorty's arguments against ahistorical senses of persons and society rehearsed thus far are sufficient to show how he would dispense with the Kantians. He is at greater pains to refute the anti-Enlightenment communitarians. He argues against three objections of the communitarians to the sort of liberalism to which he, Dewey, and (so he argues) John Rawls adhere.

The first objection is that democratic societies will not survive without an ahistorical grounding of a sense of "common good." The second is the assertion that the personality types associated with the rise of individualistic democracies are decidedly undesirable. The third objection is that Enlightenment-based liberalism is heir to a false sense of human nature—the self as rational, individualistic, and ahistorical— and that pragmatic liberalism seeks to replace this view with a historicist understanding which is presupposed but not articulated.

Rorty dismisses the criticism which calls for an ahistorical grounding by noting that even the failure of liberal democracy would not in itself argue for the need for foundations since there is no essential connection between the collapse of democratic institutions and the loss of consensual assent to transcendent ideals. Whether democracy survives, and whether human beings can get along without foundational beliefs, are two separate questions, each to be decided solely on empirical grounds.

With regard to the claim that democratic liberalism has created undesirable personality types, Rorty simply asserts that what has been gained by way of freedom and privacy is worth what has been lost. Thus Rorty does not seek to refute MacIntyre's claim that liberal culture is dominated by the Rich Aesthete, the Manager, and the Therapist,[95] he merely responds that this development ought to be welcomed "so long as *everybody* who wants to gets to be an aesthete (and, if not rich, as comfortably off as most, as rich as the Managers can manage . . .)."[96] This is the same response Rorty gives to Weber's criticisms of secularization, bureaucratization, and the "disenchantment of the world." Indeed, Rorty believes any real reenchantment of the world would be a threat. "For it is hard to be both enchanted with one version of the world and tolerant of all the others."[97]

This is somewhat puzzling. After all, Rorty does argue that the narratives we construct cannot do without heroes. Our heroes will not presumedly be the undesirable personality types Rorty acknowledges might accompany the rise of liberal democracy. It is difficult to see how telling stories of the "mighty dead" is not an attempt at world enchantment. And wouldn't it be hard to be both enchanted with one set of heroes and tolerant of all the others? I grant that the heroes of Rorty's narratives often seem rather wooden and pale. But even if there is little chance that Rorty's heroes would enchant the world at large, the point remains that he is caught at cross-purposes here and ought to consider which of the two possible ways he wishes finally to lean.

As for the third criticism of the communitarians, the view that traditional liberal democracy presupposes a discredited, Enlightenment view of human nature and, by extension, that pragmatic liberalism ought to own up to the vision of human nature presupposed by its practices, Rorty concedes that there are views of the human being that comport much better with his form of liberal democracy than others (the view, for example, that the self is a "centerless web of beliefs and desires"). Still, he wants to argue that pragmatic liberalism can get along quite well without a theory of human nature. An implication of the belief that democracy is prior to philosophy is that the communitarians' claim that political institutions are no better than the philosophical principles that ground them may be reshaped into the pragmatic claim that the philosophical ideas used to articulate liberal institutions are constructed by reflection upon those institutions. It is the institutions that justify such reflections, not the reverse. Thus, another way of saying, as Rorty does, that democracy is prior to philosophy is to say that the need for freedom takes precedence over the search for truth.

Rorty's nonconventional understanding of the relations of principles and praxis is an important aspect of his social and political thought. Far from merely inverting the relationship between principles and their practical implementation, Rorty treats principles as "reminders of practices, not supports for them."[98] In this way he is permitted to avoid articulating the relationship between his actions and his reasons for acting. In a liberal democratic society, such articulation can lead to conflict due to the fact that alternative justifications for a practice are possible. What was relatively harmonious at the level of action can lead to real ideological conflict.

Attainment of the absolutest clarity is a romantic ideal of the reasoning creature. Clarity of the logical and semantic sort is associated with univocal definition which guarantees unambiguous usage. Normally, clarity may be contrasted with the state of unarticulated ideas or feelings we call confusion, but if we are to make sense of our hyperconscious era, I think it is important to contrast clarity not only with confused or muddled ideas but with "vague"[99] notions or feelings as well.

Muddled ideas are essentially unarticulatable because potential senses of the notion cannot, for whatever reason, be sorted into meaningful units. Vague ideas, on the other hand, are richly determinable in the sense that a variety of meanings are associated with them. Leaving muddled thinking aside, we may distinguish two primary senses of vagueness.

A concept is semantically vague by virtue of its possession of a number of actual or potential interpretations. A concept is said to be pragmatically vague when a number of discrete actions are occasioned by it. The vagueness of an action is a function of the number of ways it might be rationalized. Semantic vagueness may be either "literal" or "metaphorical". Literal vagueness is the consequence of our contemporary metamentality. Notions such as "freedom" and "love" are literally vague in the sense that a number of stipulatable senses, derived from a variety of theoretical contexts, may be unpacked from the locution. Metaphorical vagueness is the sort of richness associated with the new uses of words. It is from metaphors that new meanings emerge.[100]

An implication of the above is that it is useful to distinguish between intratheoretical and intertheoretical forms of vagueness and clarity. In the first instance, terms are either stipulated or not within the context of a single theoretical context. In the second instance the putatively same locution is provided alternative stipulations by appeal to two or more theories.[101]

No one is more sensitive than is Rorty to the fact that, for the sophisticated intellectual in late modern culture, terms are almost always both semantically and pragmatically vague. That is, both with respect to the meanings of one's ideas, and the practices associated with them, vagueness reigns. There are "one to many" relations among ideas and their definitions, and "many to one" relations among practices and the ideas that are presumed to initiate or to interpret them.

It is useful to consider pragmatic and semantic versions of vagueness in terms of historical and intertheoretical varieties:[102] Historical vagueness is a complex form of pragmatic vagueness resulting from the co-presence of alternative narratives accounting for the relation of the present to the past. With regard to the subject of intellectual culture, these narratives may begin with Plato or with Kant; with respect to our political culture they may begin with Plato or the French Revolution. Historians of modern scientific culture might wish to begin with Kepler or Newton or Bacon.

There is a relation between Nietzsche's idea of active forgetting and my use of the term vagueness. One sense of active forgetting would require either a suppression or a strong misreading of any narrative which would threaten one's own creative agency. A second sense involves the foregrounding of all perspectives upon an object which establishes the truth about the object as the sum total of interpretations. In the latter sense, the burden of the past is not felt since there is no single best manner of interpreting. Thus by denying the exclusivity of a particular meaning or meanings, maintaining the sum of interpretations as a vague cluster, we can achieve the ends of active forgetting.

Intertheoretical vagueness is a type of semantic vagueness occasioned by the refusal or inability to employ a term in a single stipulated sense. Gregory Bateson discusses what I am calling intertheoretical vagueness under the rubric of "Learning III,"[103] which involves an awareness of the context of theoretical contexts leading to an experience of the parity of theories. The self as "a habit of acting in contexts and of shaping and perceiving the contexts in which [it] act[s]" is radically redefined by such experience. Ch'an or Zen Buddhism seeks the dissolution, or decentering, of the self by the employment of the *kung-an* or *koan*—a conceptual puzzle that requires the compresent entertainment of inconsistent meanings.

To the reasonably aware, reasonably well-trained philosopher, intertheoretical vagueness is a species of literal vagueness in which ambiguated concepts have a variety of stipulated senses attached to them, much as barnacles to the hull of a ship. To the squinting eye of reason these are nothing more than mutated grotesques, but to a more open gaze they are seen to be perhaps the most representative artifacts of our hyperconscious age. They are "cluster concepts."

Now, if we ask about the effects upon the acts of communication of the loss of the metaphysical comfort of a final essence and the historical comfort of a single narrative thread, the simplest response is that, under the conditions of having to operate in a context in which the principal self-descriptive and communicative vocabularies are vague, the self is *permanently ambiguated* (or, in Rorty's language, *decentered*). The entertainment of a vague notion involves the sort of self-ambiguation associated with the decentering of ideational, practical, or affective modalities of the personality. We are all little Hamlets, urged from within to substitute "and" for "or" at the crucial moment in our soliloquies.

I don't mean to suggest that this is what most of us who call ourselves intellectuals believe we are doing. It is, rather, what we perforce must do. To state the case as baldly as possible: When we assert, we often do so oxymoronically. When we *mean*, we often mean *inconsistently*. We cannot avoid asserting or meaning more than we consciously intend.

I have probably overdrawn Rorty's point in my attempt to contextualize his message concerning the relations of principles and praxis. I have done so in order to demonstrate that there is an important issue here. The refusal to articulate a presumedly strict relationship between praxis and the principles which serve as reminders of those practices is often based upon a recognition of the intransigent vagueness of both our principles and practices.

One of Rorty's more thoughtful critics, Milton Fisk, objects to Rorty's penchant for vagueness with respect to the relations of principles and praxis in this manner: "Reminders are not enough when the issue is not a uniform and unchallenged practice but recruitment to a practice in a world of conflicting practices. Reminders suppose hegemony but do not build it."[104] Fisk wants to distinguish the sort of metaphysics external to practices from that internal to practices. The latter is a properly pragmatic metaphysics which owns up to the principles involved in its commitments even while recognizing that those commitments and the practices which elicit them may change. Pragmatic metaphysics of the sort recommended by Fisk is not based upon representation or correspondence with reality. "The truth of metaphysics has to do with the validity of a practice it makes feasible."[105]

Rorty would hold the disagreement between him and Fisk to be primarily an empirical matter. Rorty's attitude toward principles suggests that settled practices do not call for justification. But the question of what is truly settled must be left open for discussion. Here Rorty flirts with bad faith. For what Rorty seems to deem settled—for example, the connection between liberalism and democracy—may not be settled after all. According to Fisk, "the liberal idea of many contending forces creating a rich social mixture on the basis of a self-interested pursuit of advantage and the democratic ideal of wide participation in social decision making irrespective of rank and riches have made an explosive pair."[106]

Fisk believes that without some sort of metaphysical constructivist apologia for liberal democracy, it will remain at best a set of practices primarily relevant to those intellectual elites who receive most comfort from them. Fisk's point is well taken. It is too easy, beginning from a desire to banish the bugbear of dogmatic metaphysical assertions, to extend one's biases to the more harmless kind of ad hoc generalizations which attempt to advertise the implications of one's admittedly contingent commitments. Rorty's methodophobia seems overly extreme, exposing him to the debilitating disease of so many would-be pure of heart—namely, *scrupulosity.*

On the other hand, one can be sympathetic with his disinclination to celebrate any theoretical commitments, especially so in the light of the mission Rorty has chosen for himself. But, given Rorty's overly fastidious distaste for theory, one can also sympathize with critics such as Fisk who claim that he should own up to the principles he believes internal to his pragmatic praxis. And though Rorty would consider such speculations concerning his thinking somewhat rude and irrelevant,[107] it would seem that, as long as we recognize that the ad hoc and ephemeral principles of nominalist pragmatism guarantee only a "metaphysics of the moment," no real harm can be done.

One may wonder why Rorty objects to generalizations of the qualified, ad hoc variety that Fisk endorses. Clarity is never completely attainable; nor would it ever, if attained, be enough. Nonetheless, it is at least a desirable goal in many situations. Indeed, Rorty's use of words like "pragmatism," "nominalism," "historicism," is much too undisciplined to reckon the virtues and limitations of his thought in the absence of some generalizing critique. That is to say, Rorty's vocabulary may not be rich enough to protect his views from being assessed in terms of individual metaphors and sentences that house them rather than as a relatively coherent whole.

But there is a deeper point here. Rorty wishes to avoid being drawn into discussions of the theoretical implications of his beliefs in order to maintain the tolerant, pluralistic character of his thinking. For example, the search for a liberal consensus on the "common good" ought go no farther than the formal claim that the co-existence of a variety of moral discourses, including at the commonsense level a variety of concrete beliefs about "human nature" and "justice," is, on the whole, a good thing.[108] A "broad intellectual tolerance," to use Whitehead's phrase, is a requisite of liberalism.

Rorty grants that one could spell out one's views and that, as a philosopher, he has a predilection to do just this. But, he would not seek any other than an implicit consensus suggested by sharing the same practices. And those shared practices alone do not suggest shared beliefs. There is a distance between practices and the reasons that we give for them. Even in the most nonpejorative sense, rationalization is likely to be in error.[109] There is too much slippage twixt the practitioner's cup and his rationalizing lip.[110]

Rorty's liberal stance requires that we maintain pluralism not only with regard to practices and to ideas which might be employed as characterizations of or justifications for those practices, but also with regard to the sorts of pairings which might be made of particular principles and practices. The chief reason for this is that semantic and pragmatic vagueness are not only socially and politically beneficial, but are unavoidable consequences of the complexity of our intellectual lives.

We should bemoan this condition only if we still believe that words are channels through which "meanings" are somehow extruded. Rorty's is a causal theory of communication. Language serves a rhetorical function. All reasons we might give for our actions, as well as all meanings we might assert as attaching to our uses of words, are rooted in the arbitrariness that the pragmatic interpretation of language as a tool, rather than a medium, requires.

I indicated at the beginning of this chapter that the aesthetic axis of American philosophy is a response to the demands of pluralism. John Rawls claims that liberal democracies are heirs to the principle of religious toleration deriving from the religious wars which followed the Reformation, and the diversity of large market economies associated with the rise of capitalism. American democracy certainly developed from these factors. Further, the peculiar sort of aesthetic pluralism associated with American thought has shaped our democracy in a distinctive manner. Thus, Rawls concludes: "As a practical political matter no general moral conception can provide the basis for a public conception of justice in a modern democratic society."[111]

Rawls' writings after *A Theory of Justice* help to clear up many of the ambiguities, and ambivalences, of his magnum opus. It is clear now that Rawls is not attempting to derive political doctrines from a theory of human nature nor is he, in Rorty's words, "attempting a transcendental deduction of American liberalism or supplying philosophical foundations for democratic institutions, but simply trying to systematize the principles and intuitions typical of American liberals."[112]

Rawl's "reflective equilibrium" of moral judgments and general principles is a continually shifting one which depends upon changes in an individual's knowledge and understanding and in the circumstances of the society. Rawl's understanding of reflective equilibrium is particularly consonant with Rorty's view of the self as a centerless web of beliefs and desires which is continually being rewoven by recourse to new perceptions, inferences, and metaphors. Indeed, such a view of the self can be seen as both cause and consequence of the pluralism of democratic societies.

There are, of course, limits to this pluralism. According to Rorty, in a Jeffersonian democracy we must avoid issues that would undermine the tolerance such a society requires. This means, of course, that some issues are simply not open for discussion and will not be tolerated. The more obvious ones are the agendas of bigots and demagogues. But the thesis that democracy is prior to philosophy, and freedom prior to truth, and that (therefore) fanaticism, not irrationality, is the chiefer evil, places the liberal in a rather silly-seeming position. Not only the strident hate-mongering prophets of the new age, but the milder, more modest seekers after truth, such as are the objectivist scientists and foundationalist philosophers, must be deemed fanatics and charged, however politely, with being (just a bit) "mad."

The priority of democracy to philosophy entails the consequence that upon encountering one who claims no qualifications for membership in, nor professes any desire to be a part of, a liberal democratic society there are no grounds for conversation or debate. To repeat a point made earlier, the liberal sees philosophical principles as generalizations from the institutions of a liberal democracy, not justifications of them. One does not question these principles without questioning the viability of democracy itself. The closest thing that one can do is to employ the method of reflective equilibrium with respect to the interplay of liberal principles and liberal praxis.

Rorty believes that there can be a number of topics which one does not discuss because there is insufficient overlap between one's liberal beliefs and the beliefs of one's interlocutor. Indeed, when Rorty claims that "not every argument need[s] to be met in the terms in which it is presented,"[113] he claims to be reiterating a basic Jeffersonian principle. Instancing Jefferson's refusal to let the Christian Scriptures provide the criteria for the evaluation of political institutions, Rorty claims that "it is not evident that [democratic institutions] are to be measured by anything more specific than the moral intuitions of the particular historical community that has created those institutions."[114]

Fortunately, the pluralism of a liberal democracy is limited only with respect to the public sphere. The view of the self as a centerless web of beliefs and desires suggests the existence of a radical variety of beliefs. Though a society of such selves will hardly be one with its center everywhere and circumference nowhere, the potential differences among individuals is likely much greater than would be the case in a society of essential selves seeking to realize their "true natures." As we shall soon see, we require a healthy private sphere to absorb much of the radical distinctiveness of the centerless selves occupying liberal democratic societies.

Were we forced to join the search for private perfection with the quest for public justice, there would perforce have to be limitations placed upon the variety of beliefs admitted into both public and private spheres. But Rorty believes that this is not necessary. He thinks liberal democracy has won for us the ability to leave the private and the public unfused. We do not look at socialization (as did Aristotle) as the use of the private sphere to prepare one for the public life of the citizen.

As Rorty has indicated, for the postmodernist bourgeois liberal, both positive laws and political principles are generalizations from the institutions of liberal democracy. The private/public distinction is a generalization from those institutions of a liberal society aimed at "letting its citizens be as privatistic, 'irrationalist,' and aestheticist as they please so long as they do it on their own time—causing no harm to others and using no resources needed by the less advantaged."[115]

Rorty's attack upon the usual manners of treating this distinction is based upon his *nominalism* and his *narrativism*. The argument is straightforward: A nominalist can find nothing either private or public to which we could give objective, essentialist definitions. The ethnocentric historicist can only appeal to the present state of wealthy, capitalistic, liberal democratic societies predicated upon individual autonomy and justice as fairness.

It is not the radical theorists but the liberal Rorty who recognizes that a central strength of the ethnocentric bourgeois liberal's inventory lies in its tools for the critique of ethnocentrism. Likewise, Rorty realizes that there is a consensus among Western liberalism to the effect that we ought to suspect consensus. The theorists narrow that consensus by seeking its essential character; they make their ethnocentrism dangerous by presuming to take an objective, universal, "God's-eye" view of things.

The pragmatic attempt to overcome the theory-practice dichotomy expressed in Peirce's notion of beliefs as "rules for action," and Dewey's understanding of ideas as tools, allows us to express the relations of private and public as two alternative spheres of praxis, one which has autonomy as the goal, and the other which aims at justice. Those, such as Dewey, Rawls, and Habermas, whose concerns are with justice offer one set of tools; those, such as Nietzsche and Heidegger, whose interests are primarily self-creation provide another set.

Rorty insists that we remain sensitive to the manner in which private self-creation can lead to cruelty. Such can occur if we seek to employ others for purposes of private gratification, or if we use more than our fair share of resources, or if the amount of time spent in self-creation excludes any exercise in the support of justice and fairness in public, or if the self we create is a dumb clod or an arrogant aesthete, insensitive to the pain and humiliation suffered by others. Alternatively, of course, it is likely that too much yielding to public need will result in a narrow, hollow, and dull personality.

Rorty addresses the problem of the appropriate balance between the private and the public spheres, in a rather oblique manner, by noting the purposes served by intellectual activities such as the reading of books. One reads books in order to extend and develop the stable, widely used vocabulary associated with both private and public purposes. Secondly, one may read in order to work out some *new* vocabulary relevant either to the private or public sphere. A private vocabulary provides answers to questions of self-creation and self-articulation; a public vocabulary answers questions about one's sensitivities and responses to other human beings. Though those who find their own perfection in service to others may combine the two, most of us require separate private and public vocabularies.

This is the essence of Rorty's "postmodernist" bourgeois liberalism. It is bourgeois by virtue of its having as its aim the "attempt to fulfill the hopes of the North Atlantic bourgeoisie."[116] It is (at least mildly) postmodernist by virtue of its anti-foundationalism, which leads Rorty to eschew (à la Lyotard) any metanarratives of the sort "which describe or predict the activities of such entities as the noumenal self, the Absolute Spirit or the Proletariat."[117]

Of course, Rorty doesn't wish to give up either narratives or metanarratives. He merely wishes to "replace both religious and philosophical accounts of a suprahistorical ground or end-of-history convergence with a historical narrative about the rise of liberal institutions and customs."[118] This narrative is one of a movement from the supposed necessity to the recognized contingency of language, morality, and social institutions. The story tells of a movement from the search for truth to the search for freedom; a movement away from the model of a scientized to that of a poetized culture.

The ideal citizen of such a utopia is a "liberal ironist." Rorty adopts Judith Shklar's definition of "liberals" as "the people who think that cruelty is the worse thing we do"[119] and defines the term "ironist" as "someone sufficiently historicist and nominalist to have abandoned the idea that [her] central beliefs and desires refer to something beyond the reach of time and chance."[120] Liberal ironists then are "people who include among [their] ungroundable desires their own hope that suffering will be diminished, that the humiliation of human beings by other human beings may cease."[121]

Rorty's "liberal utopia" is one in which the strong poet and the revolutionary are the agents of change. But change is sought not by protesting on behalf of an abstract idea of humanity but against those elements of a society which contradict its general self-image. And this protest does not take the form of *Ideologiekritik*, but of creative expressions of the imagination.

The closest Rorty comes to getting specific about political issues is in his discussions of the more "utopian" of the political thinkers such as Roberto Mangabeira Unger and Cornelius Castoriadis,[122] whose visionary politics comport well with the social meliorism of Rorty's aestheticized pragmatism. Rorty accepts the Brazilian Unger's claim that contemporary American society has become cynical and morose, and has yielded itself up to a kind of whimpering "Alexandrian" apocalypticism which flies (lamely) in the face of the expansive optimism of the newly born American spirit. We have forgotten our roots, become embarrassed by Whitman's celebratory poems, and have enrolled in what Harold Bloom has termed "The School of Resentment," founded by Heidegger, Althusser, and Foucault.

Rorty admires Unger's unabashed appeal to imagination and strength of will in order "to enlist the intellectual resources of the North Atlantic world in the service of concerns and commitments felt more keenly elsewhere."[123] He praises Castoriadis' claim that "the *only* thing that is not defined by the imaginary in human needs is an approximate number of calories per day."[124] Rorty believes, with Unger and Castoriadis, that if there is to be any significant change in politics and society, it will not be by extrapolation from past or present trends, nor will it be from a generalized critique of past or present social ills. We must engage in "describing the future in terms which the past did not use."[125]

Using "an imaginary, lightly sketched future" as one's starting point will preclude getting bogged down in argumentation. And though this attitude seems irresponsible at best, Rorty's claim is that utopian politics is the only real politics of change, since the non-utopian variety is "frozen politics" which "serve to legitimate . . . precisely the forms of social life . . . from which we desperately hope to break free."[126]

There is, of course, a direct connection between Rorty's notions of incommensurability (and the causal theory of communication that serves as its principal consequence) and his appeal to the rhetorical function of imagination in the service of political change. The situation in North Atlantic democracies is such that "normal" political science is unproductive. Business as usual will not work. A paradigm shift of the sort achieved on a grand scale by the French revolutionaries of 1789 is the model to which Rorty appeals. That he sees this shift as a change in imagination, rather than as a reasoned response to a set of unacceptable circumstances, is consistent with his view of how *any* aspect of human social or cultural life (not merely the political) changes.

I wish Rorty had included in his discussions of political theory some reflections upon the relationship between liberal democracies and their economic determinants. As I argued in the preceding chapter, the economic strand of modernity is significant in contextualizing a range of issues concerning the relationship of personality and property. Rorty's failure to treat these issues in any argumentative detail makes his reflections on political life seem somewhat detached. Viewed in the light of his endorsement of the idea that "cruelty is the worst thing we do," his programmatic interests come off as rather thinly urgent at best.

In spite of this criticism, the sheer enthusiasm with which he seconds utopian theorists such as Unger and Castoriadis might lead some of his readers to say to Rorty, and through him to the utopians whose cause he so eloquently champions, "Almost thou persuadest me . . .". For it is arguably an open question as to whether we shall better motivate ourselves by rehearsing, as does the School of Resentment, the worser of our possible futures than we shall by echoing again Whitman's words that the theme of "the great psalm of the republic" is "creative, and has vistas."

HEROES (AND VILLAINS) OF THE NEW PRAGMATISM

Rorty has got to make distinctions between the heroes and villains of his piece in order to make the narrative work. In *Philosophy and the Mirror of Nature* the good guys and bad guys were sorted into edifying and systematic thinkers. Plato, Descartes, Kant, Husserl, Russell, the early Wittgenstein, and Whitehead are systematic, while Nietzsche, Dewey, the later Wittgenstein, Heidegger, Gadamer, and Rorty are edifying thinkers.

Rorty distinguishes his contrast of edifying and systematic philosophers from the contrast of "normal" and "revolutionary" thinkers. The former distinction is in fact between two types of revolutionaries. One sort, the systematic, wishes to see his novel vocabulary institutionalized, made into the standard normal discourse. Edifiers, on the other hand, struggle against becoming a part of any tradition. Edifying thinkers recognize their merely seasonal relevance and maintain an intentionally peripheral stance with respect to the mainstream tradition. "Great systematic philosophers are constructive and offer arguments. Great edifying philosophers are reactive and offer satire, parodies, aphorisms."[127]

The type of revolutionary who wishes to replace current normal discourse with a new vocabulary is revolutionary only with respect to the current status defining that discourse. He is in agreement with his predecessors that "we must have rules." He is as fearful of anarchism as his political counterpart. In fact, for the systematic thinker, philosophical anarchism is more fundamental than the political variety. To be an-archai is to be without principles as determining sources of order since, with Aristotle, we believe that an arche is that from which a thing can be known, or that from which a thing first comes to be, or that at whose will that which is moved is moved or that which changes changes.[128]

The edifying philosopher is a philosophical anarchist who attacks the status of the current rules defining normal discourse. Moreover, he attacks a meta-rule as well—namely, the rule that rules may be exchanged only when one believes that they have been found inadequate and are to be replaced by rules which better accord with "the world." Such metaphilosophical anarchism is hard to achieve. It is difficult to "decry the very notion of having a view while avoiding having a view about having views."[129]

Rorty would like to avoid the irony of self-reference edifying philosophers subject themselves to by claiming that criticizing the self-referential inconsistency of the edifying philosopher shows "poor taste," or "a lack of tact." He thinks that the judgment when to hold someone to the moral obligation to advertise his views and when to be tactful and not discuss the matter of views at all should be based on the desire to maintain a truly conversational relationship. What conduces to conversation is to be enacted; what impedes it is to be avoided. "Edifying philosophers can never end philosophy, but they can prevent it from attaining the secure path of a science."[130]

I like this idea. One can sympathize with Rorty's desire to avoid subjecting edifying philosophers to the self-referential critique. I believe that we would all be better off without this, the sleaziest weapon in the philosopher's arsenal. But, as we shall see in the following chapter on Rorty's use of irony, it seems that Rorty himself cannot get along without this misguided missile. His use of "foundational" and "systematic" as scare words to apply to a selection of the big names in the history of philosophy (Plato, Descartes, Locke, Kant, Russell, Husserl, Whitehead) may be deemed as tactless as the attempt to assay the "views" of Wittgenstein and Heidegger.

Of equal significance is the fact that Rorty's judgments as to which thinkers are edifying and which ought be confined to the museum of philosophical oddities is—even on his own terms—highly questionable. Many of those on his hit list may be considered systematic or foundational in the Rortyan sense only if we refuse to offer them the basic courtesy of treating them as *gesprächspartneren*.

To cite the most notable example: Who really reads Plato as a foundationalist thinker? *Pace* Karl Popper and Richard Rorty, does anyone care whether Plato *seems* to have or want a system? Most read Plato, I believe quite rightly, for inspiration and the ennobling of affect, or for interesting approaches to particular questions, or (most importantly) as an ironist par excellence whose literary employment of Socrates self-consciously places limits on his own systematic ambitions.

Platonic philosophy continues to be taught to undergraduates primarily as an evocative vehicle of humanist culture, with only the vaguest of specific principles suggested as essential to his thinking. And surely the persistence of Plato depends upon such a reading. Plato's philosophy is a lure toward knowledge; Platonic eros is the desire for understanding.[131] Plato's use of Socrates as a literary device placing limits on any systematic aspirations one might read into his thinking serves much the same purpose as Nietzsche's or Wittgenstein's or Heidegger's devices for avoiding being coopted by the champions of normal discourse.

Surely, if one had to assess the single most important effect of Platonic discourse on our culture, it would be in the continued stimulation toward conversation. It is a sign of the yawning gap that all too often opens among philosophers that I, for one, am simply unable to see how *anyone* could think otherwise about the cultural role of Platonic thinking.

Again, it is precisely the *incoherence* of Descartes' mind/body dualism, not his substantive or methodological claims, that has been most philosophically stimulating. Granted Descartes' desire to "get it right" once and for all, there is perhaps no thinker more productively used

and abused by strong misreaders—from Leibniz to Samuel Beckett—
than René Descartes.

Bertrand Russell is certainly a harder case. But at least this much
can be said on behalf of Russell the Edifier: it is a peculiar kind of foundationalism that leads to the changing of one's ideas every second book.
Further, the self-assessments found in his autobiographical writings
show that he well recognized the ironies, both constitutive and dramatic, that had beset him as a philosopher.

In spite of its explicit appeal to system, Whitehead's definition of
speculative philosophy as "the endeavor to frame a coherent, logical,
necessary, system of general ideas"[132] is best read with a heavy emphasis on the sense of "endeavor." Doing so allows one to argue for anti-
foundationalism in a manner that leaves the conversation open.[133]

I believe Rorty to be somewhat tactless in his readings of many of
the philosophical greats as "systematic thinkers." Further, it seems that
Rorty's rather tendentious isogesis ("strong misreading") of Dewey's
thinking which makes of him a hero of anti-foundationalism can easily
be seen by Dewey's naturalistic disciples as at least as far off the mark in
the opposite direction.

If Rorty is correct in assuming, as he at least implicitly must, that a
responsible reading of philosophy must involve *mis*reading, the interpretations of those putative foundationalists I have just given must be
assessed on other than the grounds of doxography and historical reconstruction. And if we are asked to forbear Rorty's misreadings, he must
(if he is to strive to treat us as conversation partners) defer, at least initially, to our misreadings as well.

One can already hear Rorty's (ironic) response to the claim that
Plato or Whitehead were certainly not foundational or systematic in
the pernicious sense that he claims, and that Dewey was a great deal
more foundational than Rorty is wont to admit: "Well, in the course of
my attempt to adapt pragmatism to a changed intellectual environment, I had to pick out some heroes and some villains and these seemed
the most likely candidates."

I find nothing to condemn here *in principle*. I am willing to agree
with Rorty that whom we treat as a party to conversation and whom we
consider beyond the pale involves a moral, not an intellectual judgment. I have stretched this subject this far for two reasons: First, to highlight one of the criteria by which Rorty creates his lists of heroes and villains. Second, I have wished to show that this criterion may be applied
in ways that significantly alter the membership on Rorty's lists.

In sum, I don't believe that there is a real distinction between those involved in getting it right and those involved in getting on with it. Over and over Rorty stresses the point that readers should not be committed simply to discerning the points intended by the author, but must try to get from a given author something helpful in their tasks of self-creation. Even if one does not go quite that far in personalizing his approach to the philosophers he reads, all but the professionally purblind can appreciate the interpretative extremes that not only exist in the history of philosophy, *but actually constitute that history*. This variety constitutes philosophical activity as effectively edifying rather than systematic. The *Geisteshistorikers*, not the doxographers, have been the caretakers of the philosophic enterprise.

In fairness to Rorty, I should repeat that my carping disavowal of his particular choices of edifying heroes and foundational villains is, from his perspective, broadly beside the point. The only value in making an issue of the suitability of his particular selections is to suggest how the decision to take one thinker with utmost seriousness and treat another with lightminded finesse (an enterprise in which all intellectuals at least sometimes engage) shapes the narratives we construct. We will elaborate upon this point in our discussion of the uses of irony in the following chapter.

A second group of philosophers qualify as Rortyan heroes by virtue of their more or less direct contributions to the beliefs defining the New Pragmatism. There are those pragmatists such as James, a part of Peirce, the Jamesian Dewey, Quine, Wilfrid Sellars, Hilary Putnam, Donald Davidson, and John Rawls, who promote the main contentions of the New Pragmatism and those, often other parts of these same heroes, who stand in its path.

The general line of argument connecting the proto- neopragmatists to the New Pragmatism is focused by Rorty's claim that the epistemological tradition from Descartes confused the process of acquiring knowledge with that of the justification of knowledge claims.[134] Wilfrid Sellars' criticism of the "the myth of the given," Quine's critique of the synthetic/analytic distinction and the "'idea' idea," and Davidson's collapse of the distinction between language and world provide the appropriate resources for overcoming this confusion.

Of course, the thinking of the later Wittgenstein lies in the background of the pragmatic analysts. The early Wittgenstein, with all mystical elements excised, had influenced the positivists, but the direct influence upon American pragmatism came when Wittgenstein abandoned the attempt to see a relationship between language and the world and moved in the direction of a holism which required the assessment of the meaning of sentences by appeal to other sentences. By doing so he effectively interpreted language as a set of social conventions. It is at this point that Wittgenstein may be said to have influenced Sellars, Quine, and Davidson.

Both Sellars and Quine[135] are epistemological behaviorists. This means that each seeks to understand knowledge by appeal to the social justification for beliefs. Sellars assaults the "myth of the given." This is the view that one can justify knowledge claims on the basis of some prelinguistic, perceptual, or intuitive "given." Quine attacks the "'idea' idea," which names the belief that there is anything internal to the language user which determines the meaning of linguistic utterance.

The most direct statement of Sellars' assault on any sort of givenness is found in his claim that all awareness is "a linguistic affair."[136] Though one may believe that response to perceptual stimuli, in infants and in nonhumans, takes place apart from language, the fact remains that *awareness* requires the classification and organization of concepts in the manner of some community of language users. Only if we forget the distinction between the acquisition of knowledge and its justification can we believe that knowledge may be grounded in some pre- or nonlinguistic state of affairs.

The pragmatism of Quine is of the Peirceian variety which holds out for a naturalistic ground for knowledge claims. Quine believes that physics provides privileged access to the way of things. Physics "limns the true and ultimate structure of reality." With science defined primarily by appeal to the character of physical science, Quine believes the basic distinction between science and nonscience to parallel the distinction between the empirical and nonempirical.

Quine's rather troubling (to Rorty) naturalism aside, practically everything else Quine says qualifies him as a Rortyan hero. Accepting Peirce's view that beliefs are "habits of action," Quine is able to avoid the "'idea' idea" that has undermined epistemological investigations since Descartes. We are not looking for the nature and structure of ideas and asking after the manner of their production; instead we are examining the behavioral ramifications of beliefs.

Quine attacks the analytic/synthetic distinction by asking after the basis for claiming that some beliefs ("core beliefs") are *necessary*, while others are contingent. The idea of necessity is held to mean that there are some beliefs we simply couldn't do without. Quine approaches the question anthropologically by asking how we would come to an understanding of "necessary" and "contingent" simply through an observation of behavior. On these grounds, putatively necessary statements

such as "1 + 1 = 2" and "There have been some black dogs" will be
assessed as related to one another by virtue of the degrees of commitment individuals express with respect to these propositions. That is,
all we shall ever be able to get is some sense of the degree of tenacity
with which a particular individual holds to certain beliefs. Once we
find that the necessary/contingent, analytic/synthetic distinction is a
matter of degree, we find that appeal to social contexts to justify degrees
of tenacity is the only viable manner of investigating knowledge claims.

In his *Philosophy and the Mirror of Nature*, Rorty used Sellars and
Quine as principal heroes of the New Pragmatism, objecting only to
their residual scientism. These two figures (and we could add others,
such as Hilary Putnam[137]) leave open the possibility for the hegemony of
scientific over literary culture. Subsequently, Rorty has found Donald
Davidson "deepening and extending the lines of thought traced by
Sellars and Quine."[138] Though there is some controversy as to whether
Rorty has gotten Davidson right, the disagreement seems to be more
from the side of Davidson's disciples than from Davidson himself.[139]
We have considered the influence of Davidson in some detail in the
preceding pages. It only remains to summarize how he has deepened
and extended the thought of Quine and Sellars.

In both Quine and Sellars there is a residue of scientism. The
residue is rather large in Quine who holds that physics limns the nature
of the real. Thus in Quine there is still a ghost of representationalism to
be found in the privileged relation of physics to the external environs.
Sellars wants to avoid any word-world relationship, but he is troubled
by the skeptics' argument that we could, after all, be wrong in our
claims about the world. Sellars would like to maintain a causal, nonrepresentational view of the relations of selves to the rest of the world,
but he allows that only at "the end of inquiry" can we know that our
beliefs conform in some substantial sense to the world. This residual scientism makes philosophy dependent upon scientific advances in the
sense that, according to Rorty, "every time science lurches forward,
philosophy must redescribe the face of the whole universe."[140]

What Davidson yields, as we have already discussed, is any vestige
of the reality/appearance distinction. With this goes the "scheme/con-
tent" relation, leaving us with no strong meaning of the activity of
"making true." A significant implication of this collapse of distinctions
is that the literal/metaphorical distinction goes by the board as well.

A final member of this list of reluctant heroes is John Rawls. As we
indicated above, Rawls' later work seems to accommodate the sort of
thinking Rorty represents. On my reading, Rawls has learned some-

thing from Rorty which enables him to say what he wants to say in a more philosophically significant manner. Rawls' refusal in his later work to interpret "the original position" in transcendental terms, and his acceptance of "reflective equilibrium" in place of the application of principles characterized in accordance with some essential human nature, places the practical, political capstone on the New Pragmatism.

The systematic/edifying distinction which leads on to hermeneutics serves as the background to the development of the New Pragmatism as a movement from mind through experience to language. Those who led us up to the promised land, such as Quine and Sellars, along with those, such as Davidson and Rawls, who can be nudged into paradise (even if at the cost of losing many of their dearest disciples) are heroes in the truest sense.

A third class of heroes are those who expressly place their historicist mark upon interpretations of science and philosophy. Beginning with the early Hegel whose *Phenomenology* Rorty takes as a paradigm of historicism, the modern age has been marked by an increasing dissatisfaction with attempts to discover transcendental truths. Blumenberg's analysis of the origins of modernity discussed above is an even more consistent rendering of the historicist turn in modern thought. But the real heroes of the historicist movement are those who have argued persuasively for the historicist character of science.

Hegel's chief contribution to modern culture was that he showed how reason might be temporalized. The temporalization endorsed by the early Hegel of the *Phenomenology* was not only a move in the direction of the dominance of historicism, "the emphasis on the mortality of vocabularies,"[141] but was also a *Romantic* movement, one which both expressed the corrigibility of principles and urged that the adoption of new vocabularies by human beings and institutions was the motor of history. This is an important point because Rorty's assault upon the emptiness of the relativist's arguments is grounded in his own Romantic belief that what matters is not that there are many alternative theories floating about as candidates for belief, but that there are alternative sets of actually entertained beliefs which serve as the justifications for an individual's decisions and actions.

The birth of "the two cultures" may with some justification be attributed to Kant's diremption of the value spheres which placed ethical and aesthetic concerns alongside the concerns of scientific understanding as viable human activities. But Rorty allows that we owe to Hegel the Romantic view that what has come to be called "literary culture," by virtue of its celebration of the mortality of vocabularies and the value of creating new ones, is superior to the culture of science. Thus, "reason cunningly employed Hegel, contrary to his own intentions, to write the charter of our modern literary culture."[142]

"Pragmatism," for Rorty, names that movement which sublates Hegel's Romanticism and historicism into a single manner of thinking allowing for the desire to perfect the self by appeal to literary sources while leaving a space, the public sphere, for getting on with the practical affairs of social life. The formula lies in the pragmatist's belief that new ways of speaking will help us get what we want. And what we want, contrary to the caricatures of pragmatism, includes the self-expansion desired by the Romantic as much as the security and comfort provided by the technician and engineer.

The two cultures have now been satisfactorily assigned stations and their attendant duties. The scientists, technicians, and engineers, with the exception of those very few who are able to serve as paradigms of self-creation, are accorded the task of easing the pains of social existence; the poet and novelist are to provide new vocabularies which can serve as models of private perfection. Thus does Rorty cunningly employ Hegel, contrary to his own intentions, to write the charter of the New Pragmatism.

From Hegel it is one small step to Thomas Kuhn's "romantic philosophy of science" and Harold Bloom's "philosophy of romantic poetry."[143] We may grant that, from any but Rorty's perspective, this could appear to be one giant leap. Kuhn is one of the foremost representatives of the movement "from epistemology to hermeneutics."[144] This is the movement from the attempt to understand the relationship between thought, experience, language, and the "world," to the attempt to engage discourses in a conversational manner in order to move toward fruitful agreement or conflict. For Rorty, the difference between epistemology and hermeneutics is expressed in terms of the Kuhnian distinction between "normal" and "abnormal" discourses. In the former there is a consensus as to the meanings of principal terms and the conventions for employing them in arguments. In the latter, such conventions are brought into question and the meaning of terms is often radically shifted away from the "norm."

The issue for Rorty is one of commensuration. Elements of a given discourse are commensurable when they are "able to be brought under a set of rules which will tell us how rational agreement can be reached on what would settle the issue on every point where statements seem to conflict."[145] Hermeneutics challenges this assumption and with it the notion that there is a common ground for discourses. Kuhn's specific contribution to the shift away from epistemology toward hermeneutics is to ask "whether science, as the discovery of what is really out there in the world, differs in its patterns of argumentation from discourses for which the notion of 'correspondence to reality' seems less apposite."[146] That is, is agreement on propositions within the humanistic disciplines such as history and literary criticism sought in a manner qualitatively different from the manner agreements are sought in science?

Kuhn addressed this issue by asking whether philosophers of science could provide rules for commensurating scientific theories and answering the question, "No." The choice among scientific theories is then placed on a par with the choices among controversial commitments in any community of discourse. This led to the discussion of "normal" and "abnormal" discourses. Normal discourse is discourse in which commensuration works. This condition obtains when all, or most, contributions to the discourse are treated in accordance with conventions in place by consensus. Abnormal discourse occurs in periods of transition from one theory to another. In this transitional or "revolutionary" stage, old terms take on exotic meanings and new words are introduced.

That the normal/abnormal distinction cuts across all cultural interests simply means that there is no discipline closer to "the way things are" than any other. Thus, there is no longer any need to presume, with the Enlightenment thinkers, that the rules of science can be extended to all areas of culture to provide universal commensurability and therefore universal agreement on the way of things.

This brief summary of Kuhn is likely unnecessary because his views have become so familiar. Even his former critics have taken up many of his once controversial conclusions. It is, nonetheless, important to note the significance of Kuhn for Rorty. Rorty is very much interested in demonstrating that, not only is science no "natural kind," its claim to cultural privilege is historically contingent, and no longer seasonally relevant. Rorty's claim that "literature has now displaced religion, science, and philosophy as the presiding discipline of our culture"[147] suggests that another class of heroes will be found among the poets, novelists, and literary critics who serve that presiding discipline.

It is not only Kuhn's Romantic philosophy of science but Harold Bloom's philosophy of Romantic poetry that cancels the cultural dominance of science and establishes the reign of the culture of literature. Though Kuhn certainly acknowledges the role of individual genius in scientific revolutions, it is the scientific community in crisis, or in its "abnormal" phase, that occupies his attention. Bloom's role, at least as a hero in Rorty's narrative, is to stress the poetic and critical function of the individual creator. As I have mentioned before, Rorty has bought into Bloom's notion of "strong misreading" not only because it is a necessary consequence of his desire to pump new life into the same-old discourses of philosophers, but also because he believes that the hegemony of literature entails a press toward private self-perfection. Thus, as I said at the beginning of this work, a kind of Oedipal overcoming of the past is essential if one is to be free of the sense of belatedness, the nostalgic feeling of having come too late to the conversation to add anything more than a few sardonic smirks and world-weary sighs.

By employing strong misreadings of texts, "the critic asks neither the author nor the text about their intentions but simply beats the text into a shape which will serve his own purpose."[148] This shaping of the text is performed not only by the critic assaying the work of dead poets, but by the would-be great poets themselves who seek to break with a stultifying past through an original act of self-creation.

The practical consequence of moving from religion, science, and philosophy as presiding disciplines, to literature and literary criticism, is that novelists and poets become the real heroes of the public life. Two of the more interesting and far-reaching of Rorty's claims are, first, that the employment of literature primarily for the purposes of private recreation trivializes the impact, both actual and ideal, of the poets and novelists, and, second, that employing philosophers as guides in one's public life is futile. We are not so much guided but goaded to action and, therefore, it is whatever sensitizes us to the pain and humiliation of our fellows that best serves the public weal.

If there is a distinction to be made between poets and novelists it would be on the basis of an informal division of labor between the makers of metaphors and the creators of narratives. Each are essential for individuals in search of private perfection and for those who would become more sensitive to the pain of other people. Rorty, following Milan Kundera,[149] thinks of the novel as the proper genre of democratic society since, in the course of novelistic narratives, any number of characters lay claim upon the reader's attentions, affections, and antipathies. "The novel is the imaginary paradise of individuals . . . where everyone has the right to be understood."[150]

Rorty draws the distinction between the novelist and the philosopher, insofar as it is most relevant to the present age, as a distinction between "curiosity" and "nostalgia." Contrasting Heidegger's view of the West with that of Milan Kundera, Rorty finds Heidegger separating himself from his subject matter in such a manner as to try to cleanse himself of the defects of the history of Being.

> Heidegger is still doing the same sort of thing which Plato tried to do when he created a supersensible world from which to look down on Athens, or Augustine when he imagined a City of God from which to look down on the Dark Ages. He is opting out of the struggles of his fellow humans by making his mind its own place, his own story the only story that counts, making himself the redeemer of his time precisely by his abstention from action. . . . Whereas Plato looks down, Heidegger looks back. But both are hoping to distance themselves from, cleanse themselves of, what they are looking at.[151]

Heideggerian nostalgia involves an encapsulation of the West which makes Heidegger's story the only story worth telling. And though it is an escape into historicity rather than into eternity,[152] it is essentially the same story that Plato told.

Contrasted with this closed-shop mentality, Kundera celebrates the novelistic utopia as, in Rorty's words, "a crowd of eccentrics rejoicing in each other's eccentricities."[153] This sort of utopia is one in which "everybody has the right to be understood, but nobody has the right to rule."[154] Kundera's utopia is open-ended, involving the creation of inexhaustible possibilities.

There is no surer way of telling the good guys from the bad guys than to note that the black hats, abetted by a brooding nostalgia, see the Western project as having exhausted its possibilities and would like to see it closed down. The white hats, on the other hand, want to open up the possibilities, to ring the variations of all the themes. And when those variations are exhausted, they wish to introduce yet other thematics, other genres, other twists in the plot.

Charles Dickens is perhaps the best illustration of the novelist in Kundera's and Rorty's sense. His novels are populated not so much with heroic protagonists as with the people such as those we pass on the street (people who would be ordinary if there were any two of them alike!). Eccentrics, loveable and otherwise, overdrawn characters like "little Nell," or "little Dorrit," force us to feel empathy, often against our sense of taste. Scrooge and Marley, Carton and Darnay, the Gradgrinds, the Dorrits, become a part of our vocabulary, and function, in place of moral principles, as the media of moral evaluations. In the world influenced by the novel, "moral comparisons and judgments would be made with the help of proper names rather than general terms or general principles."[155]

The purpose of Dickens' work is to highlight the foibles of his characters in such a way as to interest us in those otherwise unremarkable people we encounter in our daily lives. In Dickens' novels we are provided models of suffering and models of sacrifice which help alleviate that suffering. Emotions are brought to the surface and serve to motivate as well as magnify the practical consequences of our moral evaluations and actions. In placing narrative above theory, curiosity over nostalgia, and proper names over moral principles, the novelist serves the cause of liberal democracy by showing us that cruelty is the worst thing we do.

Specifically with respect to the issue of pain, Rorty shows how the work of two novelists, Vladimir Nabokov and George Orwell, serve to sensitize us to the sufferings of others. The distinction between Nabokov and Orwell relevant to Rorty's argument lies in the private reference of the former and the engagement of the latter in the throes of public life. In this they differ from other novelists such as Marcel Proust, whose concern is not with cruelty but with self-creation.

"Nabokov wrote about cruelty from the inside, helping us see the way in which the private pursuit of aesthetic bliss produces cruelty. Orwell, for the most part, wrote about cruelty from the outside, from the point of view of the victims."[156] Nabokov's *Lolita* (1955) and *Pale Fire* (1962) concern "the *special* sort of cruelty of which those capable of bliss are also capable."[157] This is the sort of cruelty committed by "pitiless poets . . . who are content to turn the lives of other beings into images on a screen, while simply not noticing that these other people are suffering."[158]

The special character of Nabokov was that, as a writer concerned with the attainment of aesthetic bliss, he had little concern for human solidarity. His best works, according to Rorty, explore the questions raised by critics who find a failure to consider human solidarity a failure of art. Having identified art with a "compresence of curiosity, tenderness, kindness and ecstasy,"[159] Nabokov explores the consequences of the fact that "curiosity" adds a positive dimension to art by permitting artists to notice, among other things, the sufferings of others. He is troubled, however, by the fact that curiosity is separable from ecstasy. Not only are they separable, but the greater artist, Nabokov suspects, may be the obsessed, the *selectively* curious, the individual who is able, when the demands of art require, to ignore the suffering of his subjects. Rorty suggests that no one before Nabokov had so effectively sketched characters—Humbert Humbert of *Lolita* and *Pale Fire*'s Kinbote—who were not only moral monsters by virtue of their *incuriosity*, but geniuses as well.

Pale Fire is structured around a poem written by "the famous American poet," John Shade. The poem, which concerns the death of his daughter, is "appropriated" by Charles Kinbote after Shade's death. The majority of the novel is presented as a commentary on Shade's poem. Kinbote is "very curious indeed about everything that effects his own desires for boys or for glory. He is bored and annoyed by everything else."[160] Still, for all his self-involvement—indeed precisely *because* of it—Kinbote shows himself a better writer, and in so doing illustrates Nabokov's concern that a final union of curiosity and ecstasy may not be possible.

According to Rorty, Nabokov believes that the search for private perfection in one's art may necessarily open one to the cruelty born of both selective indifference and selective curiosity. A further consequence of this recognition of the tension between tenderness and kindness, on the one hand, and the realization of aesthetic bliss, on the other, is that Nabokov thought of those writers who consciously sought the alleviation of suffering through their art as having been thereby disposed to write mere "topical trash."

Orwell's *1984* receives an extremely sensitive analysis by Rorty; one which shows two contributions of Orwell to the liberal cause of becoming sensitive to human suffering. In *Animal Farm* and the first two-thirds of *1984*, Orwell provided "an alternative context, an alternative perspective, from which we liberals . . . could describe the political history of our century."[161] His second contribution was his description of O'Brien, who believes that "the object of torture is torture," and his persuasive suggestion that such as he are *possible* in the twentieth century. Thus Orwell "helped us formulate a pessimistic description of the political situation which forty years of experience have only confirmed."[162] Orwell showed the contingencies of our political history, both in terms of what the liberal would take to be its positive and negative possibilities. "Socialization . . . goes all the way down, and who gets to do the socializing is often a matter of who manages to kill whom first."[163]

Nabokov and Orwell, writers with different gifts and different predilections, shared the ability to sensitize readers to unnoticed cruelties in private and public. Thus, they are heroes of Rorty's liberal utopia. But there is a further use of literature besides sensitizing us to the sufferings of others and the possible cruelties of which we are capable. One can employ the act of writing as a means of furthering the search for private perfection and as a means of avoiding humiliation by insulating oneself against the threat of "forced redescription."[164]

Marcel Proust is perhaps the most fortunate example of a writer who succeeded in freeing himself from the power of others' descriptions of him.

> Proust became autonomous by explaining to himself why the others were not authorities, but simply fellow contingencies. . . . At the end of his life and his novel, by showing what time had done to these other people, Proust showed what he had done with the time he had. He had written a book, and thus created a self—the author of that book— which these people could not have predicted or even envisaged. . . . He turned other people from his judges into his fellow sufferers, and thus succeeded in creating the taste by which he judged himself.[165]

Presumably, then, we can employ Proust's novel as a model of self-description. This model is at variance with that of Nietzsche and Heidegger, who want to do the redescribing of others in such a manner as not to be themselves victimized by redescription. Proust, according to Rorty, is open to such redescription. Once autonomy has been achieved it cannot be taken away by becoming a part of someone else's description. Proust and his ilk seek beauty, not sublimity. "Beauty, depending as it does on giving shape to multiplicity, is always transitory."[166] Once new elements are added to the multiplicity, the former beauty will be destroyed. On the other hand, "to try for the sublime is to try to make a pattern out of the entire realm of *possibility*."[167] Thus to try for the sublime is not to be satisfied with merely creating the taste by which one judges oneself. It is necessary to prevent anyone else from judging one by any other standards.

The functions of literature are to be found in the provision of models of self-description which avoid humiliation and promote sensitivity to the sufferings of others. Thus literature, particularly the novel, can serve as a principal medium of a liberal democratic culture, the members of which recognize that cruelty is the worst thing we do.

A final criterion Rorty employs to select the heroes or villains of his piece involves the use of irony. Kierkegaard claimed that irony "masters the moment," and that is precisely the sense Rorty attempts to give the term. Those who employ the recognition of the corrigibility of our final vocabularies as a means of attaining private perfection, without at the same time allowing that ironic sense to undermine processes of socialization, are heroic indeed. Those, on the contrary, who take themselves too seriously, and fail to see the salvific power of the ironic sense, or who apply irony beyond the private sphere in such a manner as to humiliate others, are arch villains.

The theme of irony is so important in Rorty's thinking that we shall reserve the following chapter to a discussion of it. There we shall have occasion to consider two of the villains of Rorty's narrative—Jürgen Habermas and Michael Foucault. But the principal focus of the next chapter will be a figure who is, for Rorty, as well as many others, at once the greatest of heroes and the most heinous of villains. I refer, of course, to Martin Heidegger.

3

IRONY'S MASTER, IRONY'S SLAVE

Given the richness and complexity of Rorty's thinking, it might seem a rather profligate use of space to devote an entire chapter to the ironic character of his prose. But Rorty's shift from logical to rhetorical modes of argumentation has rendered the standard literary tropes such as metaphor and irony central to his project. Irony is particularly important because one of the primary means of classifying the thinkers Rorty engages is in terms of the presence or absence of irony in their thinking. I want to consider the sense Rorty gives to irony, and his "offensive" use of the ironic gesture, and then, in the last three sections of this chapter, I will discuss the manner Rorty employs both the seriousness and lightmindedness that irony permits to engage the thought of three thinkers important to his enterprise: Habermas, Foucault, and Heidegger.

A STRONG MISREADING OF IRONY

According to Rorty, every reflective individual has a "final vocabulary." This self-justifying vocabulary contextualizes and shores up one's beliefs and actions. A final vocabulary is constituted by words used for moral praise and blame, and for the creation of the heroes and villains of the self-narratives one constructs. The vocabulary is final in the sense that it forms the final court of appeal when accounting for one's values, choices, and actions. Since it cannot be grounded in anything more fundamental, either internal or external to the person, the vocabulary can only be justified by invoking some portion of itself.

Irony is best understood as a peculiar kind of attitude one takes up with respect to one's final vocabulary. The ironist is defined by Rorty as fulfilling three conditions:

> (1) She has radical and continuing doubts about the final vocabulary she currently uses . . . ; (2) she realizes that argument phrased in her present vocabulary can neither underwrite nor dissolve these doubts; (3) insofar as she philosophizes about her situation, she does not think that her vocabulary is closer to reality than others.[1]

The doubts that plague the ironist are the result of having been exposed to a variety of alternative vocabularies and having no sense of an extramundane reality to which vocabularies are adequate to a greater or lesser degree. She thus realizes that her final vocabulary is largely the result of having been socialized in a particular manner, and that, had she been born into a different culture, things might all have been otherwise. Final vocabularies are poetic achievements, dependent upon the cultural resources from which they are constructed and, as such, are always fragile and vulnerable. The ironist's doubts do not allow her to take herself with absolute seriousness. Since her self-description is ultimately ungrounded, that description may certainly change through comparison with other vocabularies.

Rorty describes individuals as webs of beliefs and desires. Thus, the contingency of vocabularies entails the contingency of the self. And the contingency of the self is in large measure a result of its centerlessness—that is, the absence of anything like a core. The centerless character of the self entails the view that one's current beliefs cannot be final in any other sense than that they are as far as one can currently go toward self-justification. But if beliefs change, the self changes and so self-justification by appeal to a final vocabulary not only justifies but formulates the self. Doubts about one's final vocabulary are serious *self-doubts*.

Rorty contrasts irony with unselfconscious common sense. Common sense is constituted by a set of beliefs which are not only free from doubt, but which are deemed adequate to employ as means of accounting for and assessing alternative final vocabularies. If common-sensical beliefs are called into question, then arguments may be formulated which seek to justify those beliefs by appeal to examples of applicability and scope, or which generalize the rules of the language game entailed by the beliefs, or, finally, the *rational* and *logical* move will be made and questions of *definition* will be raised.

Rorty here is indicating the likeliest source for the peculiar sort of rational argumentation associated with the Western metaphysical tradition. When Socrates chided his interlocutors for not having given a definition of "courage" or "justice," but only *examples* of these virtues, he (aided by Plato's strong arm) took a first step toward the development of a metavocabulary in terms of which all vocabularies may be assessed. The metaphysician was born.

Metaphysics is the refined extension of common sense which takes a single final vocabulary with ultimate seriousness, offering it as suitable for all individuals. Thus, the metaphysician cannot be a true ironist. On the other hand, the true ironist, since she is incompletely socialized, alienated to some degree from the common sense of her community, is insecure in her own final vocabulary. This insecurity is articulated in terms of nominalist and historicist beliefs.

An important implication of the discussion thus far is that intellectuals may either be "metaphysicians" or "ironists." If the latter, their irony is, likely, a function of their nominalism and historicism. The situation is otherwise with the nonintellectual lay public. The publicly relevant common sense of ordinary folk may be expressed either in metaphysical and objectivist or nominalist and historicist terms.

The nonintellectual can be commonsensically nonmetaphysical (that is, can be nominalist and historicist) without being an ironist. Rorty believes it possible to accept the contingency of one's commitments without feeling doubts about these commitments. The culture of the common sense nominalist and historicist "is one in which doubts about the public rhetoric of the culture are met not by Socratic requests for definitions and principles, but by Deweyan requests for concrete alternatives and programs."[2]

Rorty believes that irony should be excluded from public life. The public rhetoric of Rorty's liberal utopia would be nominalist and historicist without being ironist. Irony ought be left to the private sphere since Rorty "cannot imagine a culture which socialized its youth in such a way as to make them continually dubious about their own process of socialization."[3]

We need to pause here to take stock of what is going on. Two questions arise: First, is it the case, as Rorty claims, that irony is, by definition, denied to the metaphysician? Second, ought we deny irony to the commonsensical nominalists and historicists who comprise the ordinary citizens of liberal democracies?

Metaphysicians are those who seek reality behind mere appearances and who believe that "'reality,' if properly asked, will help us determine what our final vocabulary should be."[4] Rorty seems to think that such a project precludes irony. This is a striking claim in the face of the usual understanding of the origins of the ironic tradition.

Irony has a central role in both the philosophic and literary traditions of Anglo-European high culture. The ironic sense emerges in our tradition as a theoretical effluence, as the consequence of recognized self-reference. When Cleanth Brooks said, "irony is the most general term we have for the sort of limitations placed upon the elements of a context by the context,"[5] he may well have uttered essentially the last word on irony concerning which Socrates' "I know that I do not know" was the first.

Rorty's Grand Narrative requires him to begin well after that first word was spoken; he must find ironist theory emerging in the post-Kantian age. The Hegel of the *Phenomenology*, Nietzsche, and Heidegger are his examples. Through the process of contextualizing his thought by appeal to his predecessors rather than by appeal to truth, "the younger Hegel broke with the Plato-Kant sequence and began a tradition of ironist philosophy which has continued in Nietzsche, Heidegger, and Derrida."[6] Rorty is determined by the plot of his Grand Narrative to begin the effective history of irony with the modern age.

There is, of course, good reason to stress, against Rorty, that ironist theory began with Plato or, rather, with Socrates as the instrument of Plato. Plato makes Socrates a representative of pure reflexivity—that is to say, pure recognition of the conditions of self-reference ultimately resulting from the fact that we have an *embodied* existence. Finitude of embodiment leads to the limitations of place and space, of time and event, which foreshadow all of the discomfitures of philosophical existence.[7]

Further, Plato's employment of Socrates can be said to render the Platonic system problematic. Socrates is made to play edifier to Plato's systematic aspirations. This involves the institutionalization of doubt. If it is true, as Emerson claimed, that "Socrates and Plato are the double star which the most powerful instruments will not entirely separate,"[8] then we may be justified in treating the two as is so often done as a single figure, "Platocrates," whose thinking is permanently ironized.[9]

Full consciousness of the dilemma of coherent thought raises philosophy to an ironic plateau which early on required a redefinition of the philosophic task. By providing a context for both edifying and systematic philosophies, irony suggests the uneasy alliance of those notions which characterize all first-rate thought. Irony is the celebration of self-reference, the advertisement of contradiction. It suggests both openness and the constraints of principled thought.

Plato associated philosophy with the drive toward completeness of understanding, which he called Eros. A more general term with which to define philosophy in this mode is *deference*. Deference is an act of ecstasy which finds the locus of value in the encountered excellence. Philosophy is unqualified deference to encountered excellences. The lover of beauty is driven by an Eros which excludes him from the beauty he seeks, thus guaranteeing that the strength of Eros is a function of distance and defect. The act of valuing is a disvaluing act as well.

Rorty wishes to characterize irony solely in terms of nominalism and historicism. But there is a real sense in which so-called systematic thinkers are fully capable of employing irony in the construction and application of their systems. Indeed, as I suggested in the last chapter, certain thinkers whom Rorty classifies as "systematic" might well be construed as edifying. To do so, one must simply take seriously the manner in which they employ irony.

For example, George Santayana, protesting all the while that he is neither a metaphysician nor a systematic thinker in the traditional sense, offers his "system" to his readers with these deliciously elliptical and acutely ironic words:

> Here is one more system of philosophy. If the reader is tempted to smile, I can assure him that I smile with him, and that my system . . . differs widely in spirit and pretensions from what usually goes by that name. . . . I am merely attempting to express for the reader the principles to which he appeals when he smiles.[10]

Or consider Whitehead's profound expression of irony toward the end of his *Process and Reality*: "The chief danger to philosophy is narrowness in the selection of evidences. . . . Philosophy must not neglect the multifariousness of things. The fairies dance and Christ is nailed to the cross."[11]

Though Rorty's irony, as we shall see, is directed toward the limitations of the narratives he tells, and the "final vocabulary" those narratives entail, while Whitehead's irony is a function of the recognition of the limitations of one's grasp of philosophic evidence in the construction of systems, the chief point lies in the recognition of irony as a substantive part of the enterprise of thinking.

From Whitehead's point of view, it would be impossible to make the metaphysician's assault upon the infinite without a sense of constitutive irony. Further, Whitehead's process metaphysics depends upon the notion of "cosmic epochs"—cosmological orders defining the general character of the world which change over time and thus relativize the order and structure of things, making it necessary for the metaphysical realist to remain ironic not only about his contingent beliefs but about the contingent cosmos as well.

Rorty would want to see not just the *content* of beliefs ironized, but the character of belief itself—particularly the belief in the search for the Good, or the endeavor to frame a system of ideas which could be used to interpret every element of experience. But I see nothing to prevent us from reading Plato and Whitehead, among many other so-called metaphysical thinkers, as owning precisely that sort of doubt. One can certainly continue to search while doubting. The courage to do just this is one of the truest by-products of the ironic sense. If Plato and his progeny are shorthand for their final vocabularies, and if we are permitted the technique of strong misreading, I would claim that whatever Plato might have meant, the predominant (mis)reading of his work has been as an open-ended, edifying philosopher. And though Whitehead's disciples have demonstrated a serious failure to appreciate his irony, an ironic reading is not only possible but extremely productive.

I am not plumping for a return to the grand metaphysical tradition; on the contrary, I am sympathetic with Rorty's unquiet disdain for the systematic, objectivist, ontological thinkers and believe along with him that this sort of thinking is rightly out of fashion. My point concerns the constitutive nature of irony which, I would hold, is as important to the metaphysical thinker as to the nominalist historicist. Indeed, it appears likely that irony cannot exist without the dialectical interactions of the "nominalist" and "metaphysician."

My second question concerning Rorty's understanding of irony was whether or not, as Rorty claims, we could have a society in which the nonintellectuals were nominalists and historicists without being ironists. Rorty claims this to be possible in much the same way that atheism, once a privilege of the intellectuals, has now trickled down to the lay public. Just so, he thinks, the nominalist and historicist aspects of intellectual life could find a home among the nonintellectuals. The difficulty here is that there seems a much closer connection between nominalism and historicism and the ironic sense than Rorty believes. I find it hard to imagine a real nominalist, even of the relatively unselfconscious sort, who, if pressed, would not be found ironical as well.

Common sense is ordinarily a serious affair. There are, however, as I have argued above, many metaphysicians who share the ironic sense of the nominalists and historicists. But if common sense were converted to the historicist and nominalist perspectives, it would be hard to imagine, as Rorty suggests, that the nonintellectuals so conditioned "would see themselves as contingent through and through, without feeling any particular doubts about the contingencies they happened to be."[12]

Rorty defends private ironism by making a "firm distinction between the private and the public."[13] The language of the private sphere is the language of individual self-creation. The language of the public is the language of pain and humiliation—how to recognize them, who suffers them most, and how they might be alleviated. The historicist (read "poetic narrativist") turn releases us from the metaphysical desire for freedom from time and chance. The contingencies thus recognized are now divided among those associated with the search for self-perfection and those involving the desire for social good.

Rorty's diremption of the private and public spheres helps to shape his normative prescriptions concerning both self-actualization and common public praxis. The value of Richard Bernstein's observation that the same conditions Weber saw as threatening autonomy and freedom (secularization and the advance of instrumental rationality) Rorty sees as realizing them, depends upon the manner in which Rorty's radicalized distinction between the private and the public spheres allows him to accept the public cost of Weber's "iron cage" in order to have the rewards of autonomous self-actualization in private.[14]

Rorty claims that irony should not be made public because the suspicion it casts upon final vocabularies would frustrate the socialization process. Also, if irony were made public, any privileging of one's vocabulary at the expense of others, perfectly appropriate in private, would be the cause of humiliation. There are myriad languages of self-creation. As long as they remain private no harm is done.[15]

Rorty himself may be guilty of making irony public through his removal of the romantic masks of the authors of books aimed at sensitizing us to the pain of others. For Rorty, persons and cultures as "incarnated vocabularies" are understood through the medium of books in which the text, not the author, is the object of understanding. "We treat the names of [authors] as the names of the heroes of their own books."[16]

I confess that for me there is something a bit offensive about the manner Rorty is willing to treat the writers of books. Moreover, the offense I take when I encounter Rorty's treatment of some of my heroes (the public ones) is pertinent evidence of the manner his irony affects my relationship to the public sphere. If the relationship between the self-image of a writer and her own particular self is contingent, so, of course, is the relationship between that image and the selves of her readers. Everything now hinges upon the meaning of contingency. If we employ the jangled neuron account of self-causation, can we gird our loins and entertain, as well, the vocabulary of self-creation? Perhaps myriads of neurons will have had to have been jangled in a particular manner, or a peculiarly complex set of kinky obsessions have been present, if one is to respond to a particular writer. If so, why does Rorty bother to offer his suggestions concerning private irony and public hope?

Rorty would say the difficulty lies with those of his readers who do not always distinguish his metatheoretical remarks about the consequences of the distinction between the liberal ironist and the metaphysician, on the one hand, and his own application of this distinction to classify and interpret individual authors, on the other. But if Rorty is worried that public uses of irony may undermine the socialization process, shouldn't he be fearful that his own severely ironic treatment of the authors of books will seep into the public consciousness and undermine our political idols? There is, after all, no nonpermeable membrane protecting us from such osmosis.

One of the odder of Rorty's claims is that, while movements such as Marxism, Christianity, and utilitarianism have all served the cause of human liberty, "it is not obvious that ironism ever has."[17] I don't see how to justify this remark. We may take Socrates as the paradigmatic example of the effect of irony upon the public sphere. Socratic thinking enables us to recognize that philosophy is born with the *polis*. The *polis* served as a form of publicity which protected the private act of thinking. Thinking, always a solitary enterprise, can only be done in the *polis*. But the very protection of privacy through public institutions and practices places the thinker over against his environs. Thought can only be possible if there is critical distance. But the thought made possible by that critical distance is only thought in accordance with principles (*archai*) serving to justify that distance as the presupposition of inquiry.

Thus the poignancy of Socrates' refusal to leave Athens to avoid death. The "death" consequent upon leaving Athens was worse punishment than the death he faced within it. Outside the environs of the city-state he had no context, no public sphere, no home for himself and his *daimon*. Inside the *polis* he was free to think, but not to live; outside the city he was free to live, but no longer would he be able to think.

Clearly, Socrates sees himself as a public figure, one whose personality was shaped by his *polis*. A large part of his mission was defined by service to the *polis* and a significant element of that service was performed through the use of irony.

When my sons are grown up, I would ask you, Oh my friends, to punish them; and I would have you trouble them, as I have troubled you,
if they seem to care about riches, or anything, more than about virtue;
or if they pretend to be something when they are really nothing,—
then reprove them, as I have reproved you, for not caring about that
for which they really ought to care, and thinking they are something
when they are really nothing. And if you do this, both I and my sons
will have received justice at your hands.[18]

Socrates, who has long served as a model for the moral activity of
the philosopher, is here making an extremely ironic statement which
effectively embedded irony in the intellectual life (both private *and* public) of Western culture. He is saying to his jury, "If you will act in the
manner I have acted, a manner which has led to my death-sentence,
then I and my sons *will have received* the justice denied me at this time
and place."

This is hardly a vain plea, since that justice has been since forthcoming by virtue of the activity of the marginalized gadflies which
Socratic intellectuals have always been. One has only to see the number
of philosophers jailed during times of social unrest in Latin American
countries, countries which take quite seriously the political role of the
intellectual, to entertain the possibility that the philosopher, as ironic
critic and gadfly, has served the cause of liberty.

I believe Rorty has overstated his case. Granted the dangers to the
socialization process of an obsessively doubt-ridden common sense,
there are really no mechanisms in place, nor ought we readily wish to
erect any, which would prevent irony from seeping into the public consciousness. The socialization process has long included something of the
Socratic bias, and there is good reason to believe that in an increasingly
nominalist and historicist culture, that bias, freed now from Platonic
excesses, can serve the cause of human liberty. And though the case of
Socrates' ironized student, Alcibiades (along with his many incarna-
tions throughout history), ought give us pause, I see no reason why a
secularized, historicized, poetized culture cannot be successfully *ironized*
as well.

IRONY ON THE OFFENSIVE

In his theorizing, Rorty finds irony emergent from self-doubt. But in
his actual employment of irony, he often directs his own doubts outward in the direction of other final vocabularies. He is the ironist whose
doubts are weapons used against metaphysicians and others with

whom he takes issue. By attempting to argue for the contingency of metaphysical vocabularies, Rorty plays *eiron* to the metaphysical *alazon*.

Rorty's offensive use of irony is a function of his recognition that the ironic sense is a conjunction of two affective extremes—*seriousness* and *lightmindedness*. If one takes the ironist's comments seriously, he is able to say: "But I was only joshing!" On the other hand, accepting his comment as humorous may lead the ironist to decry his target's insensitivity. Thus the ironist on the offensive sends not one but two arrows from his bow: One, from Eros, which will enable not destroy; the other, guided by Apollo, is aimed at Achilles' heel. If one responds as if attacked, Cupid has his feelings hurt. If one invites Cupid's arrow, he discovers his mistake only when the mortal wound is opened.

Rorty, a master of irony, is aware of this characteristic of irony and uses it, as all ironists do, for purposes of attack and defense. He chooses to take seriously philosophic theories when such a response is crucial to the construction of his narratives and he takes up a lightminded stance toward them when that serves his purpose.[19]

My main purpose in the remainder of this chapter is to demonstrate the manner in which Rorty employs irony as a critical tool in his narrative constructions. Before I explicitly address this issue, however, I want to say a bit more about the nature of irony as an alliance of seriousness and lightmindedness.

Theoretical understandings of the sort most often associated with philosophic activity are inseparable from the specific intellectual prejudices which, properly ramified, permit the theoretician to be classified as this or that *kind* of thinker. Thus we have materialists, idealists, existentialists, whose various theories construe worlds intellectually inhospitable to individuals holding significantly different points of view. The paradoxes thinkers perforce confront at the very beginning of theoretical constructions must be dealt with summarily if any coherent thought is to follow. The problems of the One and the Many, being and becoming, substance and process, universality and particularity, spontaneity and determination, form and flux, are the two-headed Hydras which stand between the nascent thinker who wants to understand his world and that act of understanding which, he must believe, justifies this desire.

The pretheoretical circumstances within which a thinker finds himself are (as all but the most dogmatic and insecure of philosophic spirits would readily confess) indifferent to any final organization in terms of firm priorities. Naively, we cannot but say yes to flux, to form, to spontaneity, to causal determination, to universality, to particularity. It's not our intuitions, but the account of them, that presents us with dilemmas. Still, it is silly to deny the value of giving accounts, if for no other reason than to pay appropriate homage to yet another form of the paradox—that of self and other, of knowing and the known. We must distance ourselves through the act of accounting from the object of our account. Philosophy, which begins in the diffuse sense of wonder, reaches its maturity only by confronting those responsibilities attendant upon the acceptance of finitude, the first form of which is the recognition that bias and prejudgment form the *via dolorosa* of the philosopher who wishes to move in the direction of truth and objectivity.

The story of philosophy is less a tale of grand dialectical interactions in which the substance of one vision occasions the response of an alternative philosophic style and method, and more the account of limited vacillations between imagination and responsibility, between the recognition of the source of thinking as the sole justification of thought and the claim, tacit but firm, that philosophic sources must be legitimated by norms presumed to pattern the imaginative flux.

Were one to seek an appropriate metaphor for the tense relationship in philosophic irony between lightmindedness and seriousness, it could be found in the pairing of delirium and hysteria, between, that is to say, the uncoordinated multifariousness of the contents of reverie and the rigidly synthesized contents of systematic thought. Juxtaposed to these more generic categories, the shriveled and pale concepts of the "analytic" and the "synthetic" may be seen still to bear the marks of their origin. Between delirium and hysteria, imagination and responsibility, lightmindedness and seriousness, edification and systematic construction, the activity of thinking finds its proper range.

Of the two extremes it is hysteria that has reigned in Anglo-European philosophy and culture. Or in less paradoxical language, it is the rigid, dogmatic, literal seriousness of systematic thinking, rather than imaginative and edifying lightmindedness, that best characterizes our mode of thinking. At its ironic extreme, this dominance has permitted, for example, Adolf Eichmann his station and its duties while denying freedom to the Marquis de Sade. Responsibility realized through the implementation of procedures without exception is safer (indeed, "saner") than pure imagination unconditioned by structures. The Sades and the Eichmanns embody the extremes of the activity of thinking between which runs a line with an excluded middle. There is no still-point, no pivot, no place of equilibrium. The thinker is faced with two equally incomplete alternatives.

The message of the ironist is that philosophy must fail. For either it will be found irresponsible in its celebration of the uncoordinated particularities which are the *terminus a quo* of experiencing, or it will be charged with hysterical rigidity in its quest for objectivity and truth. The obvious rejoinder is futile: one may grant that the extremes I have characterized are seldom if ever achieved—and then only by default. This is, however, no defense against the one-sidedness of the philosophic enterprise. Attempts to balance the paradoxical extremes only obscure the fact that one of the two must be affirmed more fruitful. For the deepest truth about philosophic speculation is that at its very heart there lies a contradiction which at one and the same time defines its character and precludes the successful realization of its function. That many philosophers of note have lacked sufficient ironic sense to recognize this bespeaks the bad faith that has haunted the caretakers of the intellectual enterprise.

The refusal to take other final vocabularies seriously often leads to redescription, which threatens humiliation. This is true of Rorty himself. In two senses, it seems, he employs redescriptions in such a manner: often his "strong misreadings" are at the very least Cain-esque, if not altogether Oedipal, and his assault upon systematic, metaphysical thinkers is an aggressive refusal to read in such a manner as to avoid dismissing these thinkers as unworthy of conversation. In either case, there is the potentiality of humiliation.

The aim of Rorty's strong misreadings is to force redescriptions. Even if he claims it is persuasion he is attempting, it is the sort of persuasion aimed at the "rising generation," not, for the most part at the targets of his redescriptions.[20] If he can persuade the younger minds to view the characters who populate intellectual culture in the manner that he does, they will be forced to see at least some of these in unflattering ways. The consequence will be to subject the villains of his narratives to the humiliation of being taken in a sense differently than they wish.

I certainly realize that I may be overdrawing this point. In the first place, it is not easy to see how any conversation can go on among thinkers without the dialectical give and take involved in playing one vocabulary over against another. And the subjects of Rorty's redescriptions, the quick if not the dead, are certainly able to take care of themselves. Further, many of Rorty's efforts are ones he would associate with his private project of self-perfection, rather than with any attempt to influence the sphere of public praxis.

On the other hand, irony is often at least as cruel as Rorty suggests, and one can sympathize with his wish that it be kept a private matter. But, unless he means to limit the public sphere to the narrowly political sphere, the realm of beliefs and actions backed by law and sanctions, it is clearly the case that Rorty himself, as well as his intellectual foils, are public figures whose publicity opens them to the threat of forced redescription.

Rorty would respond that he does indeed wish to keep irony a private matter, reserved for intellectuals. And he would accede to the fact that he treats other intellectuals, those who have written books at least, "not as anonymous channels for truth but as abbreviations for a certain final vocabulary and for the sorts of beliefs and desires typical of its users."[21]

Were one to accuse Rorty, as I am, of humiliating the authors of books which he dismisses or gives a strong misreading, he would defend himself by saying that he is not aiming at the concrete historical individual but the persona created by the books. There is the individual who wrote the books and the work of art in accordance with which the presence of the individual is transformed. There is the real live Nietzsche, the "utterly lonely man" (whom Stefan Zweig describes as sitting and writing for hours amidst books and "a frightful arsenal of poison and drugs . . . the only helpers in the empty silence of [the] strange room in which he never rests except in brief and artificially conquered sleep"[22]), and the Nietzsche created by *Beyond Good and Evil* and *Thus Spoke Zarathustra*. There is the Heidegger of *Being and Time* and "The Question Concerning Technology" and the arrogant and petty, ambitious party member.

But surely there is a problem here. The private individual is contrasted with the books he writes. Are the books his public personage? If so, do Rorty's strong misreadings constitute public uses of irony? Further, if the writers of books, such as Nietzsche and Heidegger, are in quest of private perfection, then the selves that Rorty attacks are the selves they wish to be in private, and he is guilty of making light of them in public. Rorty could certainly say that his strong misreadings are merely a part of his own quest for private perfection, but that still seems to leave the redescription of the individual an illustration of humiliation.

Were one able to make as clear a distinction as Rorty sometimes wishes to make between novels aimed at the alleviation of pain and humiliation and philosophy texts as models of private self-creation, irony might be kept a private matter. But the humiliating consequences of redescription have to do not so much with Rorty's views of the relations of private and public life, and the functions of philosophy and literature, as with the self-descriptions of those whom he redescribes in order to make them fit his distinctions.

We might speak here of Rorty's abuse of irony. But of course irony cannot be abused anymore than punning can be abused. I suppose one might be moved to complain, "OK, Professor Rorty, you can't have it both ways!" But, of course, Rorty is not only the master of irony, but its slave as well. *He can only have it if he has it both ways.*

Rorty does have a point, even though it is only the (oxymoronic) point of irony: our strongest beliefs, our firmest convictions, are seldom held in thought with great clarity. The clarity and rigor of our ad hoc commitments are often the result of being goaded into finally realizing what we mean to say or do. A narrativist poetics serves this purpose rather well. And Rorty would never claim himself immune to the ironist ploys of others. Indeed, one can't help wondering if he is not continually disappointed at being so often, by so many, taken *so seriously.*

The problem is that philosophy has been such a serious enterprise for the greater part of its history. The strong application of ironic light-mindedness from time to time provides the only real exceptions to the general humorlessness of Philosophy's Long March to Truth. Of course, saying that philosophy isn't funny is not the same thing as saying one cannot make fun of philosophers. Philosophers have continually been the objects of humor on the part of nonphilosophers who take a superior stance toward philosophy and its practitioners, or on the part of one philosopher taking a superior stance with respect to the thought of another. This interpretation will hardly support the view that philosophers are themselves necessarily ironic creatures, since serving as the potential object of someone else's irony is hardly the same as having an ironic sense of one's own.

Philosophy does not primarily comment upon the ironic character of existence and circumstance, but, rather in the course of attempting to plumb the depths of being and meaning, the philosopher makes an ontological or methodological slip and falls on his face. His critics, both philosophers and nonphilosophers alike, all laugh while the compromised thinker and his disciples try to maintain whatever dignity they can while proceeding to cover up the mistake. Philosophy, then, becomes ironic by virtue of its everlastingly unsuccessful siege upon the infinite, the sole motivation of which is to arrest truth and bring it home dead or alive.

Were one to claim that there is real, constitutive irony in philosophy, it would have to be based on the fact that there are real incongruities in the world which, if noted by the philosopher, serve an ironic purpose. The difficulty here is that such irony still serves the didactic purpose of one philosopher attempting to show up a colleague or a member of the lay public. Philosophic irony really works if it is based upon parity. The direct or implied target(s) of the irony must be a matter of indifference.

This is but to say that the incongruities of things, or one's understanding of them, would be ironic only if at least the following conditions obtained: First, these incongruities must be truly constitutive of the way of things and not merely, for example, consequences of the formulation of philosophical issues which makes philosophy, in part or as a whole, incongruous with the world it seeks to describe and or interpret. Second, the philosopher ought have no privileged path permitting escape from the consequences of these incongruities.

Rorty recognizes that irony depends upon the coexistence of an irreducible plurality of ways of thinking about the world. The world is a serious place, immune to the ironic sense, if we presume it to be *the* world—that is, if there is but one, single-ordered, rational, coherent, internally consistent cosmos. Even if there are many ways of conceiving things, as long as there is any hint of a logical or axiological priority given to one or some orders vis-à-vis another or others, the ground of philosophic irony is undermined. This is the case because the notion of a privileged order implies a superior stance, and such a taint of superiority cancels true irony.

Thinkers may be ironic in this sense only to the degree that they are not interpreted as taking up a superior stance. But if we provide a coherent theory for a thinker's doctrines we risk constructing a platform from which he may proclaim (implicitly) the superiority of his doctrines. Thus the instrumental, strictly didactic exercise of irony renders irony in the strictest sense relative to the teaching. Such instrumental exercises make the ironic sense anecdotal rather than intrinsically, constitutively valuable. Only if we presume that the ironic sense depends, as Rorty claims, upon a recognition of the contingency of one's commitments which, nonetheless, does not undermine those commitments, can we avoid making irony parasitical upon the "true" philosophical enterprise construed as the defense of a particular way of envisioning things.

Irony plays upon the sense of the contradiction between one perspective and myriad others. Irony can goad or tease one into the recognition of the variety of perspectives, each one no more or less contingent than one's own.

Mainstream Western philosophy can easily be construed as a rather serious enterprise by virtue of its single-minded search for a capital "T" Truth. The only philosophic positions that allow constitutive incongruities are those that permit the coexistence of alternative perspectives. Further, the mere noting of such incongruities will not in itself be ironic. There must be commitment on the part of the perceiver of and/or the commentator upon the incongruity. If the commitment is merely to *the fact that* the world is incongruous, there can be no irony, for this is simply another theoretical claim that renders the world a *seriously* plural affair.

Irony cannot serve merely as a method for the discovery of an incongruity that advertises the superior insight of the discoverer. If the lesson is one known by the critic but not by the objects of his criticism, where is the irony? Irony isn't funny, but cruel, if we do no more than *make fun* of the unaware. Such irony is tainted by smugness and must be ruled out of court.

A truly aware, well-read, reasonably sympathetic thinker such as Richard Rorty can find occasions for the exercise of irony everywhere. Everyone he reads must lead him to ask, "Can it be that he has a point I have overlooked in the formulation of my beliefs and desires?" He must, however, be careful in his response. For if he directs his irony outward by demonstrating the contingencies of alternative vocabularies rather than his own, then he has employed irony in a less than fruitful manner. In fact, in the truest sense, he has failed to be consistently ironic.

In sum, I believe that Rorty's understanding of the uses of irony, though a distinct improvement over most, is defective for two reasons: first, because of his insistence that irony ought be kept private; second, because, against his own intentions, when he uses irony in the interpretation of alternative philosophical visions, he divides the serious from the lightminded uses of irony in so strict a sense as to effectively lose its beneficent effects. The systematic/edifying distinction is a direct reflection of this diremption.

Thus, when Rorty employs the serious side of irony to critique his fellow thinkers, as we shall see him doing with regard to Habermas and Foucault, he ignores the possibility of providing an edifying (mis) reading that saves them as conversation partners. The result is hardly better when, as in the case of Heidegger, Rorty takes up the lightminded stance, ignoring the serious downside of Heidegger's presumedly edifying thought.

We should not blame Rorty overmuch. Philosophers traditionally

have not been able to sustain the ironic sense. Socrates might have succeeded, but since Plato was pulling the strings he was always able to
step in when necessary to move Socrates on to the serious business of
philosophy.

Philosophic seriousness has as its principal forms either systematic
construction or critique. One may attempt to resolve an incongruity
either by dissolving the incongruous propositions or by synthesizing
them into a putatively more general view. Irony is not lost here, however. For, while in the role of constructive or destructive critic the
philosopher cancels one set of incongruities, his superior stance necessarily leads him to fall into another set. In this case irony is still present,
but it is *dramatic* irony—the irony of unrecognized self-reference. This
process of generating irony through the attempt to cancel it shows the
constitutively ironic nature of the philosophic enterprise. It is the basis
for the claim that "making fun of philosophy *is* philosophy."[23]

I agree with Rorty that irony requires both commitment and the
recognition of the contingency of one's commitments, and that any
strongly theoretical justification of either the commitment or the contingency would cancel the irony or transfer it to the dramatic mode.
Theoretical or methodological commitment muzzles the world; its
incongruities then no longer have a bite. An implication of these sentiments is that the bite, the punch, of irony is a result of our being committed to one among the many possible outcomes while entertaining the
alternatives as something other than the wild fantasies of others who
fail to understand the real truth of things. Accepting both the parity of
alternative sets of beliefs, and our own commitment to one or more of
the multifarious outcomes in the world, would lead to self-referential
inconsistency, the ground of dramatic irony.

All irony is a celebration of the limitations of embodiment. This is
the reason philosophers, who are presumed to be experts in the con-
ceptualizations and contextualizations attendant upon theory construction, are so often objects of ironic jibes. It is her ability to raise this
fact to the level of consciousness in a special way that permits the
philosopher to create irony as well. The theoretical context that allows
the theorist to discern the nature of irony makes her a victim of that
recognition. It is this that finally saves the philosopher from successfully
assuming a superior stance. The sine qua non of philosophic irony is
that the joke must always be found to be on the joker.

In support of this claim, consider the text from Whitehead quoted
earlier: "The chief danger to philosophy is narrowness in the selection of
evidences. . . . Philosophy must not neglect the multifariousness of

things. The fairies dance and Christ is nailed to the cross." As long as
our principal focus is upon just the fairies' dance, or only upon the cru-
cifixion, we can hold to either the comic or the tragic elements of existence. Only if we are able to celebrate the dance of the fairies at the foot
of the cross, will we be prepared for philosophic irony. For the philosopher, nothing can be really appreciated if one ignores its context. Recall
Byron's confession: "And if I laugh at any mortal thing 'tis that I may
not weep."

As usually understood, comedy is twice removed from reality. It is
the mask of tragedy; that makes it the mask of a mask. The comic mask
hides us from the pain of loss; the tragic mask hides us from the fact that
reality is a vast indifference, a blessed multifariousness. Irony is solely
therapeutic for those who hold to a tragic sense of life that charts the
reality of pain, the intensity of suffering, hunger, and lovelessness. But
such irony is merely instrumental and cannot be constitutive of the task
of philosophy per se.

Beyond the sorts of incongruities that allow us to laugh in temporary ignorance of the tragedies of existence, lies the incongruity between
life's tragic and comic, its serious and lightminded, elements. The experience of this incongruity leads us to the ironic sense. It is certainly true
that Western philosophy has provided us all too few illustrations of
true irony. Philosophy, purged of the taint of superiority, presents a
vision that would allow for the constitutive employment of the ironic
sense. A principal virtue of Rorty's recognition of both the lightminded
and the serious side of irony is to urge us in that direction. But I believe
that Rorty's tendency to separate these dimensions too often forces him
into the stance of superiority. Then his irony fails him.

In the following sections I want to show how Rorty's diremption of
the serious and lightminded dimensions of irony leads him to contextualize the thought of three representative thinkers whom he engages in
both positive and negative manners.

PHILOSOPHY WITHOUT IRONY: JÜRGEN HABERMAS

Rorty employs the serious side of irony to position the thought of
Foucault and Habermas relative to his own. He characterizes Habermas
as "a liberal who is unwilling to be an ironist" and Foucault as "an ironist unwilling to be a liberal."[24] Thus, in spite of some very real similarities between his thinking and that of these two figures, Rorty will find
himself finally unable to include them in his family of liberal ironists.

Somewhat paradoxically, while Rorty and Habermas are much farther apart philosophically than are Rorty and Foucault, Rorty is much more appreciative of Habermas' work than he is of Foucault's. This fact well illustrates the importance to Rorty of his belief in the priority of democracy to philosophy.

> [The] shift from epistemology to Politics, from an explanation of the relation between "reason" and reality to an explanation of how political freedom has changed our sense of what human inquiry is good for, is a shift which Dewey was willing to make but from which Habermas hangs back.[25]

It is precisely that shift that qualifies Dewey as a liberal ironist and makes of Habermas a "mere" liberal.

Rorty's position with respect to the nonironic could be illustrated with regard to any of the reconstructionist thinkers. Proponents of reconstruction fall into three main camps, all of whom seek the wisdom in Antoni Gaudí i Cornet's *mot*: "Originality is a return to the origins." The principal returnings that establish the reconstructive stance of contemporary philosophy involve the three great constructive thinkers of the Western tradition—Plato, Aristotle, and Kant.

Habermas wishes to return to Kant to reconstruct the project of modernity on grounds responsive to the changed conditions of culture. Alasdair MacIntyre develops an extremely subtle reconstruction inspired by a return to Aristotle, one which bypasses the orgies of indifference associated with the systematic pluralists who employ Aristotle as the source of taxonomies born of the Happy (Self) Consciousness.[26]

The third stream is associated with the reconstructive Platonists. This reconstructive effort, represented by thinkers such as Robert Brumbaugh, Robert Neville, and George Allan, has touched Rorty only indirectly through his studies with Brumbaugh. The reason the new Platonists are left out of the conversation is twofold. One may be either systematic and historicist, as is Habermas, or historicist and nonsystematic as is MacIntyre, but to be both nonhistoricist and systematic, as are the new Platonists, precludes engagement with Rorty's project. Further, none of the heirs of Platonic tradition employ irony in a constitutive manner.

In telling the story of philosophy since Kant, both Rorty and Habermas begin with the Kantian diremption of the value spheres; both are concerned with saving aspects of the project of modernity, the Enlightenment project. As regards MacIntyre, there is a strong disagreement over the value of modernity. MacIntyre finds modernity to be cause and consequence of the collapse of community and of individual excellences. Nonetheless, there is a real agreement on the inescapably historicist character of thought and culture.

I intend to deal here only with Habermas. It is Habermas who offers one of the strongest challenges to Rorty because of the shared affirmation (on different terms) of the modernist project, and the influence of pragmatism (Peirceian in the case of Habermas), and because of the emphasis upon the act of communication, which leads both to engage the full range of philosophical speculation and scholarship. And because Habermas has some sense of a need that Rorty has long since abandoned—namely, the need to "get it right"—he is even more concerned than is Rorty to respond to criticisms. A final point of engagement between these two thinkers is that each sets out a narrative, a *geistesgeschichte*, which tells the story of the modern age.

According to Habermas, the modern age comes into its own with the Kantian articulation of the value spheres of science, art, morality. Kant was *the* philosopher of modernity precisely because he articulated the autonomy of the ways of knowing involved in the aesthetic, moral, and scientific impulses. At the same time, Kant may be said to provide the schema with which we willy-nilly must set out to bring coherence into our discussions of modernity.

Hegel was first to seek to distinguish modernity from norms in the past. The self-definition of modernity exists in terms of *the principle of subjectivity*. And the forms of cultural life as defined by this subjectivity obtain by virtue of the knowing of the self-conscious idea. This vision of the cultural norms implicit in Descartes is spelled out in Kant, and their unity is made a central concern of Hegel's philosophic project.

Habermas points out that Kant's diremption of experience and culture was not seen by him as at all pernicious, and that he felt no need to defend the autonomy of morality, art, and science. This, however, became Hegel's chief problem. And the fragmentation resulting from the collapse of Hegel's system led to three alternatives:

> *Left Hegelian* critique, turned toward the practical and aroused for revolution, aimed at mobilizing the historically accumulated potential of reason . . . against . . . the one-sided rationalization of the bourgeois world. The *Right Hegelians* followed Hegel in the conviction that the substance of state and religion would compensate for the restlessness of bourgeois society, as soon as the subjectivity of the revolutionary consciousness that incited restlessness yielded to objective insight into the rationality of the status quo. . . . Finally, Nietzsche . . . related to reason as a whole: Reason is *nothing else* than power, the will to power, which it so radiantly conceals.[27]

Habermas claims that, after Nietzsche, the critique of modernity went in two principal directions: Heidegger and Derrida instituted a critique of metaphysics; Bataille and Foucault continued the unmasking of the will to power. Meanwhile, the neo-Marxists continued a tradition of theoretical critique of modes of praxis, while neoconservatives tried to avoid theory either as the ground of normative critique or as a grand metanarrative. Habermas would see Rorty as a paradigm illustration of the neoconservative attitude.

Habermas seeks to return to Kant, not in a substantive way, but in the sense of going back *before* the decisions made by Hegel and the young Hegelians in order to critique the idea of subject-centered reason, replacing it with reason as intersubjective, grounded in the notion of "communicative competence."

It is clear enough where the disagreements lie between Rorty and Habermas. First, there is a different assessment of the value of Kant for the development of viable criticisms of contemporary culture. Second, they disagree on the importance of theory in determining the effect of philosophy on its culture.

Habermas wants to defend the sort of distinction between philosophy and literature that Rorty and Derrida seek to collapse. He does this by maintaining a Kantian-like distinction between alternative functions of language—that of problem-solving and that of world-disclosure.

> The polar tension between world-disclosure and problem-solving is held together within the functional matrix of ordinary language; but art and literature on the one side, and science, morality and law on the other, are specialized for experiences and modes of knowledge that can be shaped and worked out within the compass of *one* linguistic function and *one* dimension of validity at a time.[28]

By maintaining a distinction between the world-disclosing and problem-solving sorts of language, Habermas is able to avoid the sort of thing Rorty promotes—namely, a *poetized* culture, one which is open to the transforming effects of the novel uses of language. Habermas finds in distortion-free communication, communicative competence, the formal structure which will bring about a fruitful interaction between the poets and the technicians in a society.[29]

The second difference between Rorty and Habermas lies in the latter's concern for some kind of overarching consensus within society capable of leading in the direction of undistorted communication. Though Habermas has given up anything like absolutist or objectivist views of nature and knowledge, he maintains a kind of Peircean universalism which seeks a convergence toward undistorted communication and defines rationality as the content of that convergence.[30] Rorty's pluralism cannot lead to convergence but *di*vergence. There is neither the expectation of, nor any necessity for, consensus.

Rorty's claim that Habermas is a liberal who is unwilling to be an ironist means that he does not entertain "radical and continuing doubts" about his own final vocabulary. In a real sense, Habermas is directing his ideas against the ironic consequences of Nietzsche's assault upon the Hegelian project. Claiming that Nietzsche's criticisms of the loss of communal cohesiveness associated with modernity are made with no regard for the need for emancipation, Habermas finds Nietzsche to be the forerunner of the various expressions of the ironic sense associated with Foucault, Heidegger, and Derrida. This irony is expressive of a failure of social hope.

By substituting intersubjectivity for subjectivity as the basis for reasoning and practice in modern societies, Habermas not only attempts to bypass the critiques associated with Nietzsche and his heirs, but he makes essential the need for a substantial sphere of public praxis both reflective and productive of the social norms which, once internalized and employed as the ground of undistorted communication, constitute rationality.

Rorty says that he and Habermas have no real political disagreements, only philosophical ones. By this he means that Habermas' notion of undistorted, or "domination-free," communication serves the same purpose as the processes of maximizing freedom and autonomy through education and political access. This purpose is that of reducing cruelty within social institutions.

The differences between Habermas and Rorty concern, according to the latter,"*only* the self-image which a democratic society should have, the rhetoric which it should use to express its hopes."[31] The self-image Habermas promotes, says Rorty, is one in which "communicative reason" embodies suggestions of some form of Enlightenment universalism and rationalism. Rorty's suggestion concerning the self-image of a democratic society is that it embody, at the level of public praxis, a (nonironic) nominalism and historicism.

Habermas wants to maintain the Peircean idea of a convergence toward rationality, while Rorty wants democratic societies to promote the increased ability to live without the comforts of the hope for universal validity. Rorty says he wants a freely realized consensus on the means of achieving common purposes to be seen against the back-

ground of "an increasing sense of the radical diversity of private purposes, of the radically poetic character of individual lives, and of the
merely poetic foundations of the 'we-consciousness' which lies behind
our social institutions."[32] Such a distinction between the private and
the public life as Rorty wishes would not suit Habermas, who would
hold that the need for undistorted communication would require not
just an "accommodation" (Rorty's word) of the private and public
spheres but a real continuity between them.

The trick in trying to maintain a distinction between private and
public life is that it requires a determination of those aspects of the *self*
which function privately and those which are suitably public.
Accommodation means essentially that one not overbalance concerns
for the private or the public aspect. That may be a sound principle, but
it is clear that, just as Habermas could be accused of modeling whatever
private sphere he would recognize after the criteria of public life defined
by undistorted communication, Rorty's desire for a poetized culture is
essentially a wish to shape the public sphere along the lines of the private. In either case there is no real balance. There is, rather, in each case,
the dominance of the concerns of one over the other.

The differences between Habermas and Rorty are, indeed, as Rorty
indicates, not directly political, but philosophical. Of course, these differences include the metaphilosophical concern for what John Dewey
called "the office of philosophy." Differences over this issue could have
significant political implications. For, if Habermas refuses to yield the
emancipatory aims of philosophic critique and construction and Rorty
claims that belief in such effects of philosophers is naive, it is easy
enough to see that there will be distinctive differences possible with
respect to questions of political socialization, and the role of the intellectuals in the origination and direction of public policy.

Indeed, Rorty's fondness for "piecemeal nudges" rather than the
development of overarching programs and policies suggests that he
would be greatly disturbed by the implications of Habermas' desire to
articulate social and political structures which would promote distortion-free communication. Still, Rorty has a point with respect to the
character of the differences between him and Habermas. And he might
become even more sanguine by virtue of Habermas' most recent
account of the role of philosophy as "stand-in and interpreter."[33]

Apparently, in direct response to Rorty's criticisms, Habermas has
clarified his relationship to Kant. Kant had attempted to provide philosophy with two strong roles vis-à-vis science and culture. The first
was as "usher"—as that discipline which placed the sciences in rela-

tion to one another; the second was as "judge." In its adjudicating role, philosophy serves as the "highest court of appeal vis-à-vis the sciences and culture as a whole."[34] After establishing a basic division between what may and may not be experienced, thus "ushering the sciences to their proper place,"[35] philosophy articulated the relations among the special sciences, defining the status and character of each.

The Kantian conception of philosophy, according to Habermas, is first that of defining the sphere of the "knowable" or "experienceable" and second, that of providing an organization of the otherwise autonomous sciences. This latter conception means that philosophy serves as *scientia scientiarum*, the science of the sciences, that way of knowing which adjudicates ways of knowing.

In place of this conception of the role of philosophy, Habermas claims that the proper office of philosophy is to function as "stand-in" and "interpreter." In the first function, the philosopher works in relation to the "reconstructive sciences" such as social psychology, linguistics, the history of science and technology, which are empirical, but which raise issues of universality both with respect to the conditions of experience and expression associated with their various subject matters and with respect to the specific claims that form the propositional content of the discipline at any particular stage of its history. In its "stand-in" role, philosophy may hold questions open which might otherwise be closed by empirical, and therefore fallible, claims to validity.

In its role as "interpreter," philosophy may mediate the discourses of the various sciences. Specifically this would involve the attempt to "help set in motion the interplay of the cognitive-instrumental, moral-practical, and aesthetic-expressive dimensions that has come to a stand-still today, like a tangled mobile."[36]

Those who compare the Habermas of *Knowledge and Human Interests* (1965, 1968) with these more recent (1987) words, might feel that Habermas has yielded much of his transcendentalist concerns and gone pragmatist. But by attempting to steer a course between the Scylla of Karl-Otto Apel's transcendentalism and the Charybdis of Rorty's strict anti-foundationalism, Habermas may be thought by each of his opponents to have foundered badly. Rorty still seems to believe that Habermas is a victim of Kant's "stubborn differentiation" of the value spheres, while there is every reason to believe that Apel would hold Habermas' description of philosophy's role as stand-in and interpreter to be a capitulation to the corrosive forces of nominalism and historicism represented by Rorty.

I am concerned here only with Habermas' relationship to Rorty and so shall bypass the issues between him and Apel. Clearly, over the past few years, Habermas has been moving in the direction of a greater appreciation of the role of the empirical approaches to language (particularly language as a communicative medium) in the evolution of human societies. His increasing distancing of himself from the architectonic of the Kantian philosophy is a recognition of the relative autonomy of the human sciences qua *empirical*. Along with this, he has maintained the position that philosophy still serves as, if not the judge, then at least the caretaker, of rationality.

Even with these changes of position, the differences between Habermas and Rorty remain significant. In the first instance, Habermas' movement away from transcendental interests toward empirical ones cannot improve his relations with Rorty very much. Rorty doesn't think that the philosopher has anything special to say to scientists; there is nothing truly empirical about the philosopher's pursuits. Habermas' movement toward empirical research in the human sciences has been matched by Rorty's move toward the poetical and metaphorical. The latter's "aestheticization" of culture cannot be well commensurated with the new empiricist emphases in Habermas.

Second, Rorty's reversal of the traditional relations between philosophy and literature precludes the philosopher per se from having any special responsibilities as caretaker of the rationality of a society. The aestheticization of culture goes along with, indeed has as one of its implications, the privatization of the intellect.

The net effect of Habermas' presumed movement away from objectivist and toward historicist and pragmatic concerns is that the distance between him and Rorty remains at least as great as before. The reason for this is that this presumed movement is only apparent to the extent that Habermas maintains an essentially nonpragmatic theory of meaning.[37] Both the "problem-solving" and "world-disclosing" functions of language presuppose that normative meanings denote an encounter with, or disclosure of, a linguistically nonconstituted world. There is for Habermas (what Rorty denies) something "out there" that makes our sentences true. Habermas' historicism and pragmatism are rooted in the play of appearances, which means they are not *rooted* at all in what he presumes to be most real.

The briefest characterization of the difference between Rorty and Habermas is that the former has a causal theory of meaning, while the latter maintains a belief in a reality beyond appearances which meaningful expressions can, in principle, confirm or disclose. It is this that allows Rorty an ironic sense denied to Habermas. Unlike Rorty,

Habermas refuses to call into serious question, not simply the present status of defensible knowledge claims in the human sciences, but *the status of knowledge claims per se*.

The failure of Habermas to accord irony sufficient weight in the construction of his arguments leaves Rorty no other choice than to treat him in a serious-minded manner. Whatever respect Rorty might have for the thinking of Habermas must be qualified by the suspicion that he may be taking himself and his proposals altogether too seriously. On the other hand, the mere fact that Habermas has engaged so many of his critics with philosophic seriousness has had the consequence of leading him to change his views significantly. The interesting irony here is the fact that it is easy enough to see the manner in which his philosophic engagements have led to changes in his views. I find it much more difficult to chart such changes in Rorty's doctrines. It might well be true that, practically speaking, the stolid Jürgen Habermas has demonstrated a somewhat greater openness to the contingency of his views than has the ironic Richard Rorty.

IRONY AND THE LIBERAL CONSCIENCE: MICHEL FOUCAULT

Rorty's thinking is in many ways much closer to that of Habermas than Foucault, the reason being that the philosophic differences that separate him from the former make for very little difference in the character of their specific values and commitments relevant to the public sphere. In other words, they are both liberals. But Rorty departs from Habermas by combining his liberalism with a strong sense of the contingency of philosophical commitments and, therefore, qualifies as liberal *ironist*.

The differences between Foucault and Rorty are much more significant. The fact that, as Rorty claims, they share a strong ironic sense is broadly irrelevant since the locus of irony for Rorty is the private sphere within which the search for self-perfection goes on, while Foucault's ironic gestures are directed toward ideas and institutions born from social complexes to which a distinction between public and private is quite irrelevant.

The telos of Foucault's thinking is what one might sometimes see as the Marxian telos—namely, the winning *for the individual* the rights and responsibilities of his own autonomous, humane praxis. On the terms of Rorty's diremption of the public and private spheres, however, the rewards of autonomy are private privileges which may have little to do with humane (public) praxis.

Rorty claims that Foucault is not a liberal. But on the definition of liberal as one who believes that "cruelty is the worst thing we do," it is hard to see why Foucault doesn't qualify. There are several reasons why Rorty thinks he does not. In the first place, the liberal ironist takes two projects to be primary: (1) the private project of self-invention, and (2) the public project of expanding the range of her "we-consciousness."[38] There is the need on the part of the liberal not simply to recognize the evil of cruelty but to participate in the development of a public moral identity with which to confront that cruelty. In addition, there must be the presence of a hope that cruelty may in fact be overcome. It is in order to protect this, often fragile, hope that Rorty wishes to ban irony from the public sphere.

Foucault not only balks at identifying himself with any "we," he seems to have little hope that anything may be done to improve the lot of human beings which he so powerfully describes. No modern philosophical writer has written so graphically and so movingly about pain and humiliation as has Foucault. But by desiring to remain a faceless writer, Foucault (claims Rorty) intentionally disqualifies himself from membership in any "we."

Rorty believes that the principal difference between himself and Foucault is that he believes "we liberals" suffices to name the appropriate we-consciousness for democratic societies and Foucault clearly does not. Rorty is doubtless correct in his claim that Foucault was suspicious of the socialization process in any of its modern forms. Foucault was, in fact, an anarchist, a perfect exemplar of one who tries to ironize public life.

Rorty's criticism of Foucault, insofar as it depends upon a private/public distinction, might be seriously misdirected. The anarchist often carries his irony to the extreme of doubting whether one can finally escape the strictures of the public life in the form of institutions functioning as "discourses of power." Such pessimism effectively cancels anything like a notion of a private sphere of self-creation. Insisting upon distinguishing the public and private spheres risks begging what for both Rorty and Foucault is the essentially empirical question of whether there is an efficacious private life for individuals in liberal democratic societies.

There is some question as to whether Foucault's writings, either by intent, implication, or default, distinguish the search for private perfection from the quest for social reforms. And if irony is supposed to be a private matter, irrelevant to public praxis, it is difficult to explain the sort of impact Foucault's writings seem to have. I can't imagine a better means of sensitizing one to the pain and humiliation of legal punishments than by reading the opening pages of Foucault's *Discipline and Punish*.[39] This work presents descriptions of the most vile and gruesome, yet legally sanctioned, punishments, juxtaposed with diagrams and drawings, all contextualized by Foucault's distant, analytic, dispassionate, clinically controlled treatments of "the body of the condemned" and "the spectacle of the scaffold," the cumulative effect of which is both to attract and repel the reader, leaving him finally in a state of chastened contempt for the cruelty of which we are all capable.

If the philosophical writer writes, as Foucault does, about the presence of pain and humiliation, and if, following Rorty's advice, we are to concern ourselves not with the connection of the person and his work but of his work and the world; and if we can distinguish those sorts of works which sensitize us to the existence of cruelty and those which could be used in our search for private perfection, how are we to assess the work of Foucault? Foucault, the ironist, wrote of pain and humiliation in a manner that could sensitize us as much as any novelist so called. Thus, it seems Rorty must allow Foucault his due as an ironist whose words have *public* relevance. For if we treat "Foucault" as an abbreviation of his final vocabulary and apply the relevant part of that vocabulary to our liberal need to become more sensitive to the possibilities of pain and humiliation, he seems a viable hero of the public sphere. If the connection between works which can sensitize us to "the pain of those who do not speak our language"[40] and the authors and readers of such is contingent, how is Rorty able to say which are so illumining and which dwell in the shadows?

Rorty's response would be that Foucault might be able to make us feel concern for the existence of cruelty, but he does not offer us any hope that such cruelty may be overcome. It is with respect to Foucault's hopelessness that Rorty finds him a failed liberal. Thus, Rorty's objections to Foucault concern the Kantian question as to what we may legitimately hope. There is a hopelessness entailed by Foucault's diagnoses that the liberal democratic Rorty cannot stomach. The grounds for Rorty's hope and Foucault's hopelessness lie in the different attitudes of these two thinkers toward the relations of the public and the private sphere.

The focal issue is that of individual autonomy. Foucault believes that autonomy to be threatened by social institutions. Rorty responds to this view by saying "autonomy is not something which all human beings have within them and which society can release by ceasing to repress them. It is something which certain particular human beings hope to attain by self-creation."[41] Foucault's response would be that the lack of autonomy is a consequence of discursive formations which shape, and ultimately define, the individual.

All human agency is shaped in this manner. We can understand the authorship of a text, a code, an institution, a law as the consequence of interactions among a number of anonymous participants. For example, the author of a book is herself authored by the critical tradition that interprets the book. This tradition is a function of the social and cultural relations associated with a set of discourses which can be analyzed only by contextualizing them within an alternative set of determining causes. And so on.

On Foucault's terms it would be futile to decry such a consequence of transcendental anonymity. The absence of "we-consciousness" in Foucault is a consequence of the unreality of any "we." This is itself a consequence of the fact that the formation of any "I" is through the agency of intersecting power discourses. Thus Foucault would insist that a rejection of authority which attempts to isolate a single agent or decision-maker—or a self-conscious "we" for that matter—as *sole* authority has missed the point entirely. Authority is always diffuse.

For Rorty, self-creation is confined to the private sphere. The public sphere serves the purpose of reducing cruelty. Attempts to reduce pain and cruelty do not require that one be autonomous in the Foucaultian sense. Here again we meet with a kind of optimism on the part of Rorty which suggests that there is nothing in the sphere of public social institutions that can preclude the development of autonomy in private, at least for some. But, as we have noted before, Rorty has, perhaps, not paid sufficient attention to the manner in which the capitalist/Marxist dialectic has shaped institutions in such manner as to affect the processes of private life.

Sometimes Rorty seems altogether too sanguine about his belief that all we have any right to expect is that a very few individuals will realize themselves. But if this is so, then there is a real hopelessness in Rorty with respect to any but the fortunate few. For what sort of democracy is it that would accede to such a low-level realization of individual autonomy? Rorty would be ready with the expected answer: it would be the sort of democracy defined by those *liberals* who believe that cruelty (not the failure to promote generally high levels of individual autonomy) is the worst thing we do. But one of the most significant refinements of liberalism in the late modern period lies in the recognition of the subtle and nuanced forms cruelty takes. A liberal might well say that the failure to include the hope for autonomy for the masses among one's hopes is the failure of truly democratic hope. Rorty's hope seems to fall short of what one might legitimately expect from a liberal.

Rorty might complain that the unrealistic hopes of bleeding-heart liberals have done little to sustain true democratic reforms. His own bleeding heart long since stanched by a realistic assessment of the limitations of democratic institutions, Rorty expresses the chastened hopes of a "clotted liberal."

I would feel better about this position of Rorty (if indeed this *is* his position) if I had some idea as to just how limited he believes the realization of autonomy might be in a viable society. On the other hand, I expect that many would have real sympathy with his professed desire to substitute piecemeal nudges aimed at the real reduction in specific instances of pain and cruelty for grand programs aimed at the realization of autonomy for all.

I think we might make a case for the beneficent effect of the public irony of Foucault the anarchist. After all, it is not just romantic nostalgia or brutish indifference or childish hysteria that leads individuals to rail against the tyranny of institutions, laws, norms, and principles. There are *responsible* critiques. Part of Foucault's responsibility lies in his recognition that any criticism which seeks to maintain critical distance suffers from the vastness of that distance which renders such critiques harmless at best and at worst guarantees that every philosophic act serves to defend the structures. This is Foucault's point when he says, "I think to imagine another system is to extend our participation in the present system."[42]

Foucault's anarchism attempts to cancel that distance by denying *archai* in all forms—the *arche* of cosmogenesis, of historical beginnings, of individual understanding and agency, and a fortiori, of any given social or political entity. The primary consideration in the critique of normative authority Foucault provides involves the recognition that the tyranny of social systems dominated by tradition is clearly a function of what he has called "transcendental anonymity." Transcendental anonymity suggests the notions of "divine origins" and "hidden meanings" associated with theological institutions which bind us to the tradition/history ellipse by underwriting a reversion to the unconsciousness of tradition as a means of escaping the rabid self-consciousness of history. Such constitutes an awakening from the nightmare of history which is at the same time a falling into the deeper, less troubled, slumber of tradition.

Foucault recognizes (and this is but one expression of his hopelessness) the futility of anarchistic attempts to escape the power relations determined, not by this or that form of historically constituted social or political system, but by the notions of action and agency in each of its possible forms. Thus the communitarian ideals of classical anarchism which determine its character as little more than wan hope are nothing more or less than fantasies.

Rorty questions Foucault's analysis of social institutions which finds power relations everywhere. Foucault's mistake, according to Rorty, is compounded by his desperate impatience with the ubiquity of such relations. That impatience is fathered by the frustration resulting from Foucault's apparent belief that societies per se cannot provide the tools essential to attacking the problem of the oppressiveness of power. One can find the lever and fulcrum but there is no place to stand.

There is, Rorty believes, a harmless, "empty" sense of power which ought lead to little objection. It is the sense in which the recognition that all relations—from interpersonal to political—are "power relations" leads parties to the relation to shrug and say, "So what?" Rorty seems to believe that Foucault suffers from the monk's disease of "scrupulosity" (which, of course, occasionally afflicts Rorty as well) and that the enflamed conscience that accompanies this illness has rendered his analyses rather exaggerated.

Foucault is quite close to Rorty in at least one regard. He recognized as well as does Rorty himself that the wholesale cannot assault the wholesale. Theory, in either its teleological or its reductive guise, cannot dissolve the structures which thrive best on theories, visions, general understandings. It is impossible to combat principles simply with more principles. What appears in Foucault to be a generalized critique of the ubiquity of power relations is in fact simply the result of an accumulation of examples of the phenomenon of power. Foucault is a nominalist and his method is perforce inductive. It may be true that he never found an instance of an autonomous individual, or a social institution that was not determined by power discourses, but that is not tantamount to saying none exist. Like the pragmatist, Foucault is a *bricoleur*. His methods can only be ad hoc, his "principles" can only be tactical, makeshift.

The wholesale assault upon authority either leads to the blind destruction with which most individuals associate anarchism in its social and political forms, or it effects that transcendental anonymity that imports onto-theological notions into the communitarian context as a means of guaranteeing harmony and stability. The intimate connection between the anarchist and the mystic is explained in this fashion. Recall the spiritualist and Anabaptist movements of the radical reformation of the sixteenth century, in which communitarian and millennial politics were fed by mystically inspired doctrines.

The value of Foucault's piecemeal assault upon power and authority is that it may hold the promise of a place to stand, not outside the structures, or above them, but amidst their ruins. These ruins are not the result of a forceful assault of the revolutionary, nor of internal collapse born of the "inevitable contradictions of class," but are the consequences of an altered perception. Just as the parking lot and shopping mall are visible ruins of the open field on which they were erected, so institutions, beliefs, ideologies, and theories are the ruins of the insistent particularities of imagination. What heretofore was seen to be the complicated tapestry of civilized culture may eventually come to be seen as the patchwork quilt which, in fact, it is. Foucault can help make Rorty's point.

DER FALL DES HEIDEGGERS

Rorty's consideration of Habermas and Foucault has addressed their significant similarities and differences with his views. In the course of his discussion of their thought, Rorty has not only addressed their attitude toward the subject of irony, he has employed irony in its form as high-minded seriousness, taking these thinkers more or less at their word, in order to position his thought in relation to theirs. In his consideration of Heidegger, Rorty often takes the opposite, lightminded, stance employing irony as a means of reshaping certain of the emphases of Heidegger's project.

Rorty finds Heidegger to be the most challenging thinker of the twentieth century. This may seem passing strange, given the nominalist directions of Rorty's thinking. There are a number of reasons why Rorty concentrates so much attention on Heidegger. First, everyone else has done so. That is, the most influential philosophers of the latter half of the twentieth century have invested much of their energies in their readings of Heidegger. He is King of the Hill and cannot be ignored by anyone who would raise himself to the eminence of "seminal thinker." Second, Heidegger's early work, *Being and Time*, expresses a kind of pragmatism that resonates with the sort that Dewey projected. And Heidegger's later turn away from that pragmatism toward the history of Being and the negative articulation of the "enframing" effects of technology provides an important foil for Rorty's thinking. Third, in the wake of the discussions of his relations to National Socialism, Heidegger has become a primary example of Rorty's views concerning the relations of a creative thinker to his creations, and of the individual and his works to the private and public spheres.

In his discussions of Heidegger, the importance of Rorty's ironic stance toward other thinkers is well advertised. It is here that the central place of irony in Rorty's thinking is illustrated. For, the sorts of criticisms, both strident and reserved, that Heidegger's Nazism has received illustrate for Rorty a failure of the liberal to realize the essentially light-minded mood with which many thinkers must be approached. The liberal without lightmindedness fails in two ways: First, there is too much seriousness attached to the search for principles employed to guide and shape public praxis. But, and this is what the Case of Heidegger illustrates, there is also the failure to appreciate the real value for projects of self-creation of those thinkers whose actual personality one would deplore and whose ideas one would certainly reject if made the ground of public actions.

Rorty's version of the early and later Heideggers takes this form: The early Heidegger of *Being and Time* was close to Dewey in his pragmatic attitude. The later Heidegger, who traded his analysis of *Dasein* for a discourse of "the history of Being," criticizes the pragmatism of his early work as one more example of the enframing associated with "productionist metaphysics," which began with Plato's attempts to see the world as a set of productions modeled after archetypal forms in much the same way as an edifice is erected by appeal to a set of architectural plans. From the Greek desire to uncover *archai*, principles, to the pragmatic desire to promote technological development, there is a need to reckon with the processes of things in terms of something that can be laid out in advance—namely, "principles" or "techniques."

Heidegger's own pragmatic leanings in *Being and Time* result from recognizing the continuity between the intellectual (believing) and the affective (desiring) aspects of human existence. By making the Being-in-the-world of *Dasein* the ground of truth, Heidegger at once historicizes truth and moves toward a quasi-Deweyan form of pragmatism. Indeed, "once understanding is de-intellectualized . . . by viewing the so-called 'quest for disinterested theoretical truth' as a continuation of practice by other means . . . most of the standard pragmatist doctrines follow."[43]

But the shift from the early to the late Heidegger brings with it a recognition that the relativity of Being to the operations of *Dasein* within a particular historical epoch allows Heidegger to tell the story of Being in such a way as to try to get beyond the technological enframing which he sees as the destiny of Being from Plato onward. This leads him to attempt to move beyond the pragmatism of *Being and Time*. Heidegger remains ambivalent with respect to the issue of the historicity of Being. In spite of the ontic/ontological distinction, the project of *Being and Time* can be read pretty much as a capitulation to the historicity of Being. On the other hand, the later Heidegger, for the most part avoiding the term "ontology," often seems to suggest that there is an ahistorical essence in accordance with which the various episodes in the history of Being are to be assessed. Rorty's view is that the early Heidegger tended toward the ahistorical option while the later accepted the view that "philosophical reflection is historical all the way down."[44] Thus there is a tension between the Heidegger who claims that all stages on Being's way are contingent and therefore are on a par one with the other, and the Heidegger who claims that the Greeks before Plato had a more *primordial*, a more *authentic*, relationship to Being.

Rorty resolves this tension by giving Heidegger a pragmatic reading. The history of Being is a history of the language which has spoken Being. This is a history of "final vocabularies." "Being is what *final* vocabularies are about. . . . [A]ll we know of Being is that it is what understandings of Being are understandings of."[45]

If Heidegger agrees that asking for greater specificity of the meaning of Being—becoming a traditional philosopher rather than a poet—is a movement in the direction of power, why is it, Rorty asks, that Heidegger often speaks as if the present epoch of Being's story has led us farther from Being than was so in the age of the Greeks?

Rorty claims that the "belatedness" and "nostalgia" of Heidegger's later philosophy can be accounted for in the following way: The Greeks were close to being because better able to sense the contingency of the specific language they used to house Being. That is, they recognized that the language they used excluded other equally viable languages. This means that enframing in one language excludes other sorts of enframing. Thus every disclosure is also a concealing of other meanings. The call of Being cannot be heard in all languages at once. "To be primordial is thus to have the ability to know that when you seize upon an understanding of Being . . . you are automatically giving up a lot of other possible understandings of Being."[46]

Rorty believes that he can appropriate Heidegger as a hero of his new pragmatic movement if he can excise the twin malignancies of belatedness and nostalgia from Heidegger's thinking without the patient dying. Can he do this? He thinks that he can by claiming that the metacriterion for uncovering the primordiality of thinking in a given epoch can be employed to show that the contemporary age is even better able than were the Greeks to understand the contingency of vocabularies.

Rorty's claim seems to involve something like an empirical question. Are we not, empirically speaking, better able to recognize our contingency than were the Greeks and their heirs, protected by their quest for certainty which produced absolutes of all varieties—*Nous*, God, Mind, The Laws of Nature? But the question is not empirical at all. It revolves about the issue of whether our contemporary recognition of cultural diversity and the possibility of revolutionary changes in art and politics constitute the recognition of the *sort* of contingency which Heidegger addresses. Rorty's metatheoretical celebration of the contingency of language, of self, and of community would, as Rorty himself recognizes, be rejected by Heidegger as a frenzy of modes of enframing which involve an exchange of one contingent method of attaining identity and meaning for another. And Heidegger's strictures against technology as enframing are precisely opposed to this frenetic attempt to meet the tyranny of form by exchanging one form for another.

Yet Rorty makes a telling point, it seems to me, when, citing Derrida's *mot*, "Heideggerian hope is the reverse side of Heideggerian nostalgia," he shows how Heidegger's wish to make of his own thinking a decisive event in the history of Being leads him to encapsulate that history and attempt to take a stand beyond it. Thus does Heidegger yield his sense of contingency, and with it his own relatedness to Being. If Rorty is right, then Heidegger finally allows his irony to fail him, and with this failure becomes one more victim of the desire to "get it right."

But we may wonder about Rorty's reading of Heidegger. For it is certainly possible to move from a sense of the contingency of vocabularies to a desire to substitute *something more final than vocabularies.* Heidegger's waiting for the Call of Being might have been more than simply waiting for another vocabulary, one more *methodos.*

Whatever one's final judgment on the details of Heidegger's thinking, it seems possible to accept the implication of Rorty's argument to the effect that he is a prime example of failed irony. He was, that is to say, *a thinker who finally refused to be either a liberal or an ironist.* I believe that the reason for this lies in the peculiar form taken by Heidegger's desire to be himself a "decisive event" in the history of Being, along with the actual historical events that preceded his attempted apotheosis.

The essential argument against Heidegger, at the theoretical level, is his connection of the history of Being with a particular epoch of German history and, at the practical level, his unrecanted involvement in the movement of National Socialism which particularized and focused the German culture and language. In his *Introduction to Metaphysics* (1935),

Heidegger identifies the *Dasein* of the German nation as the center of Europe and the context within which the question of Being is to be addressed. The collectivism of communism and the autonomy and individualism of capitalism provided no way out for the modern world. National Socialism, as a movement associated with a community of language and ethnicity held out promise. It was not until Heidegger finally saw the commonalities between fascism, communism, and capitalism as all a part of the same technological frenzy that he detached himself philosophically from National Socialism. It was then that he worked out the holistic theory of technology as having universal effects through the notion of *Gestell* or "enframing."

It makes good sense to me to say that Heidegger's *Kehre*, which involved a movement away from the pragmatics of *Daseinanalysis* toward a poetic, quietistic mysticism was a direct result of Germany's loss of the war.[47] If "the destiny of a language is grounded in a nation's *relation to being*,"[48] then the failure of National Socialism is an event of real philosophical importance.

One of the effects of Heidegger's philosophy which Rorty would certainly endorse is to indicate the effete status of metaphysics as anything other than a historicist enterprise. The explication of Being must occur within a specific language and culture, otherwise the concreteness of *Dasein* is lost. But the move to universalize the story thus told, making it a story of all *Dasein*, is an attempt to make all beings speak the same language, and thus to make them a part of a single culture. These are clear culturally imperialist, totalitarian, implications. Rorty holds that "although Heidegger was only accidentally a Nazi, Dewey was essentially a social democrat."[49] Contrary to Rorty, however, I would say that, in the same manner that Dewey was *essentially* a social democrat, Heidegger was *essentially* a closed-shop totalitarian.

Habermas seems to agree with this sort of interpretation when, commenting upon Heidegger's application of his *Daseinanalysis* to the *Dasein* of the German nation, he says: "Because he identified 'Dasein' with the Dasein of a nation, authentic capacity to be with the seizure of power, and freedom with the will of the Führer . . . an internal and not easily touched up connection between his philosophy and contemporary events was established."[50] The consequence of this was that changes in the fate of National Socialism shaped Heidegger's specifically philosophical conclusions.

Hannah Arendt has provided a defense of the totalitarian predilections of Heidegger by appeal to what she held to be a *deformation professionelle* of philosophy per se.[51] Arendt cites Plato and Heidegger as primary examples of philosophers who, upon entering the public sphere, turned to tyrants and Führers and claims that the "attraction to the tyrannical can be demonstrated theoretically in many of the great thinkers."[52]

But this defense of Heidegger fails to see the radical difference in the proposals of Plato (and indeed most of the other sorts of thinkers who were attracted to tyrants) and Heidegger. Plato's thought may have been implicitly culture- and language-bound, but he sought principles that were not associated with a single language or culture. Heidegger historicized and thereby enculturated Being in a most explicit manner.

Rorty's approach to the Case of Heidegger is to be distinguished from almost every other[53] in that it does not depend upon either an internal analysis of Heidegger's thought or upon an assessment of biographical events. (Though Rorty is certainly knowledgeable enough about Heidegger to have done both.)[54] Rorty's "defense" of Heidegger is in the spirit of Oscar Wilde's *mot*, "The fact that a man is a poisoner doesn't affect his prose."

Rorty advises us to "hold our noses, separate the life from the work, and adopt the same attitude to Heidegger's books as we have to other people's. We should test them not against our moral intuitions but against competing books"[55] One reason for doing this is because the story Heidegger told of the history of Western philosophical thought tried "to explain why we use the words we do, and thus, among other things, why we have the moral intuitions we have."[56]

The conclusions Rorty ultimately draws concerning the increasingly infamous Case of Heidegger largely depend upon his view of the self as a centerless web of beliefs and desires. Following Freud's view of the contingency of moral sensibility, Rorty claims that "a person's moral character—his or her selective sensitivity to the pain suffered by others—is shaped by chance events in his or her life. Often, perhaps usually, this sensitivity varies independently of the projects of self-creation which the person undertakes in his or her work."[57]

That may be so, but one can easily question Rorty's lightminded interpretation of Heidegger at this very point. If the sorts of connections between Heidegger's admittedly questionable moral character and his philosophical projects noted above are taken into account, it becomes plausible to see a close relationship between that character and his philosophical proclamations.

We should grant, however—again consistent with Rorty's notion of the decentered self—that the works of anybody whose mind was complex enough to make his or her books worth reading will not have an "essence," that those books will admit of a fruitful diversity of interpretations, that the quest for "an authentic reading" is pointless. One will assume that the author was as mixed up as the rest of us, and that our job is to pull out, from the tangle we find on the pages, some lines of thought that might turn out to be useful for our own purposes.[58]

There is certainly some wisdom in Rorty's urging us to look more closely at the connections between books and other books than between books and their authors. Especially is this so since in the vast majority of cases we have very little information about the biographies of the authors of the books we read. Were we required in every case to assess the character of the author before evaluating his writings, we should be in seriously dire straits.

But this really isn't the problem. For years, most of the readers of Heidegger's works hadn't any other information than the texts themselves from which to develop their opinions. Nonetheless, they might well have found some of the implications of Heidegger's language, particularly the language of *Introduction to Metaphysics*, to be suspect.

There is also some value in Rorty's pointing out that any claim to the effect that Heidegger wrote something like Nazi metaphysics needs to be weighed carefully in the light of the Nazi criticism of Einstein to the effect that he wrote "Jewish physics." But mutatis mutandis there is every reason to believe that a philosophy employing *Daseinanalysis* and the assessment of the phenomenon of advancing technology will affect provincial political ideologies in a manner that notions of space, time, and matter-energy cannot.

Rorty is perhaps somewhat disingenuous when he says that "if you know that the very idea of 'authentic existence' or of 'harkening to the voice of Being' is inherently fascistic, you are spared the trouble of comparing Heidegger's account of the history of Western philosophical thought with, for example, Hegel's, Popper's, Dewey's, or Blumenberg's."[59] After all, it is not notions as vague as these that trouble Heidegger interpreters, but the sort of statements alluded to in the quote from Habermas above, statements which make German language (after the Greek) the most metaphysical of languages and then proceed to tie a nation's destiny to its relation to Being, the story of which is, of course, best told in the language that presently speaks Being best—namely, the language of the German nation.

The Case of Heidegger highlights further problems in Rorty's use of the public/private distinction to shore up his concept of irony. In fact, the controversy surrounding Heidegger's *Fall* seems to have brought out all of the frustrations and strangulated passions of philosophy in decline. If Heidegger's thinking both follows from and leads to the aberrations of Nazism, what are all his disciples, commentators, and annotators to do? Ought we ask them to apologize for their commitments on Heidegger's behalf?

Alternatively, what happens to the morale of the philosopher wishing to take his profession seriously if Heidegger's Nazism is shown to be, not a *deformation professionelle*, but a mere accoutrement, a contingent phenomenon, like a passion for stamp collecting—a mildly interesting fact about the individual, but one which doesn't say all that much about the man's character? Or (and this is Rorty's position) what if the man's nasty character was in fact advertised by his Nazi connections, but this character itself has little to do with his thought, which makes its primary contribution not to the public sphere of social and political praxis but to the private and intimate realm of self-articulation?

The dichotomy of the intellectual and the moral virtues derives from Rorty's radical separation of the public and private and his belief in a centerless self. How do these distinctions fare when put to the acid test of the liberal's desire to see the reduction of pain? Should we allow, even in the cases less equivocal than that of Heidegger, that the public nasty, by defining himself as an "intellectual," can justifiably escape censure for his public actions? What happened to the liberal ironist's desire that pain may be reduced? Is silence in the face of Heidegger's tawdry ambition the best way to reduce the pain of the events associated with the World War II period, events which Heidegger often explicitly, always tacitly, endorsed? Are there really any liberal ironists besides Rorty (among whose ungroundable hopes is the hope that pain will be diminished) who believe that the only thing we ought say about the Case of Heidegger is that "one of the century's most original thinkers happened to be a pretty nasty character"?[60]

Rorty may be right. Theory might well have become so divorced from public praxis as to be irrelevant to it. But there is still a serious problem here that Rorty cannot help but see. If, as Rorty says, Heidegger believes that "attempts to feed the hungry, shorten the working day, and so forth, just do not have much to do with philosophy,"[61] then does it matter whether or not his thinking lacks specifically *totalitarian* implications? For certainly his thinking has specifically insensitive, selfish, elitist implications which could only serve to subvert solidarity. That's probably bad enough.

I would claim that even if Heidegger was only accidentally a Nazi, the fact that he owned an awesome insensitivity to the pain of others is hardly accidental but is a direct implication of the elitist character of his intellectual life. I find it difficult to believe that the instinctive disrespect many feel toward the moral failings of intellectuals has any less destructive consequences than would the ironizing of our political rhetoric. Yet Rorty's lightmindedness toward Heidegger won't permit him to appreciate these points.

What do we learn from Rorty's approach to *der Fall des Heideggers*? Perhaps there is not much to be said other than that one of America's most intelligent philosophers is as capable of blindness as are the rest of us when his final vocabulary is at stake.

4

EXCURSUS AD HOMINEM

It is embarrassingly difficult to present a balanced assessment of Rorty's thinking. An exposition of his views is easily enough accomplished, but once one recognizes that he has plausible reasons for believing that vocabularies are closed to internal critique and that changes in beliefs are not, therefore, open to rational analysis, assaulting his inferential moves, challenging the coherence of his "first principles," or appealing to alternative sources of evidence becomes both impertinent and irrelevant: thus "critique" must take on an unusual meaning.

Eschewing historical and rational reconstructions in favor of *geistesgeschichten* permits Rorty, by recourse to a series of strong misreadings, to insulate himself against standard philosophical criticisms. His quite plausible claim that beliefs change not only rationally through perception and inference, but causally, as well, through recontextualizations stimulated by novel metaphors[1] renders this insulation well-nigh complete.

Rorty's exegetes, therefore, require both sympathy and license. It is most difficult to catch a poetic nominalist in a contradiction. And even if one did, it is even more difficult to get an *ironic* poetic nominalist to feel remorse. Criticizing Rorty's views is often much like responding, "No, 't wasn't!" to the line of Lewis Carroll's *Jabberwocky*, "'T was brillig . . .". Thus any critique of Rorty is bound to present itself, at least in part, as an *excursus ad hominem*.

LONELY PROVINCIALISM

There is a strangeness about Richard Rorty's prose, at once impersonal and private, and yet revealing of a inner complexity that, like Kierkegaard's, Nietzsche's, and William James', invites psychological analysis. The resonance with Nietzsche is found in the fact that, like Nietzsche (sans the hysterical bravado), Rorty writes as if he sees himself as "a destiny," as if he is to serve as *terminus ad quem* of classical philosophy as the claim to capital "T" Truth and *terminus a quo* of a postphilosophical world. Rorty could be seen as a "destiny" and a "casualty" in the same sense as Nietzsche claimed to be. His thoughts are certainly as unseasonal as Nietzsche's, his nihilism as defiantly courageous.

Perhaps the comparison with Nietzsche is overdrawn. James, whose warring tender toughness left him more morose and fragile than his published persona ever seemed, might be as good a model. Yet the characterization that comes to mind reading Rorty is basically one that, for moderns at least, is resourced in Nietzsche. Like Nietzsche, Rorty is a Benign Nihilist. And that nihilism expresses itself directly in Rorty's provincialism, ethnocentrism, and heroism. It also shapes his attitudes towards poetry and prophecy—issues central to his narrativist posture.

Consider the ubiquity of the theme of *loneliness* in Rorty's writing: he accepts the condition of a "lonely provincialism" born from the "admission that we are just the historical moment that we are, not the representatives of something ahistorical,"[2] as well as from the recognition that "there is nothing deep down inside us except what we have put there ourselves."[3] Under such conditions "what matters is our loyalty to other human beings clinging together against the dark."[4]

Rorty characterizes the postmodernist bourgeois liberal ironist as a lonely provincial beset by doubts about her own final vocabulary, that set of words and propositions which evoke the sentential attitudes comprising the self. This vocabulary contains both a private and a public element. The private may be well refined and even idiosyncratic, while the public side can be unsophisticated and relatively simple-minded. The focus of the private vocabulary is *sublimity*, while the public supports the aim of *decency*.

There are no discernible transformation rules guiding the movement between the private and public aspects of one's vocabulary any more than between the vocabularies of different individuals. This being so, when there is sufficient contrast between the private and the public beliefs we might as well speak of two final vocabularies. Likewise, when the individual seeks satisfactions primarily in either one or the other of the spheres there is convergence toward a single vocabulary. Rorty finds the liberal ironist to be one who hopes that "she will not be limited by her own final vocabulary when faced with the possibility of humiliating someone with a quite different vocabulary."[5]

The lonely provincial is insecure in her moral identity. That moral identity is what gives her some sort of contingent guidance concerning what she expects of herself vis-à-vis others. It is the recognition that "socialization . . . goes all the way down, and who gets to do the socializing is often a matter of who gets to kill whom first."[6] This is the rock upon which liberal hope founders, when it does. It is the other side of the coin from "Thank God I was born in a free America!"

In addition to the doubts about that aspect of one's final vocabulary that defines moral identity, there may be doubts concerning that element which defines the private idiosyncratic self. And if the idiosyncrasy runs deep enough, one comes to doubt one's sanity. There being no core self, no rules for establishing normalcy, sanity is determined by the functionality of one's beliefs. Whether we think ourselves sane or not has more to do with how well we match the consensual vocabularies associated with the descriptions of inner life we encounter in literature or how much hope we have that we will be able to make the narrative of our inner life, as weird as it might currently seem, influential as a resource for others' self-creation. Because of these doubts, the lonely provincial finds that he "desperately needs to *talk* to other people, needs this with the same urgency as people need to make love . . . because only conversation enables him to handle these doubts, to keep himself together, to keep his web of beliefs and desires coherent enough to enable him to act."[7]

In deciding what sort of person you will become, there will be questions directed to both the private and the public side of your enterprise. With regard to the public sphere, you ask with which communities you should seek solidarity. The question concerning the private aspect of your existence "is (to adapt Whitehead's definition of religion): what should I do with my aloneness?"[8] This latter statement sets the context for Rorty's thematic of loneliness. Rorty's adaptation of Whitehead's definition of religion ("Religion is what the individual does with his own *solitariness*"[9]) replaces "solitariness" with "aloneness" and by so doing recalls Paul Tillich's existential problematic which contrasts "essential solitude" with "existential loneliness"[10]—the former suggesting the singularity and uniqueness of the finite particular being, the latter expressing the absence of connectedness with other finite beings. One senses in Rorty's worry over his "aloneness," something of the pain that comes from the loss of a sense of solitude.[11]

This loneliness and loss of solitude is the loss of metaphysical comfort. The two metaphysical comforts concern the identity of the individual and the persistence of the community. Rorty does not consider the issue of identity in terms of the concrete particular individual, but it is implicit in statements such as: "A post-Philosophical culture . . . would be one in which men and women felt themselves alone, merely finite, with no links to something Beyond."[12] And again, the loyal citizens of a liberal democratic state might well be "ruefully grateful that their private senses of moral identity and the models of the human self that they develop to articulate this sense—the ways in which they deal with their aloneness—are not the concerns of such a state."[13]

Loneliness comes in three forms: there is the biological sense to which "human nature" provides the comfort; there is the sociological sense for which hope for the persistence of the human community defined by our ethos provides the comfort. Beneath these there is one's own peculiar, centerless web of beliefs—chaotic, erratic, always bemused, often confused—for which comfort has often been sought in the mystical sense of God whom Whitehead describes as "the great companion—the fellow-sufferer who understands."[14]

The belief that our biological similarities guarantee us certain rights and that, moreover, these similarities "entail the possession of something nonbiological, something which links our species to a nonhuman reality and thus gives the species moral dignity"[15] is the ground of our notion that there is a human nature which defines what we essentially are.

Rorty notes that Nietzsche's charges against the entire philosophical tradition from Plato onwards—that it constituted a nihilistic appeal to a "Reality" behind "Appearance," a set of objective principles which ordered the flux of things—was grounded in a fear of contingencies, a resentment at the disordered character of things. Such an appeal denied the truth of things, the truth that there are only *interpretations*. Rorty wants us to face the Nietszchean truth without the need to react as did Nietzsche and the post-Nietszchean thinkers such as Heidegger and Foucault. For all of these thinkers believed that there was a connection between the metaphysical and the political refusals to face contingency. The first refusal led to God and Eternal Ideas; the second led to the faith in science and technology and the belief in human progress.

Rorty looks to Hans Blumenberg who argues[16] that one can separate the desire for self-grounding, which has motivated the philosophical and theological traditions from Plato onward, from the Baconian desire for self-assertion. As a philosophy of self-assertion, pragmatism is "a philosophy of solidarity rather than of despair."[17]

The resentful belatedness characteristic of nostalgia philosophies such as Heidegger's, or the cynicism of faceless philosophies such as Foucault's, or of the sophisticated relativists comprising our intellectual elites, come from an inability to avoid the pain of loss attendant upon the failure of the metaphysical and theological traditions. As a practical matter, the appeal to transcendent others to secure and legitimate ourselves and our values hasn't worked. Rorty looks beyond such despair over the failure of the Enlightenment project to a mature acceptance of our contingency.

Rorty's claim that our sense of community has "no foundation except shared hope and the trust created by such sharing"[18] is not grounded in any cosmological or epistemological arguments about the character of things, but is simply the result of a recognition of the failure of objectivist appeals. But the ubiquity of the theme of loneliness in Rorty's writings, and the poignancy of his descriptions of the lonely provincial, suggest that he himself has not quite moved beyond nostalgia and the sense of belatedness.

What sort of criticism is this? Certainly not a logical one. It is worth considering whether, since there is no firm strategy for deciding when to go public and when to devote oneself to the private projects associated with self-perfection, the best one can hope is that there will be some sort of balance. Rorty, however, trained as a philosopher, recognizes that "philosophy has become more important for the pursuit of private perfection rather than for any social task."[19] The bookish Rorty is more private than public. His aloneness, therefore, is rather more acute than that of the public person. Solidarity, after all, offers its strongest comfort to the public side of the person.

This would be of no consequence were it not the case that the pervasive tone of loneliness in Rorty's writings is part of the rhetoric of his enterprise. And for the anti-foundationalist Rorty, rhetorical persuasiveness is essential to his philosophical program. There are no rational shifts among vocabularies, only causal ones. Rorty's web of beliefs, though perhaps significantly overlapping with those of others, is not rationally related to any other. He is in a real sense always outside, alone even in the intimate relations with those closest to him. Rorty claims that he can "live with the Freudian thought that everything everybody does to everybody else (even those they love blindly and helplessly) can be described, for therapeutic or other purposes, as manipulation."[20] This is largely because, on Rorty's version of Freud's view of the self, "there are . . . too many selves for 'selflessness' to seem a useful notion."[21] The loneliness, in other words, goes "all the way down." For we are no more or less apprised of the character of our own internal alters than those constituting our friends and intimates.

On this view it is hard to trust that there will be sufficient motivation to move beyond one's private life and the pursuit of self-perfection to reduce the pain of others. But Rorty believes the most important hedge against loneliness to be found in the search for public solidarity. This is the realm of justice as opposed to love. This contrast is important since, for Rorty "*all* human relations untouched by love take place in the dark. This is an extended sense of 'in the dark' analogous to the extended sense of 'alone' in which we mortal millions live alone."[22] Were this not so, were we to be continually apprised of the environmental influences of those we judge in society, we would find it difficult to reconcile the claims of justice over love in the public sphere. "All-seeing love" could always find reasons to excuse the antisocial actions of others. Justice must be blind.

The fundamental character of loneliness Rorty uncovers is that associated with the in-the-dark nature of most human interactions. This darkness pervades not only the public world but casts its shadow as well over the private sphere. Given the complexity of selves as centerless webs of desires, a belief in "all-seeing love" as anything more than an inspiring slogan would be seriously naive. We are as often cut off from our other selves as from our intimates and from our fellow citizens.

Still, the sense of solidarity, even though it will touch only our public selves, is important for Rorty. Its efficacy lies in the hope or belief that "our community cannot wholly die."[23] That is to say: the peculiar sort of value we represent—we Greeks, we heirs of the Enlightenment—will persist. This theme leads us beyond the privacy of the lonely provincial into the realm of ethnocentrism.

SINCERE ETHNOCENTRISM

Languages have no natural demarcation one from the other—no universal grammar or logic, nor any transcendental signifiers. The basic units of language are neither structural nor semantic in the narrow sense. A language is a congeries of overlapping vocabularies. Ultimately there is only one "language"—not in the sense of a universal set of semantic and syntactical structures, but as a congeries of gestures, sounds, words, and vocabularies which don't really add up to anything coherent. It is a contingent fact that languages do sort out along ethnic and political lines. A language user is focused by a tradition of language use. This tradition is expressed as the literature of the language. One learns one's language by mastering the literature of one's tradition. One then argues from that base. This is Rorty's *ethnocentrism*.

Many of the strongest criticisms of Rorty's thinking are directed against his avowed ethnocentricity. Though much of the animus motivating these criticisms is, I believe, misplaced, there are some hard issues Rorty has yet to confront to the satisfaction of even his most sympathetic critics. Richard Bernstein accuses Rorty of a historical "myth of the given" by writing about "our tradition," "our practices," as if they were "historically given."[24] Bernstein is, of course, correct. Rorty is not just passively ethnocentric, he is *ethno-focal*. This is Rorty's "principle of sincerity." Everyone has the right of "insisting that the beliefs and desires they hold most dear should come first in the order of discussion. That is not arbitrariness but sincerity."[25]

Rorty's narrativist, poetic historicism is not one which dispassionately charts the manner in which ideas and institutions are passively determined by time and circumstance, but one which reckons the manner in which some privileged few (selected by him from among a sizeable cast) were capable of shaping events through the creation of novel and efficacious vocabularies.

Ethnocentrism is, in one sense, *culturally* conservative. If "socialization goes all the way down" (at least all the way to the bottom of the public self), then we must be concerned with the socialization process in the sense that we want individuals in society to be able to share a substantially common discourse. The later and earlier generations, and those coevals separated by wide geographical distances, ought to receive somewhat the same socialization process. Rorty explicitly supports E. D. Hirsch's program of "cultural literacy," which involves teaching students to recognize literary, scientific, and historical allusions as a means of providing contexts in terms of which to understand important texts within their culture.

The presumption is that primary and secondary schools would be the place for such socialization. Here students should receive "the standard, patriotic, upbeat, narrative about our society, its history and its values."[26] The place for reformism is in college. This means, of course, that half of the population will be left out. But, on the other hand, if it is stable, democratic change that is sought, denying to those who will not go to college "the recognitional capacities necessary to function as a part of the electorate"[27] is more important than sowing seeds of discontent.

One of the truisms to which the young are apt to be subjected in their admittedly ethnocentric socialization process is the belief that ethnocentrism is a really bad thing. By the time young people are able to recognize that this anti-ethnocentric belief is a function of their peculiar form of ethnocentric enculturation, they will be prepared to move beyond the mere claim to universality associated with the Enlightenment rhetoric in order to accept the contingency of their beliefs.

The same liberal democracy which becomes aware of its ethnocentrism can highlight the elements in its institutions which mitigate any negative, exclusory effects of that bias. Rorty wants to divide the moral responsibilities of liberal democratic societies between "the connoisseurs of diversity" and "the guardians of universality." The former direct our attention to the ignored or otherwise unenfranchised members of our society, while the latter guarantee "that once [these people] have been shepherded into the light by the connoisseurs of diversity, they are treated just like all the rest of us."[28]

It is difficult to see how one could really believe, as have so many of his critics, that Rorty supports "hegemonic discourse" or spends his time plumping for the status quo. These charges would be easier to support if his qualified cultural conservatism were backed up by *political* conservatism. This does not, however, appear to be the case. Ethnocentrism only involves taking one's language, beliefs, desires and the interests of one's community as a *starting point*. In this Rorty agrees with C. S. Peirce:

> True conservatism, I say, means not trusting to reasonings about important questions of vital importance but rather to hereditary instincts and traditional sentiments. . . . Thus true conservatism is sentimentalism. . . .
>
> The conservatist need not forget that he might have been born a Brahmin with a traditional sentiment in favor of *suttee*—a reflection that tempts him to become a radical. But still, on the whole, he thinks his wisest plan is to reverence his deepest sentiments as his highest and ultimate authority.[29]

Conservatism is consistent with a resort to common sense, intuitions and hunches which are, as Peirce well knew, the clothing of evolutionary survival mechanisms. These are notoriously inertial. But if, as Rorty claims, metaphysics is the extension of common sense, there is an inherently conservative character to it. Indeed the more systematic "final vocabularies" against which the nominalist Rorty rails might turn out to be essential to any conservatism.

A more telling criticism of Rorty's presumed conservatism comes from the communitarian, John Wallach: "Rorty's perspective favors the rulers, however they may be defined, as opposed to the ruled, empowered public and private officials rather than the citizens themselves."[30] I believe Rorty would be justified in asking this critic to accept the fact that his conservatism is neutral with respect to the issues of rulers and ruled and that even if in cases of a tie the wearer of the badge or crown retains his advantage, this doesn't settle the issue. The neutrality of a general perspective doesn't require that the individual proponent of it remain neutral. It precisely leaves open the choice of action. One may not like the fact that the vision doesn't rule out nastiness in all its forms, but at this point Rorty would simply say that no one has been able to do anything like this before and his view simply makes a virtue of necessity. Thus, we ought to get rid of (among other such futile gestures) "the Marxist idea that a philosophical super-science can tell the working class their true situation, and . . . Heidegger's idea that the fortunes of philosophy determine the fortunes of mankind as a whole."[31]

Rorty's nominalism makes him supportive of the connoisseurs of diversity, "specialists in particularity" such as novelists, historians, and ethnographers. As long as we stress the importance of these types rather than those who dispense *Ideologiekritik*, we should be continually open to expanding the sense of our ethos.

Part of the reason Rorty trades the language of the philosophers for that of the poets is that it is too easy to chart the permutations of the philosophers' efforts and demonstrate that nothing new is conceivable. Metaphors are resourced in the imagination—a particularistic, nominalistic repository. Nominalism insures novelty by denying the sameness of particulars construed as members of a class or instances of a universal. Thus the nominalist perspective is essential for those who might otherwise be jaded by their knowledge.

Within the context of the ethnos we share with Rorty, there is plenty of room for liberal and radical beliefs and actions. In our society ethnocentrism entails the acceptance of a democratic context as the beginning point of discussion (and thus entails "the priority of democracy to philosophy"). But this is consistent with a radical critique which appeals to the reigning self-image of the culture.

Further, ethnocentrism is intellectually or socially or politically

defective only if it advertises a "closed-shop" mentality. Rorty's ethnocentrism is not closed since it is quite consistent with seeking practicable ideas and programs beyond one's culture.

> Part of the force of Quine's and Davidson's attack on the distinction
> between the conceptual and the empirical is that the distinction
> between different cultures does not differ in kind from the distinction
> between different theories held by members of a single culture. . . .
> The same Quinean arguments which dispose of the positivists' dis-
> tinction between analytic and synthetic truth dispose of the anthro-
> pologists' distinction between the intercultural and the intracultural.[32]

The fluidity of the distinctions between intracultural and intercultural, and between one language and another, implies that our beliefs
and desires, if not an unbroken web across cultures, may contribute to a
fabric which can be productively woven together with elements that
come from a variety of different cultures. This belief certainly renders
Rorty's ethnocentrism less open to attack from the cosmopolitan left.[33]

There is still the question as to the manner in which the utopian
revolutionaries and strong poets who would serve the dynamic of social
and cultural change are able to take up a critical stance toward their
own societies. The proponents of *Ideologiekritik* are able to employ programmatic proposals which purportedly transcend the particular society whose interests they serve.[34] The sincere ethnocentric in his role of
strong poet or revolutionary cannot make his claims on behalf of "universal rights" or a "common humanity." Changes are enjoined by members of a segment of society in order to move the entire society closer to
its own self-image.[35]

The "principle of sincerity" invoked by Rorty as the ground of this
ethnocentrism will then support not only the priority of democracy to
philosophy, but (what may amount to the same thing!) the priority of
rhetoric to philosophy (in its more traditional senses) as well. Philosophy
becomes a kind of forensics aimed at giving specific character to a liberal democracy and justifying an individual's role within it.

The belief in democracy is not primarily formal. Rorty does not
simply want to see individual self-determination through the exercise of
conversation, debate, and the ballot. Clearly there are substantive issues
about which debates ought or ought not take place wrapped up in his
vision of democracy. The range of allowable values is part of Rorty's
heritage. It is where he must begin if he is to be sincere.

The best way of understanding the consequences of Rorty's ethnocentrism is to assay his attitudes toward other cultures. He has not spent a great deal of time on questions of cross-cultural comparisons, but what he has written is most provocative. In "A Pragmatist View of Rationality and Cultural Difference,"[36] Rorty distinguishes three distinct meanings of "rationality" and "culture." The former carries the following senses: (1) the sort of technical reason associated with environmental adaptation, (2) that wide intellectual and practical tolerance associated with the promotion and exercise of freedom and persuasion in developing "syncretic, compromise, ways of life," and (3) the objectivist, transcendent means of establishing an evaluative hierarchy which sets the human being apart from the brutes.

Culture has the following meanings allied to the sense of rationality: (1) shared habits of action, (2) the refined, noninstrumental modes of civilized beliefs and actions associated with the economic and intellectual elites, and (3) the product of objectivist rationality—those values and institutions that promote the realization of what is most essentially human.

Rorty, of course, rejects the objectivist sense of rationality and the meaning of culture that goes along with it. He then plays the remaining pairings of culture and rationality against one another to determine some guidelines for cultural interaction. Rorty focuses his sense of ethnocentrism, which he believes he shares with John Dewey, in the following narrative: The first and second senses of rationality have had productive interactions in the modern period. That is, efficiency and tolerance have grown together. Scientists and technicians were increasingly encouraged to look beyond the presumed wisdom of the high priests and philosophers for productive ideas. Modern technology developed in societies imbued with the rhetoric of Christian brotherhood. Religious pluralism associated with immigrations to early America ramified the need for tolerance.[37]

There is no necessary connection between efficiency and tolerance, of course, but neither is there any reason to believe (with Heidegger and the Frankfurt school) that technology is intrinsically dehumanizing. Were one to believe this it would have to be because she were possessed of an objectivist sense of rationality and a universalist understanding of culture. The alternative is to attempt to provide "a utopia in which humans caused each other far less suffering than they presently do."[38] This decrease in suffering would be sought within a society which balanced that need against the need for a maximum of tolerance for different ways of living.

Now Rorty asks what the consequences of this sort of ethnocentrism would be. The most important response is that it would lead to piecemeal, wholly experimental, and essentially nonprogrammatic, interactions. There would neither be the desire to save cultural values simply because they were there, nor would there be the attempt to define in advance what would constitute "suffering." Rorty doesn't stress this point in this context but it is clearly an implication of his belief that "cruelty is the worst thing we do." Cruelty has as one of its most painful forms the exercise of humiliation. Humiliation results from "forced redescription." Such redescription occurs when one insists that some other individual or group accept one's description of them rather than being free to describe themselves.

The exercise of persuasion associated with rationality-as-tolerance cannot go on at the global level. One must get down far enough into specifics to compare descriptions in order to offer specific, concrete, and testable alternative beliefs or modes of action. The presumed total-itarian, colonial, and missionizing character of Western technocratic societies would dissolve if the truly pragmatic, pluralistic character of liberal democracies were realized.

Rorty acknowledges (what he believes Dewey acknowledged in his later work) that rationality-as-tolerance will likely be aided by look-ing away from science and technology and toward art. The poet, not the scientist and technician, then, may be the proper heir to the high priests either of religion or of science. Here we see that the aesthetic pluralism of American thought discussed earlier has two positive contributions to make to the liberal democratic utopia which serves as the form and substance of Rorty's ethnocentrism: first, it provides a model of the sort invoked by Emerson and James to accommodate real difference in the most tolerant of manners, and second, it provides the model of the artist, the poet, rather than the scientific or technical expert, as the source of cultural creativity.

Movements which turn away from science and find norms in reli-gion as a means of seeking transcendent values, such as those associated with certain contemporary cultural critics in India,[39] are not piecemeal enough for Rorty's tastes. *Contra* Rorty, however, it should be said on behalf of the Indian culture that religion (implicated with art) has served to promote a high degree of tolerance in a society which is, arguably, far more pluralistic than that of the North Atlantic democracies.[40]

Rorty hopes by appeal to the artist to reinforce the piecemeal and occasional character of cultural change.

> The real work of building a multi-cultural global utopia, I suspect, will be done by people who, in the course of the next few centuries,

unravel each culture [as shared habits of action] into a multiplicity of
fine component threads together with equally fine threads drawn from
other [such] cultures, thus promoting the kind of variety-in-unity characteristic of rationality [as tolerance].[41]

This is the project of the novelists, the ethnographers, the journalists—
the connoisseurs of diversity, the specialists in particularity. In the promotion of cross-cultural understanding, therefore: "We need to be on
the lookout not just for Japanese Heideggers, Indian Platos, and Chinese
Humes, but for Chinese Sternes and Indonesian Rabelaises . . . people
who enjoyed unweaving the tapestries which the saints and sages had
woven."[42]

I think Rorty is right here. Philosophers seem increasingly aware of
the pale abstractness of much of their work, especially when applied to
questions of intercultural understanding. Still, it would be well to keep
in mind that "abstractions" come in two varieties: formal and selective.
In the effort to avoid the formal abstractness of the philosopher, we
shouldn't altogether yield ourselves up to excessive selectivity of those
who muck about in the exotic particularities of this or that culture.

One wonders how the ethnocentric Rorty might handle a case such
as the following: In 1989, at the Sixth East/West Conference held in
Honolulu, Hawaii, a paper was delivered which concerned the relationship between mythical and philosophical interpretations of history.
Accounting for the meaning of historical narrative by appeal to mythical resources is a common convention of religion, literature, and politics
and is in itself quite unexceptional. In this instance, however, a rather
dramatic incident occurred during the discussion of the paper.
Ramchandra Gandhi, grandson of Mahatma Gandhi, responded to the
presentation in something like the following manner:

"You have given us a myth," he said. "I will offer another one. Very
briefly. Suppose Brahma allows, indeed encourages, the violence of
human beings one to the other. . . . Suppose Brahma allows, indeed
encourages, events such as the holocaust, and all the terrible violence
witnessed in Europe in this century. . . . Suppose this is true . . . and suppose Brahma does this in order to sensitize us to the pain human beings
cause the animals."

My recollection is that these remarks occasioned only silence—a
bemused, for some an embarrassed, silence. Yet I think Gandhi's myth
made its point rather well. It is conceivable that the Anglo-European
interpretations of pain, and of history itself insofar as it is punctuated by
terror, cruelty, and suffering, would constitute an entirely different

accounting were we to take seriously the most uncontroversial consequences of this narrative. Human beings may be inured to the pain of
their fellows to some degree by remaining deaf to the squeals and
moans that come from the slaughterhouses.

Can we who "are born in another's pain and perish in our own"[43]
and who live lives which in part owe so many of their pleasures to the
pain of animals[44] feel altogether justified with the defense of our attitudes provided by the parodies of Samuel Butler and the somber
advices of the medical establishment concerning the need for protein?
Or should we seek vindication from mythical resources, appealing to
the Genesis narrative which makes the human creature lord over the
beast of the fields and birds of the air, supplementing our apologia by
appeals to the Platonic association of soul with reason and reason exclu-
sively with the human being?

Gandhi's myth would have to seem silly to those of us Westerners
who weigh its advices against cold economic, gastronomic, and psychic realities. The rational individual easily reduces such thoughts to
absurdity by asking such scrupulous questions as "Well, after all, plants
are living, perhaps feeling, creatures. Would you really condone the
consumption of vegetables? And why stop with the organic realm? The
destruction of the inorganic structures which increases entropy is
strongly analogous to cruelty, is it not?"

Indeed, where does it end? Must we have a concept of cosmic *adi-
aphora* to get us off the hook? Or does the ecological movement, which
ultimately is aimed at a resolution of the human being's responsibility in
the entropy-producing environment, preclude moral holidays? Such
reductios miss the point. That we should consider silly certain valua-
tions of the phenomenon of pain merely begs the question since that
judgment is dependent, as is all thinking to some degree, on the specific
character of our understanding of pleasure and of pain.

As Samuel Johnson noted, "We do not disturb ourselves with the
detection of fallacies which do us no harm." And Hume's more than
casual identification of good and evil with pleasure and pain[45] suggests
that insofar as reasonings are moral they are conditioned by the parameters of pleasure and pain. Every pragmatist, especially Richard Rorty,
must consider thinking and pain to be associated since the problematic situation from which thinking emerges is a more or less painful
mixture of the stable and the precarious.

The only way a nominalist historicist such as Rorty can approach
this issue is through a widening of the reference of the term "we." The
question is whether he would be willing to include those Indian indi-

viduals who so broaden the reference of "the ability to feel pain." Including them in the phrase "one of us" would lead to an increased awareness of the fact and character of the extralinguistic phenomenon of pain, and would ultimately lead to the inclusion of other living things in what Albert Schweitzer called "the community of those who bear the mark of pain." But can liberal Western individuals who owe so many of their transient pleasures to the pain of cows and chickens applaud the consequences of such awareness?

Rorty claims that "pain" is an extralinguistic phenomenon. But he also claims, in another context, that "Dewey should have dropped the term 'experience' . . . and should have looked elsewhere for continuity between us and the brutes. . . . The only relevant break in continuity is that between non-language users . . . and language-users."[46] There is a real tension here: On what grounds might Rorty exclude animals from his desire to reduce pain? Apparently, on the grounds that they do not use language. But that is to ignore an extremely relevant continuity ("pain") and employ instead *the break in continuity* as the means of excluding the brutes from the concerns of those who would reduce pain. If Rorty wants to defend a certain class of entities that experience pain, he has moved far beyond a simple appeal to an extralinguistic datum. He is forced to say something like: "It is the pain of those who (on other grounds) are deemed to be *like me* with which I am concerned." I don't see why one ought not employ the criterion of the ability to experience pain as one's grounds for establishing continuity and then appeal to that continuity when defending the brutes from pain.

One might say that the sort of ethnocentrism Rorty preaches has the potential to significantly alter our social and cultural practices. For if, as Rorty suggests, part of the content of our peculiar ethnocentrism is a suspicion of ethnocentrism, the liberal ironist, plagued by doubts over the value of her final vocabulary, will be open to conversations with those who share a different ethos. And, sometimes, as in the case of the illustration just cited, that openness can lead one to broaden the application of one's (ethnocentrically derived) beliefs.

PALE HEROICS

As Lonely Provincial Rorty recognizes the existential problematic of private life in liberal democratic and technological societies. As Sincere Ethnocentric, he recognizes the contingency of the starting point for any conversation he might have with those whose thought and values are shaped by a different ethos. Together these recognitions serve to mitigate any resort to radical or revolutionary action. But, as we learned in chapter 1, we can't dispense with heroes. Contrary to the import of his ethnocentrism and provincialism, Rorty's heroism suggests some sympathy for revolutionary action. Rorty's heroes are, as we have seen, drawn from the world's strong poets, and utopian revolutionaries. In chapter 2, I listed some of the heroes of Rorty's particular narrative—philosophers, poets, and critics. These are the individuals whom Rorty would hope to surpass and, by surpassing, take upon himself the hero's mantle.

There are a number of curious things about Rorty's understanding of the hero in history. The first is that his heroes are not to be found in received mythical, literary, and political traditions of his culture, but are protagonists of his own peculiar narrative. Rorty has personalized the art of creating heroes. In fact, many of his heroes (Martin Heidegger is a signal instance) are self-consciously attempting to constitute themselves as heroes.

Rorty's reading of the history of ideas requires that we recognize the utility of a thinker only after the consequences of his thought have played out. This version of Hegel's Owl suffers from the same problem as its original—namely, it is often too discomfiting to believe that the heroes of history remained unaware of the meaning of their grandest efforts. Once we raise to the level of consciousness the poetic, ironic recognition that later generations will determine what sort of utensil one has created or has become, we develop a sense of things at a level (the metalevel) which former generations did not have.

Hegelian apocalypticism infects philosophers who read too much, who become too aware of the texts of their tradition, who are too sensitized to the conflicting senses of nature, knowledge, freedom, power, and law. This apocalypticism leads those surfeited with knowledge to sense that, in some manner or other, "it's over." Having finally gotten here from there, there is no place else to go. After Hegel (a fortiori, after Freud) heroes are very hard to come by.

To be efficacious our heroes must be genuine. They must be individuals who struggle and prevail on their own merits. They must have, or be thought to have, more than ex post facto identities. Rorty's heroes are antecedent, self-consciously created constructions whose status is narrative-dependent. Such heroes are contingent ciphers whose value is an accidental consequence of someone having polled a later generation.

This may indeed be the manner heroes come into being. However, if it is recognized to be such, it will be impossible for any but hypersardonic sophisticates to celebrate heroic deeds. It is impossible to truly marvel at the release of a rabbit from a hat into which we have just witnessed the poor creature being stuffed.

If Rorty is correct in saying "Newton did not know that his purpose was modern technology,"[47] then what did he know? $F = ma$? or *Every body in the universe is attracted to every other body by a force directly proportional to their masses and inversely proportional to the square of the distance between their centers*? It may be subsequently said of him that he did. But until the seeds of his new metaphor, *gravitas*, blown by the winds of contingency, found fertile soil in the minds of subsequent thinkers, blossoming finally into the unforced flower of rationalized technology, his metaphor was merely a candidate for public knowledge. What follows from this (to say the least) is a "nonteleological view of intellectual history."[48]

Contrary to Rorty's blasé account of the emergence of Aristotle's *ousia*, Saint Paul's *agapē*, and Newton's *gravitas*, in terms of jangled neurons or obsessional kinks, if one is to sustain a heroic view of history, *it matters how the trick was done*. If we have all been backstage and watched the makeup going on, if we have examined the mirrors: our heroes are goners for sure.

Ours is a disenchanted world and Rorty wishes to be an agent furthering that disenchantment. But heroes are far better fitted to an age of enchantment. Whether they can survive hyperconsciousness is a serious question. Certainly we cannot allow our heroes to be conscious of their wiring. We can, perhaps forgive them everything but hyper self-consciousness. For once the intellectual tradition is infected by such awareness, thinkers will increasingly attempt to develop their various theories in response to the theories of others rather than by beginning with the data of experience and reason. One of the dangers of the past is that it burdens us with predigested perspectives and problems, tempting us away from the more open and naive approach to thinking for its own sake.

Hegel responded to this sort of situation by developing his peculiar doctrine of the Unhappy Consciousness.

> In Stoicism, self-consciousness is the bare and simple freedom of itself. In Scepticism, it realizes itself, negates the other side of determinate existence, but, in so doing, really doubles itself, and is itself now a duality. In this way the duplication, which was previously divided between two individuals, the lord and the bondsman, is concentrated in one. . . . Hence the *Unhappy Consciousness*, the Alienated Soul which is the consciousness of self as a divided nature, a doubled and merely contradictory being.[49]

Hegel finds the Unhappy Consciousness to be the consequence of an attempt, which Descartes took for granted, to mediate the external world through the self's relationship to itself. But the contemporary synthesis of (meta) stoicism and (meta) skepticism is the hyperconsciousness of metamentality. Consciousness is unhappy when it desires complete knowledge of itself but cannot obtain it. Hyperconsciousness produces unhappiness because, having desired complete self-consciousness and having obtained it, one discovers that Hegel was wrong in assuming that the character of mind and that of reality are congruent. Such knowledge leads to frustration and, potentially at least, despair.

Until Rorty came along, the principal antidotes for the pain of hyperconsciousness were those of the taxonomists who organize the details of the long-since spent philosophic enterprise, or the obscurantist and antirationalist who take seriously the advice to engage in that "active forgetting" Nietzsche encouraged with the grandest of ironic gestures. For those unable to forget, the taxonomists' happy acceptance of cultural crystallization has served as an antidote to this phase of cultural awareness. Those who have contented themselves with collecting, coveting, preserving, and admiring the crystalline structures of intellectual culture do seem, at least for the time being, to have been spared the most debilitating effects of hyperconsciousness.

But it is difficult to avoid these effects for long. Can Oedipus survive as hero after *Tom Jones* and the writings of Sigmund Freud? Are we post-Freudians really able to appreciate the pouting Achilles, or the blustering Heathcliff? The world is too much with us for the epic sense to survive. Ours is no longer an epic age, and lyric poetry needs no heroes. Plays and novels get along quite well with mere protagonists. For a while we are satisfied with antiheroes—K., Bloom, Willy Loman, Humbert Humbert. Now we are likely to be more inspired by the absurdist language and situations of Beckett and Pinter than by any of the so-called protagonists that stray, shadowlike, through their works.

Indeed, postmodernists such as Borges, Calvino, and Vonnegut make continual resort to romantic irony to raise the process of writing to the level of consciousness, making the protagonists aware of their participation in a narrative.[50] Heroes can hardly survive that much awareness. Nor are they meant to survive; postmodern literature is one vast machine for recycling heroes into degradable refuse.

The world is too much with us for the epic sense to survive. Nietzsche's proposal of "active forgetting" as a response to the "excess of history" could conceivably maintain the morale of intellectuals by avoiding the worst consequences of relativity. Taking their cue from the classical beginnings of scientific rationalism, thinkers could proceed by canceling history, by refusing to open their speculations to historical reduction, sublation, or dialectical articulation.

Presently, reconstructive efforts in philosophy which hope to reground the discipline, whether they be found among analysts, phenomenologists, or speculative thinkers, have taken the route of active forgetting. The sense of novelty and the hope of systematic certainty are much easier to sustain if one is freed from the debilitating effects of perfect historical recall.

Nietzsche did not in fact follow the path of active forgetting. His real solution was to accept the whole congeries of the past and present ideas, when summed into a totality, as the truth. The only adequate sense of truth is that associated with the totality of perspectival interpretations constituting that which is. *Everything*—in the sense of all perspectives added together into a chaotic totality—is true.

As we have seen, Rorty's response to the problem of metamentality is to tacitly accept the Nietzschean claim, at least to the extent of allowing an initial parity to the congeries of interpretations that constitute the inventory of intellectual culture, but then to move in the direction of constructing a narrative which has, he freely admits, no more than a rhetorical adequacy.

But for those of us who still wish our heroes to emerge with some spontaneity, this is not a satisfactory response. Heroes require strong emotion, creative imagination, and the affirmation of the absolute centrality of personal vision. Two out of three is not enough. Rorty is heroic, but without the dynamic emotions of rapture, nostalgia, reverie, and delirium associated with the heroic spirit. By his continued resort to philosophic and literary imagination, and his affirmation of personal vision against the norms of objectivity, Rorty rises to the status of hero . . . if only barely.

Though Rorty claims to need heroes when he tells historical narratives of the mighty dead, he treats heroes and heroines somewhat differently when concentrating on the sorts of ad hoc narratives one gives of one's own life. Recognizing public and private meanings of morality—the first referring to the just or unjust treatment of others, the second concerning "the search for private perfection"—Rorty deems the private side of morality to be "the search for character, the attempt of individuals to be reconciled with themselves (and in the case of some exceptional individuals to make their lives works of art)."[51]

The search for character has as its goal either purity or self-enlargement. One seeks either the *ascetic* or the *aesthetic* life. Rorty espouses the search for self-enlargement, which places him in the company of de Sade, Byron, and Hegel. Rejecting the options of de Sade (sexual experimentation) and of Byron (political engagement), he buys into Hegel's approach which involves the enrichment of language, "the acquisition of new vocabularies of moral reflection"[52]—"tools for criticizing the character of others and for creating one's own."[53] But if the strong poet is to be listed among Rorty's heroic types, it is difficult to see how Rorty intends to separate the search for character from the possible realization of a heroic stature. The paradox is resolved through the recognition that many of Rorty's public heroes (the heroes of his Grand Narrative) are those whose message to the world (as Rorty reads it) is that of the importance of the desire for self-enlargement in the private sphere. For example, Rorty finds Sigmund Freud's contribution to be that "he opened up new possibilities for the aesthetic life . . . (helping) us become increasingly ironic, playful, free, and inventive in our choice of self-descriptions . . . (and making) the desire for purification seem more self-deceptive, and the quest for self-enlargement more promising."[54]

The vocabulary employed in the search for self-enlargement is one that is woven into narratives. But unlike the narrative one uses when telling the story of public events, the stories about our private selves must be accounts of centerless matrices of belief and desire of the sort discussed in chapter 2.[55] Such accounts threaten our dignity "only if we think we need *reasons* to live romantically, or to treat others decently, or to be treated decently ourselves."[56] So in place of the attempt to find a coherent self-image that will fit the whole species, we substitute "the ability of each of us to tailor a coherent self-image for ourselves and then use it to tinker with our behavior."[57]

But what is the relationship of the historical narratives Rorty gives, complete with heroes and villains, to the ad hoc personal narratives he might provide of himself for himself? Rorty claims that larger historical narratives can provide resources for vocabularies of moral deliberation and that we are quite right in attempting to see the (heroless) narratives of our own lives as a part of the larger (heroic) narratives.

This is most confusing. For Rorty suggests that one's private vocabulary includes proper names such as Julien Sorel and Becky Sharpe,[58] and we know that his own Grand Narrative includes names such as Martin Heidegger and Jacques Derrida. But if philosophers (particularly these) are primarily tools for the search for private perfection, then Julien Sorel and Martin Heidegger and Jacques Derrida and Becky Sharpe share common functions. And, certainly, if we want to tell a story which incorporates Thackeray and Stendhal in a larger narrative (not unlike the way that Rorty has spoken of Orwell and Nabokov[59]), there is no reason why the characters of their novels might not serve heroic functions. And reverting to the function of stories of the "mighty dead" which are aimed at making "our hopes of surpassing them concrete," we will need such stories only if we need *reasons* to imagine, to create, to think in ways that might lead to such surpassing. These reasons may not be present in the novels themselves, but in more formalized philosophic discourse.

I think Rorty is caught in a dilemma much more serious than is initially apparent. For if he wishes to substitute narratives when argument fails (and, as we shall see,[60] his strategies of "recontextualization" and "circumvention" depend upon this substitution), these have to be persuasive narratives. It is difficult to know how to shape a narrative without protagonists who serve as the foci of the interpretations of ideas, events, or institutions. If we wish to call such protagonists heroes when we are discussing public events, but deny that even the function of protagonist is essential to the search for private perfection, we require a reason.

The only reason I can find is that Rorty believes we must avoid the application of irony to the public sphere. Just as the socialization process expected of children must involve the initially rather uncritical patriotic accounts of their political culture, so the socialization required of the citizens of intellectual culture proceeds by exposure to nonironic renderings of how we got to the point at which we have arrived.

In chapter 3 I gave reasons why I believe this sort of limitation placed upon irony, based as it is upon a strict division of public and private life, is a bad solution to one of Rorty's central problems. The problematic status of Rorty's appeal to heroes further ramifies those difficulties. I agree that Rorty needs heroes in order to keep his narratives from degenerating into temporalized theories which stand blandly beside other such accounts, waiting for the taxonomist to put them in their place. Heroes provide the personalization and dramatic import necessary for a narrative to have persuasive force. But, granting that Rorty needs heroes, does he himself wish to attain heroic status? There is a real irony here. For Rorty to become a hero he must be part of someone else's narrative or else he suffers Heidegger's fate, which Rorty deplores, of attempting to write a personal narrative in which he identifies himself as hero not only for himself but for the history of the West. But if Rorty is a hero in someone else's narrative, it will only be in order to render concrete that narrator's hopes of surpassing Rorty. Given

Rorty's Bloomian-Oedipal sense of the movements of history, it is understandable that he would not like too soon to be a heroic protagonist.

Richard Rorty is a pale hero by choice. For he realizes that his acceptance into someone else's heroic pantheon, doubtless an event to be expected, will constitute not only his apotheosis but his demise.

A BASHFUL PROPHET

Rorty is most emphatic in his claim that philosophical pragmatism applied outside the strictly philosophical arena is rather banal. For example, most lawyers in liberal democratic societies are pragmatists who need little or no assistance from pragmatist philosophers.[61] Once philosophical pragmatism has made the point that legal theory per se has little efficacy in insuring just decisions, there is little specifically the legal profession might learn from the pragmatic thinker.

Rorty believes that the primary work of the philosopher is that of clearing the philosophical underbrush created by other philosophers. He does admit, particularly with respect to the work of John Dewey, that there is sometimes more than a banal pragmatism to which one might appeal. For, in addition to Dewey the pragmatist, there is Dewey the *prophet*, "the Emersonian visionary rather than the contributor to *The Journal of Philosophy*."[62] This romantic side of Dewey, however, is not *essentially* prophetic. Rorty believes that Dewey's prophecies are broadly irrelevant to his pragmatism, and vice versa.

Rorty's point is that neither prophetic visions nor the practical activities of the nonphilosophical professionals need philosophic support. There are thus many specific activities in a liberal democratic society the philosopher might endorse, even though they will not be backed up by general theoretical argument.

Rorty admits that, traditionally, the term "pragmatism" has meant more than a set of philosophical arguments. The term has applied, as well, to a prophetic, visionary tradition. During the time of James and Dewey, there was "still some relation between pragmatist philosophical doctrines and attempts to overcome racial prejudice, to make labor unions seem morally respectable, and to subordinate property rights to social needs."[63] This was due to the fact that, at the turn of the century, the intellectual right employed objectivist arguments to justify oppressive institutions. The pragmatists' critique could be brought to bear with some efficacy against these arguments. Today, however, the "right" is as pragmatic as the "left"; neither are inclined to employ argument. Thus the philosopher is not called upon to assault oppressive conventions. It is the judges and lawyers who perform the practical tasks once vouchsafed to the philosophical prophet. Indeed, for Rorty, professorial pragmatism renders the term "prophetic pragmatism" little more meaningful than "charismatic trash disposal."[64]

In his nonpoetic, mundanely philosophic guise, Rorty's motivation is the same as he attributes to John Dewey who claimed that "a chief task of those who call themselves philosophers is to help get rid of the useless lumber that blocks our highways of thought, and strive to make straight and open the highways that lead to the future."[65] But there is a problem here. The work of the underlaborer in removing the obstacles to the practical progress of the poet's new metaphors is not the principal work of Rorty's recontextualizations. The method of "redescribing lots and lots of things" is much the same as employed by utopian politics or revolutionary science. And the method of recontextualization is not only that of the utopian prophet; it is the method of the strong poet as well.

In a review of Cornel West's *The American Evasion of Philosophy*, Rorty says, "I do not think that professorial pragmatism is a good place to look for prophecy, or for the sort of rich possibilities which the prophetic imagination makes visible."[66] Rorty contends that the social role of the professional philosophers ought be that of junior partner to the prophets. Professorial pragmatism can only function in today's climate if it can attach itself to prophetic movements. But often prophets can get along quite well without such support. Rorty instances Martin Luther King as one who managed quite well without philosophic support. "The philosophy professors cheered from the sidelines, but were of no great use to the civil rights movement."[67]

Rorty asserts the need to recognize that prophecy is no more closely connected to philosophy than to any other discipline. He does believe that the American left is in need of "some sense of a utopian American future,"[68] but seems convinced that professorial pragmatism is not a very promising place to look for such a utopian sense.

His demurrers to the contrary notwithstanding, I believe that one could argue that Rorty serves both as a real American prophet as well as an auxiliary to other prophets. With respect to the first role, the picture of a liberal democratic utopia discussed above is arguably such a prophetic project. Rorty would likely say that this doesn't count because his presentation lacks sufficient detail; but such a denial would seem to be coyness on Rorty's part. One should grant, of course, that it is bad form in the late modern age to claim the authority of the prophet; this is the sort of thing that must be accorded you by others. Nonetheless, I believe Rorty's refusal to recognize his prophetic role when he is in the business of continually arguing for a utopian vision is no less ironic than his claim to be an underlaborer when in fact he is accused, as often as not, of being an *underminer*.

There is a sense in which Rorty is more the prophetic pragmatist than John Dewey ever was. According to Rorty, Dewey's Keatsian vision of a society comprised by a "grand democracy of Forrest Trees" is not specifically pragmatic since these visionary passages do not let the reader know how it *feels* to be a pragmatist.[69] But I would suggest that many of Rorty's rich descriptions of his poetic utopia do in fact let his readers know something of how it might feel to be a New Pragmatist. In the course of reading Rorty, one certainly might experience the anxiety born of a sense of contingency, the burden of challenges to self-creativity, the lonely, in-the-dark situation of a centerless nexus of beliefs spinning its web without the hope of metaphysical comfort. What more can prophecy do?

Even if we were to limit Rorty to the role of auxiliary, however, it is clear that he has provided strong, if unsolicited, support to what he considers to be the single movement in America which has a chance of maintaining a prophetic stance: the feminist movement. The difficulty with the movement is that its white middle class orientation is hard to overcome. Rorty anticipates little assistance from philosophers per se in the endeavor to broaden the basis of the movement.

In his Tanner lecture, entitled "Feminism and Pragmatism,"[70] Rorty provides an important apologia for political pragmatism while making some specific suggestions as to the sort of aid feminists might expect from pragmatism. One reason the New Pragmatism has a great deal to offer feminism is that many within the movement focus upon the linguistic influences that signal, promote, and sustain the oppression of women by a male-dominated society. Rorty's notion of humiliation as "forced redescription" is most relevant to this sort of focus.

Commenting on the feminist proposals of Catherine McKinnon[71] and Marilyn Frye[72] among others, Rorty shows the importance of pragmatism to feminism by arguing that the language of the pragmatic nominalist and historicist is superior to that of the universalist. Rorty believes that feminists such as McKinnon and Frye need to provide new data for moral deliberations concerning women rather than to overcome presumably "distorted" communication which somehow "masks" the true reality of women. Pragmatism allows us to take account of new descriptions which will evoke novel emotional responses and solicit novel practices. The "moral reality" the universalist believes to be masked or distorted is in fact a reality in the making. Thus pragmatism has something to offer feminism that *Ideologiekritik* does not. "Pragmatism redescribes both intellectual and moral progress by substituting metaphors of evolutionary development for metaphors of progressively less distorted perception."[73]

The sort of evolutionary development which involves contributions of novel metaphors ought be controlled in large measure by those who are most concerned with its outcome. Maintaining the same old argumentative contexts associated with radical critique, and the rhetoric of unmasking, may not promise much for there is the suspicion on the part of some feminists that "realism" and "universalism" are themselves expressions of phallocentric language. Those feminists who seek to add a new voice to the conversation might well look to pragmatists who are able to accommodate such a voice, rather than to the universalist who believes the only voice we require is that of reason and objectivity.

It is certainly true, as many feminists have pointed out, that in a male-dominated society the choices of what constitutes a viable subject for debate as well as the ground-rules of debate are decided in advance by the accepted language of rational discourse. It does appear that it is Enlightenment rationalism rather than pragmatism which is to be charged with conservatism and accession to the status quo.

Rorty's defense of pragmatism against the charges of conservatism is persuasive: For the pragmatist, personal identity is focused by a description. This description is one shaped by the linguistic resources of the community of which one is a part. Segments of a society—minorities, social outcasts, women—may historically have been described in manners which they themselves, upon reflection, found illegitimate. If forced by political, social, or interpersonal oppression to accept that illegitimate description, then members of these groupings experience humiliation. The pragmatist encourages the unrestrained development of new vocabularies of self-description.

This is hardly conservatism. For though, as noted above, Rorty's ethnocentrism recognizes (along with that of C. S. Peirce) the need to begin with one's beliefs in any consideration of important issues, this recognition does not involve an endorsement of the status quo. Rorty wishes only to admonish those among the social critics who underestimate the inertia of beliefs.

Actions aimed at the rectification of oppressive social conditions may lead one to use the Enlightened universalist rhetoric which appeals to a moral reality beyond the distorted appearances of present social practice. In this case, one may wish for a radical transformation of society such that one's laws and institutions promote and sustain that reality. The problem here is that if this desire is realized the moral reality is apt to look quite a bit like the present sense of what the dominant members of the society feel to be most desirable. In the case of feminism, women will end up getting "a piece of the action," "equal opportunity," and so forth. But if the action is male action and the opportunity one wins is the chance to be just like the boys, little may be thought to have been gained by those who feel the name "woman" is meant to designate a moral identity at variance with the Enlightenment norms.

For the pragmatist, a liberal society is meant to provide a context within which the tools for self-description may be developed. The self as a centerless web of beliefs might become something radically different from its present status by virtue of the acquisition of alternative beliefs. For women, this means that, though distinctively female identity might not yet exist, such could be created in the future through the actions of women themselves. Psychology is not destiny.

It is easy to see how this might look tame compared to the totalizing critique sought by proponents of *Ideologiekritik*. In a real sense, however, we can leave the issue open to empirical justification. Radical social critics assume that we ought to root out the evils of society; utopians claim we should plant new seeds. It may be possible to see the activity of uprooting and that of sowing as complementary contributions to a feminist utopia.

The Rortyan pragmatist would object to the employment of ideological critique in part because the aggressive, totalizing language of the critical philosopher is most open to the charge of being masculist to the core. The ad hoc, piecemeal advices of the pragmatist seem rather more neutral. Ironically, feminists are drawn to ideological critique because "masculism seems so thoroughly built into everything we do and say in contemporary society that it looks as if only some really *massive* intellectual change could budge it."[74] And it is precisely these large-scale changes *Ideologiekritik* promises. But Rorty claims that "masculism . . . can survive almost as well in an anti-logocentric as in a logocentric philosophical environment."[75]

The issue is joined between the Rortyan pragmatists and the critical philosophers at the point at which one asks after the priority of philosophy and politics. Rorty believes in the priority of democracy to philosophy; the critical thinkers believe that any political system depends upon prior deep-linguistic or metaphysical grounding.[76]

For my own part, I believe that the aims of the New Pragmatist as Rorty expresses them are more consonant with the desires of feminists who seek to gain semantic authority over themselves. Understanding culture as habits of action which can refer to any solidarity grouping within society with enough self-consciousness to want to give itself a name and a status suggests that women ought create their own culture. This might be done (in fact many, Rorty included, think this could be necessary) through *separatism*. That is to say, self-selected groups of women could retreat into private communities long enough to develop new and autonomous vocabularies. Such groups could "build their moral strength by achieving increasing semantic authority over themselves, thereby increasing the ability of those members to find their moral identities in their membership [in] such groups."[77] This sort of suggestion is consonant with Rorty's view that we ought to construct a society and a world order "whose model is a bazaar surrounded by lots and lots of private clubs."[78]

Only if one could call endorsing separatism of the sort Rorty discusses "conservative" could Rorty's views be called conservative. Many critics of Rorty fail to realize that those who appeal to the status quo of Western democracies are pernicious only if they go on to spell out the character of that status quo in terms of *theoretical* or *ideological* descriptions of the content of that consensus and then presume that, in the main, this is the best we can expect from our present society.

Pragmatic utopianism critiques the actualities of some segment of society on behalf of the potentialities of some others; it chastises the realized present in the name of an imagined future. This not only argues for change, but enriches the language in terms of which the arguments for change, and the sort of changes sought, might be characterized. This is a good illustration of Rorty's narrativist claim that one ought respond to argumentative impasses by telling "stories about why we talk as we do and how we might avoid continuing to talk that way."[79]

On the pragmatist view, the most seriously oppressed have been denied semantic authority over themselves. And since "a human being, for moral purposes, is largely a matter of how he or she describes himself or herself,"[80] the freedom from oppression is freedom to *invent* oneself. For this reason, "we pragmatists have to identify most of the wrongness of past male oppression with its suppression of past potentiality, rather than [with] its injustice to past actuality."[81]

For me, the most attractive feature of this style of thinking is that it allows us to take seriously the oppression advertised by minorities and feminists. There is something a bit disingenuous in the universalist's claim that this or that group of people has suffered greatly but that deep down its members haven't been seriously scarred. This amounts to the claim that the oppressed have not been *so* oppressed that they cannot indicate who they truly are and lay claim to that identity—as if the slave is perfectly capable of having suffered the oppression of the master and of maintaining an accurate picture of who he truly is. Far better that the oppressed, recognizing the depth of the oppression, seek to create a language which communicates who they wish to be, rather than accept one that expresses, in the subtlest ways, the inevitability of their oppressed condition.

If Rorty is not taking the stance of prophet in his presentation of this program for altering the status of male/female relationships in contemporary society, it is difficult to understand what, on Rorty's terms, prophecy might be.

A DIFFIDENT POET

There is certainly nothing in Rorty's thinking that requires us to make a hard and fast distinction between a poet and a philosopher. Nonetheless, if metaphors are the motors of linguistic growth and if the philosopher has as a principal responsibility to help living metaphors become dead ones as quickly as possible in order to "reduce them to the status of tools of social progress,"[82] then the distinction between poets and philosophers is well enough defined to ask at any particular moment who is doing what. There is nothing to prevent philosophers such as Heidegger or Derrida from serving primarily as poets, while others such as John Dewey are philosophical in the more political sense. In either case, (pragmatic) poets and (pragmatic) philosophers act in such a manner as to alter the webs of beliefs and desires, the "sentential attitudes,"[83] we human beings are.

Rorty's narrativist perspective suggests that, overall, he is writing more in the guise of a poet than a philosopher, even a *historicist* philosopher. This may mean that when Rorty employs a traditional philosophic vocabulary in a typically philosophic manner, he has, nonetheless, maintained his poetic guise. For just as Marx's thinking was no less theoretical for being a theory of praxis, so Rorty's poetic narratives are no more philosophical (in his positive sense of the term) for being stories of the perils and promise of philosophy.

Rorty would attempt to dodge this broadside by claiming that a writer not only can but *does* continually shift back and forth between "literary" and "philosophical" moments as the context requires. With some qualification, he approves of Geoffrey Hartman's designation of literary language as "a diction whose frame of reference is such that the words stand out as words (or even sounds) rather than being, at once, assimilable meanings."[84] Rorty prefers to speak of two sorts of conversational situations, one in which there is a general consensus on what is at issue, the other in which "everything is up for grabs at once." This refers to the contrast of inferential and imaginative discourse.

Now Rorty may well wish to leave on his reader's shoulders the burden of discovering when he is writing in a poetic mode and, therefore, is perfectly free to say the anti-methodological things he wishes to say and when he has shifted into a philosophic gear and would be well-advised to fess up to the principles and methods internal to his favored practices, but this is surely to invite misunderstanding.

There may be more at stake here than a failure to express himself clearly. The lack of any clear signals as to when he is functioning poetically and when philosophically is an implication of his ironic stance. It permits Rorty to have it both ways. If he is attacked as a bad poet, he can protest that he is in fact but a humble philosophic underlaborer with no poetic pretensions; if assaulted as a "fuzzie" philosopher, he can claim he is, of course, dealing not in concepts but in metaphors and, thus, is acting within a context of imagination not inference. This means of having it both ways is another illustration of his ability to shift back and forth between the sweeping generalizations associated with historicist narratives and the specific, concrete nudges warranted by his nominalism.

My reading of Rorty is that he would be much more comfortable as a poet than as a philosopher for the simple reason that he has been so long engaged polemically in the task of casting off the old descriptions of the philosophical task. And given his belief (strained as I have argued) that prophecy is not much in evidence in liberal societies, and that there is little for the philosopher as underlaborer and auxiliary to do, the poetic side of intellectual activity must seem quite appealing.

These facts bring Rorty into alliance with an individual whom he believes an unlikely colleague—namely, Michel Foucault. Foucault was trained as a philosopher but felt, for reasons much different than Rorty's, that there was little hope for the philosopher functioning in the public sphere. Rorty is sympathetic to the fact that "Foucault, like Nietzsche, was a philosopher who claimed a poet's privileges."[85] Those privileges include the permission to dismiss demands that he provide objective norms or principles characterizing where he stands. The philosopher as poet can say things like, "I'm not about to offer philo-

sophical grounds for being on your side in public affairs, for my philosophical project is a private one which provides neither motive nor justification for my political actions."[86] The prophet and underlaborer roles
are contingently connected with the philosopher, but the poet as poet
and the philosopher as poet are more intimately connected with the
activity of self-creation.

On balance, I think one would have to say that Rorty not only
thinks the creation of private autonomy more seasonally relevant for
people like himself and Foucault than the role of public philosopher, but
that he is also much more personally disposed to such a role. The shy-
ness associated with his occasional prophetic utterances well matches
the diffidence with which he approaches the poetic task. He chastises
Foucault for occasionally falling into the trap of offering his search for
private autonomy as a model for society. Only if one firmly holds to the
distinction between public morality and the search for private autonomy will the latter be a harmless quest. Foucault, as a "knight of autonomy," was at his best when refusing to see connections between his
political actions and his private project of self-creation. His *poesis* was a
making that was wholly private.

In an odd sense Rorty and Foucault do seem to be colleagues.
Rorty's criticisms of Foucault's "dryness,"[87] produced by his refusal to
identify himself with any social context, and his objections to Foucault's
attempts to protect his private autonomy by becoming "a faceless, root-
less, homeless stranger to humanity and to history,"[88] may be read as
Rorty's overreaction to the felt similarity between himself and his fellow
"knight of autonomy."

Part of the response may be due to Rorty's fear that he might be
out-nominalized by Foucault. For as Rorty says, Foucault has inverted
the traditional Platonic reading of the consequences of writing the soul
large. Society being a psychic projection for Foucault means that the
contingency of the self is to be read into the public sphere with the consequence that social institutions have no more justification than the
shape of any individual personality. This is the basis of Foucault's anarchism. And it is, of course, nominalism with a vengeance.

In one sense Rorty provides the tools for radicalizing this
Foucaultian position when he claims "that societies are not quasi-persons, they are (at their liberal, social democratic best) compromises
between persons."[89] For this is also what Rorty says *persons* are—namely
"compromises between persons." Rorty, no less than Foucault or Plato,
is writing the soul large to find the structure of society (or, consistent
with his belief in the priority of democracy to philosophy, writing soci-

ety small to find a model for the self). In any case, there is isometry between the self and society. And the interactions that take place between individuals in public are the same causal, in-the-dark interactions that take place among the relatively coherent sets of beliefs and desires forming the inventory of persons constituting an "individual."

To move productively beyond Foucault's anarchism, Rorty must tell a story of the difficulties Foucault encounters when he employs "self-assertion" in the absence of a firm distinction between the private and the public world. But Rorty's narrative of the privatization of the search for autonomy is incomplete without another denominalizing element. Rorty agrees with Charles Taylor that in his role as knight of autonomy Foucault abandoned the Augustinian tradition of inwardness which says that "one's *deepest* identity is the one which binds one to one's fellow humans."[90] Rorty says that our *deepest* identity is wrapped up in our ability to feel pain and experience humiliation, and that this is precisely what binds us to other humans. Pain may be nonlinguistic, but humiliation is not. It is our recognition of pain and humiliation as potentially experienced by all other human beings that prevents us from being indifferent to the claims of the public world. And it is this that not only mitigates the purity of our nominalism, but prevents us from remaining comfortable in our poetic projects.

Rorty is right, I believe, in claiming that Foucault responded to the pain of others without thematizing his reasons for doing so. In this he was consistent with the nominalist stance. But Rorty, reading his philosophic principles from off the pages of pluralistic American liberalism, is less jaded, perhaps, than his French comrade. He finds Foucault's poetic refusal to account for his public actions to be irresponsible and suspect.

Rorty contends that Foucault would likely be troubled by the fact that, willy-nilly, he was a useful, well-intentioned member of a democratic society. That may be so. Rorty, however, suffers the opposite discomfort. He is himself a "knight of autonomy," somewhat embarrassed by his own, not inconsiderable poetic influence.

We needn't wonder whether Rorty is a poet since his support of a poetized culture in his Grand Narrative, a culture characterized by a vocabulary "which revolves around notions of metaphor and self-creation rather than around notions of truth, rationality, and moral obligation,"[91] make it almost essential that he be so. It would be odd indeed if Rorty could eschew the role of poet for himself and still be able to describe liberalism as "the hope that culture as a whole can be 'poeticized',"[92] and to claim that the goal of a liberal culture would be "the

creation of ever more various and multicolored artifacts,"[93] and to assert
that liberal society is one that "recognizes that it is what it is . . . because
certain poets and revolutionaries of the past spoke as they did,"[94] and to
urge further that such a society has "no purpose except to make life
easier for poets and revolutionaries while seeing to it that they make life
harder for others only by words, and not deeds."[95]

Were Rorty as ideologically ill-disposed to revolutionary tactics
and as professionally unprepared to take up the poetic stance as he tacitly claims to be, he would find himself betwixt and between, a self-
benched philosopher, capable of little more than cheering on the
strong(er) poets and revolutionaries still in the game, while entertaining
the vague fantasy that he might express himself in terms that are "at
least marginally his own" and hoping then, in spite of his having so
blatantly confessed his intentions, to "tempt the rising generation" with
his words.

I understand that the manner in which I have raised the issues in
this *excursus ad hominem* may not seem philosophically respectable and
that, though my remarks have, on the whole, been positive, Rorty might
feel condemned by the skewed character of my praise. I do insist that
this perhaps overly lightminded excursus has had, as do all such gestures, a serious intent. My primary purpose has been to render plausible
the claim, first made in the subtitle of this book, that Rorty is (with the
ironical senses adhering to these terms in this particular context) both
prophet and poet of the New Pragmatism.

CIRCUMVENTION AND CIRCUMLOCUTION

Rorty believes that the important changes in one's beliefs and desires are not traceable to any particular operations or procedures; they take place in the interstices untouched by "method." In this he seems to agree with Plato:

> After practicing detailed comparisons of names and definitions and visual and other sense perceptions, after scrutinizing them in benevolent disputation by the use of question and answer without jealousy, at last in a flash understanding of each blazes up and the mind, as it exerts all its powers to the limit of human capacity, is flooded with light.[1]

Of course, Rorty cannot be truly sympathetic with the mystical flavor of the nonmethodological Plato. For Plato is perfectly sanguine about method leading one through all but the final steps in the quest for knowledge. Unlike Plato, Rorty finds method useless from the start. But there is a problem here. After all, in one important sense, method is simply manners; it is the consideration one thinker gives another, allowing him to anticipate and check out the arguments with which he is to be presented. The denial of method—however well-motivated, however justified— leaves critics with nothing but rhetorical evaluation.

In this chapter I wish to discuss Rorty's attitude toward method, claiming that though he seeks a philosophy without method, his steadfast efforts to de-methodologize his thinking are finally unsuccessful. In the course of the chapter, I will say what Rorty's method is, compare his method with that of another who unsuccessfully seeks to avoid method, Jacques Derrida, and then close the chapter, and the argument of the book, by showing how his peculiar method underwrites Rorty's search for private perfection.

RORTY'S METHODOPHOBIA

In his *Phaedo*, Plato decries the condition of misology—the hatred of arguments based upon a sense of having been let down by them on numerous occasions. "Misology and misanthropy arise in just the same way. Misanthropy is induced by believing in somebody quite uncritically . . . and a little later you find that he is shoddy and unreliable."[2] Just so with misology. Having experienced the corrigibility of argumentative methods, one finally throws up his hands and becomes skeptical of argument per se.

Misology is a common condition of our late modernist culture. Having raised to the level of consciousness the principal methods employed since the beginnings of rational thought in the West, and having witnessed the rehearsal of each in a variety of different contexts only to see these arguments relativized by alternative methods, the philosopher becomes a misologist.

Throughout this work I have stressed the effect of Rorty's metamentality on his philosophical activity. Though "misology" is as much a name for a mood as for a doctrine, it is an important element of Rorty's anti-foundational stance. In late modern culture, however, misology is not so much due to the failure of individual arguments, as to the undisputed success of which a variety of methods is capable, each within its own narrow sphere of applicability. The conclusion is the same, however: no single truth is to be won.

The disappointments Rorty has suffered are by no means exclusive to him, though he is perhaps more candid and courageous in his recognition of the failure of argument, particularly the arguments of philosophers, to provide a meaningful consensus with respect to any topic of interest or importance. As I argued in chapter 1, the effort to hold the contemporary period in thought is frustrated by the presence of so many construals of the nature of the times, each defended by rigorous analytic or dialectical argumentation. Rorty's misology is all the greater since he has opened himself to discussions with a wider selection of thinkers than almost any other contemporary philosopher. As a consequence, he has become even more aware of the scandalous inability of this type of engagement to lead anywhere.

Rorty's anti-methodological stance is determined by a combination of factors which conspire to define the condition of philosophical discussions in contemporary intellectual culture: First, the "default nominalism" resulting from the failure of systematic philosophical speculation to achieve worthwhile results underlies the sort of misology Rorty expresses. Further, the logic of argumentation is relativized by appeal to alternative logical and semantic contexts, both within and beyond our Western cultural milieu. As a consequence of the collapse of the broad foundational sense of philosophy, logical arguments, as opposed to broadly rhetorical ones, have been reduced to absurdity through the demonstrations of the theory-bound and, therefore, arbitrary principles from which they begin. A related factor is expressed by the fact, well advertised by the systematic pluralists who chart the varieties of theoretical perspective, that the terms of any philosophical vocabulary have been intransigently ambiguated by virtue of the theory-bound character of all terminologies. The recognition of the theory-boundedness of philosophic terms forces Rorty to accept a causal rather than a rational vision of intertheoretical communication. It is this fact, above all, that requires him to deny the significance of methodology.

Were one to take the broadest view of the Western philosophical tradition, the present anti-metaphysical stance, in either its positivist or postmodernist form, would be seen in terms of the emergence of the default nominalism which pervades the thinking of most who bother to look beyond their provincial perspectives in order to "hold their time in thought." The search for either a general ontology (*ontologia generalis*), which advertises the unity and coherence of the world by expressing the Being of beings, or a science of first principles (*scientia universalis*), which characterizes things by appeal to general principles ordering the whole and underwriting our knowledge of it, has collapsed into a resigned anarchy embarrassed by any invocation of "essences" or "objective principles." The beginnings of contemporary misology are to be found in the frustration of any attempts to find a sense of the whole through either an ontological or a cosmological route.

As we shall soon see, Rorty's dismissal of method often appears somewhat offhanded. He is not really interested in accounting for his misology by rehearsing the grander sorts of embarrassment to which metaphysical thinking has been subjected in the past few generations. I do, however, believe that such a rehearsal provides the proper context for understanding the real depth of his suspicion toward any conscious resort to method. I intend, therefore, to spend a few pages discussing the relation between the failure of our tradition's metaphysical aspirations and the growing distaste for philosophical method which Rorty so well represents.

The Western philosophical tradition really gets started when thinkers begin to ask after the difference between the "whatness" and the "thatness" of a thing. Asking *what* a being is is a cosmological question; considering *that* it is involves an ontological appreciation. A natural object—a "lump" as an item related with the other items in its ecosystem in complex spatiotemporal manners—is a *cosmological* entity. That the object is—its "isness"—indicates its *ontological* character.

The contrast of cosmological and ontological characters cannot be imagined without the cosmogonic tradition out of which it arises. The creation and maintenance of order from out of and over against the threat of chaos is the fundamental fact establishing our sense of beginnings. Speculative philosophy, both as general ontology and as universal science, attempts to explain the fundamental fact of *order*. The ontologist asks the question: "Why are there beings rather than no beings?" Or "Why is there something rather than nothing at all?" The cosmologist asks: "What kinds of things are there?" The cosmogonic tradition in the Hellenic West has thus determined that cosmological speculation must be *metaphysical* in the sense that it involves the search for that Being or those principles which, as transcendent sources of order, account for the order(s) experienced or observed.

The ontological question is traditionally thought to be prior to the cosmological concern. One might, of course, defend the reverse claim on the grounds that the question "What kinds of things are there?" may receive a Nietzschean answer such as: There are only interpretations, perspectives, the sum of which is truth. For if, as seems to be the case, the ontological question presumes an ordered or ordering ground, that question entails an assumption that the cosmological question may avoid.

In fact, the claim that the ontological question is somehow prior to the cosmological is a peculiar bias of those who privilege the Indo-European understanding of "being." Our bias toward unity over plurality, toward the *being* of beings rather than the insistent particularity of the beings themselves, is an accident of our linguistic and cultural dispositions.

As traditionally interpreted, both the cosmological and ontological questions presuppose an *ordered ground*. This presumption makes Western Philosophy "logocentric"—that is, concerned with the articulation of the source of order and structure in things.[3] The cosmological question simply asks about the character of things themselves, without the presumption of any single order or coherent set of orders. With Democritus, the cosmologists can ask, "How many and what kinds of *kosmoi* (worlds) are there?" As most often understood, the ontological question, grounded as it is in the logocentric motive, may be thought to mean, "Why cosmos rather than chaos?" The cosmological question in its most radical form must ask the opposite question: "Why chaos (*kosmoi*) rather than cosmos?" It asks this question because it does not presume the existence of a single-ordered world.

The argument favoring the priority of the cosmological question is that it better meets the strictures of Occam's razor since the acceptance of chaos does not require any additional principle in the form of cosmogonic activity responsible for the creation of an ordered world. There is only this and this and this. And the *whatnesses* of these *thises*—the idiosyncratic particularities of these particular things—are the only characters the order(s) own.

Obviously, on this understanding of the relations between cosmology and ontology, the issue of ontological difference (the difference between Being and beings) is more complex than a mere exegesis of Heidegger and his epigoni would suggest. We may distinguish at least the following ways of raising the question of difference: First, one might ask (as does Heidegger) after the difference between the cosmological and ontological character of things (between beings and Being) presupposing the *Being* of beings as ontological ground. Second, one might formulate a radically cosmological vision which eschews ontology altogether and assesses differences among the beings themselves. Third, there is the strictly ontological vision which begins with the maxim grounding Parmenides' *Way of Truth*: "Only Being is . . .".

A radical cosmology of the sort that Nietzsche expresses with the claim that "Truth is the sum total of interpretations" is the ground of the default nominalism characteristic of so much contemporary philosophical speculation. Rorty's nominalism is, in fact, a variety of this radical cosmological stance. The denial of a single-ordered world entails the sort of radical nominalism Rorty promotes. This denial leads to Rorty's appeal away from logical to rhetorical modes of argumentation.

Rorty's misology is directed against "rational" methods of argumentation, those that for the most part may be defined with respect to a logic based upon the division and synthesis of the subject matters of one's thinking about the world into natural kinds, and the acceptance of "p and not-p" as radical disjuncts. Such methods involve procedures which permit argument from part to whole (synthetic, dialectical) or whole to part (logistic, analytical). It is these that undergird the procedural rationalism of methodological thinking.

More simply put, there are three principal types of argument which can shape a methodological posture: analytical, dialectical, and analogical. In the West, which presupposes a single-ordered cosmos as the ground and goal of knowledge claims, these argumentative forms are based upon a part-whole model, which means that argumentation involves movements from part to whole or whole to part, or (as is the case with analogical thinking) part to part. Though analogical thinking in its purest sense does not require any resort to an overarching unity, the strictly rational employment of analogy always proceeds by appeal to a primary analogate (God, the Absolute) which guarantees that argumentation has a coherent cosmos as background.

Analytical arguments normally begin with stipulatively defined terms, theoretical propositions, or ordinary linguistic usages. In logical analysis, the appeal is to logical rules and principles involving consistency, correct logical form, soundness (truth or falsity). In ordinary language analysis, the appeal is to the syntactical and semantic requirements of the language in use. Logical analysis involves a capital "R" Rationality. Ordinary language philosophy appeals to a more modest standard of "reasonableness" expressed in the common sense of a consensual community.

The dialectical mode is usually divided into two principal variants: First, the constructive type. The implications of the principle of identity ($a = a$) and the principle of contradiction (not-[p and not-p]) permit constructive dialectic. Thus Leibniz can begin his philosophy from the principle of identity, and Hegel from the principle of contradiction, each drawing implications through dialectical argumentation. Or, more familiarly, Plato can employ the dialogical method to dramatize the patterns of *sic et non* thinking that reason entails.

The second dialectical procedure functions critically. Critical dialectic involves either *debate* or *dialogue*. The dialectic employed for purposes of debate enjoins the translation of the concepts of a theory under investigation in accordance with the theoretical assumptions of the critic. At least since Parmenides' employment of logical dialectic in his *Way of Truth*, the critical form of the dialectic (which Aristotle considered the operative sense of the term) has been in vogue among certain thinkers.

The history of Western philosophy can be read in terms of dialectical debates. The interaction among thinkers is not guided simply by formal logical procedures or principles, but is a function of semantic analyses which critique the sensibility of an alternative thinker in terms of the semantic context presupposed by the critic. Dialectical interchange of this variety generally results in intertheoretical confusions occasioned by the misconstrual of each thinker by the other.

The dialogical form of dialectic is based upon an attempt to compare semantic contexts presupposed in the engagement of alternative theoretical contexts. Taking into account the *intra*theoretical significances of the primary concepts of one's "opponent" permits one to begin to think sympathetically with him and to elicit that same sort of sympathy from him.

This form of dialectical argumentation works particularly well to illustrate that communication often requires active engagement predicated upon the recognition of otherness or difference. Dialogue also demonstrates that the interaction between alternative semantic contexts, while it yields greater intellectual clarity, may permit little progress toward consensus. That is to say, the sincerest attempt to communicate *inter*theoretically results in the recognition that alternative semantic contexts form closed systems resistant to rational communication. This recognition undergirds Rorty's claim that alterations of one's beliefs result from causal rather than rational engagement.

Analogical arguments dominate theological discourse, and both creative and critical literary expression. It is a common mode of argument in the development of scientific theories as well. In its rational form, the analogical mode begins with a fundamental image, metaphor, or model and, through an extension of its explanatory power by noting similarities of structure or function among the various elements comprising the context, one seeks to interpret the fundamental metaphor or analogate.[4]

Analytic, analogical, and the debate form of dialectical arguments are those most frequently stressed in the our intellectual communities. Attempts to define terms and concepts involve the discrimination of elements which are then recombined to form the definition. Exercises involving resort to grammatical and syntactical rules are essentially analytic. Analogical argumentation, though perhaps the most difficult to perform rigorously, is supported through the use of simile—a skill commonly exercised in the writing of prose and poetry. The debate form of dialectic is also well represented in most exercises in critical interpretations of texts. The dialogical mode of the dialectic is, perhaps, least exercised in our intellectual culture, though it is the primary method of many taxonomists.

An important consideration here is the manner in which our tradition's stress upon the significance of truth claims has shaped all three types of logical argument. Analytic arguments require "least units" of analysis with respect to which objective claims may be made. Dialectical arguments presume a putative whole in accordance with which claims of systematic coherence might be made. Analogical arguments are determined by a primary analogate serving as source and ground of analogical argumentation.[5]

Default nominalism denies the need for any unifying ground or goal. Nominalist arguments are grounded upon a part-part model which does not require resort either to objectivist principles defining a cosmological whole, or to a "ground" of Being. Nominalism in fact turns the analytic, dialectical, and analogical models of argumentation away from rational to rhetorical ends. And it is with regard to the traditional rhetorical modes of argument that we are likely to encounter the expository style of argument which approximates Rorty's "method."

Traditional rhetoric classifies arguments into those that appeal to "reasonableness" (logos), those appealing to the emotions of the audience (pathos), and those that attempt to establish the authority of the speaker or writer by persuading an audience of his/her knowledge, character, or sincerity (ethos).

The rhetorical sense of the logos style of argumentation is distinct from the strict philosophic sense. The sentence which begins Protagoras' treatise, *On Truth*—namely, "Man is the measure of all things . . ." means that human beings establish what is *reasonable* along with everything else. If there are no natural or supranatural laws or principles to which human beings must conform in order to be reasonable—laws which transcend the human being, or which at the very least are transcendental with respect to human beings—then reasonableness has no naturalistic ground. Reasonableness is, thus, conventional.

There may be no strict separation of the three rhetorical modes, of course. All three processes are likely to interact. An argument must have a minimum of interest or no one will attend to it. And the most reasonable argument will accrue a patina of unfeasability if the authority of the presenter or the context of its appearance is called into question. There can be argumentative processes whose persuasiveness is due to an audience unthinkingly acceding to the putative authority of the author of the argument or the emotional appeal of his rhetoric.

For a pathos- or ethos-based style of argumentation to be effective, meanings would have to be somewhat fixed by appeal to communally entertained subjective connotations. That is, meanings do not have to be fixed by objective reference if the connotations, or emotional baggage, of the crucial terms are not left to chance. The consistency of emotional response and dispositional activity can be depended upon to insure that words are communicable in an efficacious and harmonious manner.

In the extreme, a community grounded in this manner would have to be reasonably uniform as regards ethnicity and language, as was, for example, classical Chinese society. It could not afford to have contact with alternative communities whose members would have different sets of emotional responses, contrasting semantic systems of meaning, or who would demand objective reference as a condition of meaning. The rationalist solution of classical Western culture to the problem of diversity and plurality has been to argue for consensual views at the conceptual level and to permit differences to operate freely only at the affective level of subjective connotations. Such connotations could be idiosyncratic and individual since, given the presumed separation of idea and feeling, they could not cause any real conflict.

This is but to say that objectivist theories of truth, concerned as they are with questions of meaning and reference, are essential to those societies confronted with the necessity of obtaining consensual norms in accordance with which to adjudicate diverse opinions and doctrines. And though the rhetorical tradition is strong within Western culture, the logos style of argumentation has more often than not been presumed to have a firmer, more objective ground than rhetoric permits.

Rorty's default nominalism requires that he be satisfied with nonobjectivist, rhetorical modes of argumentation. But there is a serious problem with respect to the pragmatic efficacy of rhetorical appeals which are based upon an affective solidarity presumed to exist in liberal democratic societies. By separating the agencies of "love" and "justice," these societies have effectively banished affect from the sphere of public praxis. Rorty's desire for solidarity over objectivity is a necessary implication of his default nominalism. But to be efficacious, such solidarity must guarantee sufficient emotional homogeneity such that the public are able to constitute a real consensual community. This may be the vainest of hopes.

Pragmatism's characterization of beliefs as "successful rules for action" leaves one with little wisdom as to how to formulate a conscious, rational method that would guarantee the acquisition of such beliefs. We have, says Rorty, "a duty to talk to each other, to converse about our views of the world, to use persuasion rather than force, to be tolerant of diversity, to be contritely fallibilist. But this is not the same thing as a duty to have methodological principles."[6]

I think Rorty is attempting to make the best of a bad thing—that bad thing being the absence of any hope for consensual principles based either upon reason or emotion. By admitting that the strong poet and the revolutionary are the real agents of social change, he has acceded to a heroic vision of history which resonates with the existentialist perspective. But with no guarantee, nor any real hope, of a community of affect underlying the responses of individuals to the heroic agents of change, there is a great deal to worry about.

The fact is that the rhetoric of Western democracies is the rhetoric of *reasonableness* which has always involved appeals to objectivity and rationality. Even if, at the extreme, these be read as resorts to "the noble lie," it is difficult to think how pluralistic societies can live without them. I doubt that Rorty's separation of the private and the public spheres is sufficient to overcome the difficulties attending the absence of affective consensus. Such radical surgery as he recommends is perhaps the most candid confession of the consequences of default nominalism.

I am certainly not saying that Rorty is wrong in his diagnosis of the chaotic malaise of Western democracies; nor do I believe his pre-scription to be anything other than what appears to be the best one can do under the circumstances. Nonetheless, it is difficult to believe that a society bred to accept the Enlightenment rhetoric of individual auton-omy can find in its intellectual or practical resources anything that will permit the creation of that solidarity which is the minimal requirement for a viable society forced to live without the belief in God, the Absolute, or the fundamental Rights of Man.

I have argued that appeals to logical and rational (objectivist) meth-ods depend upon an explicit or tacit belief in the validity of an intellec-tual sensibility shaped by the ontological and cosmological concerns of the Anglo-European tradition expressed either in concepts such as Being, God, the Absolute, or norms such as Laws of Nature or the Principle of Sufficient Reason. The failure of the metaphysical tradition either in the form of a science of Being (*ontologia generalis*) or of princi-ples (*scientia universalis*) has dissolved the context within which objec-tivist appeals are made viable. The failure of metaphysics has, of course, been expressed in various ways: "the Death of God," "Positivism," "the Forgetting of Being," "the Rise of Modern Technology," "Deconstruction." Each of these names ideological implicates of the default nominalism characteristic of our contemporary coming of age.

The upshot of this discussion of Rorty's misology as a response to the presumed failure of metaphysics is to demonstrate the futility of any resort to rational, objectivist methods. The idea that there is some-thing *objective* that permits us to decide among vocabularies makes no sense "when the notion of 'description of the world' is moved from the level of criterion-governed sentences within language games to lan-guage games as wholes, games which we do not choose between by reference to criteria."[7] The important term in this citation is, of course, "criterion-governed." Presumably, it is the irrelevance of any appeal to criteria when yielding to one or the other vocabulary that makes the metaphor of "choice" inapplicable, and renders this sort of activity non-methodological in any real sense.

But what of moves within a given vocabulary? Couldn't we have an in-house method for the use of those already persuaded by a particular vision of things? It is doubtful whether, except in the case of formal axiomatic systems, one can successfully distinguish between moves within and moves among vocabularies. Granted that intrasystematic communication, to the extent that it is possible, would be noncontroversial from Rorty's perspective, real communication is not concerned with the algebraic transference of information. The Pythagorean theorem is a powerful tool for the manipulation of numbers and spatial relations, but it is not the sort of stuff that is most often communicated. Communication, even with one's self, involves the recognition and effective expression of difference. This is always causal.

One problem with attempts to employ formal method is that there is always more than a single such method. The content of one method's "already-known" may be precisely that which another method encounters as problematic. A method defined by principles which shape the enterprise of thinking sets the rules for debate. Only arguments which take place within that arena formed by a single method or set of principles may be adjudicated. But there may be family quarrels in which the arguments presume an internal problematic, and feuds which take place among different families. If we accede to the use of the language of our combatants, we are well on the way to looking silly.

Rorty believes we should learn to "brush aside questions like 'How do you *know* that freedom is the chief goal of social organization?' in the same way as we brush aside questions like . . . 'How do you *know* that Yeats is an important poet?'"[8] For these decisions are not made with reference to principles or rational criteria, and "there is no practicable way to silence doubt on such matters."[9]

In addition to "brushing aside," Rorty also employs the technique of "joshing." This resort to playfulness and lightmindedness is based upon "the willingness to view matters aesthetically—to be content to indulge in what Schiller called 'play' and to discard what Nietzsche called 'the spirit of seriousness'."[10] Rorty believes there to be no reasons (only causes) for shifting from one vocabulary to another. Therefore, when one encounters an individual whose questions or problems are such as to advertise that she is working out of a different vocabulary, there are two likely responses for the pragmatist: either to refuse to discuss the issues opened up and avoid interaction, or to circumvent the discussion by attempting to shift the ground.

If the second alternative is taken, one owes one's potential interlocutor some explanation as to why the ground must be shifted. If this explanation takes the form of a rational argument that points up the weakness of the opponent's viewpoint and the strengths of one's own, the question has been begged since one has employed criteria of strength and weakness found within one's own vocabulary. Alternatively, one's response might take the form of a narrative, a story of how we got to where we are and why we might consider moving beyond this point. This contextualizes the opponent's vocabulary in such a way as to point up its contingency—a contingency, of course, shared by every other vocabulary.

Rorty's replacement of the "'idea' idea" by the "'metaphor' metaphor," combined with his disavowal of anything that smacks of essentialism, and his rather consistent resort to the construction of narratives, makes of his claim to have absented strict methodology from his thinking a plausible one. By dissolving "objects into functions, essences into momentary foci of attention, and knowing into success at reweaving a web of beliefs and desires into more supple and elegant folds,"[11] pragmatists are able to treat everything as a function of contextualization.

I do believe, however, that Rorty's New Pragmatism shares a great many things with the "old existentialism." Rorty is a heroic existentialist who seeks to "redescribe lots and lots of things" in order to tempt the rising generation to employ his vocabulary. Solidarity must come about through conversation. But by claiming that not every argument needs to be met on its own grounds, Rorty limits the parameters of that conversation to those expressed in nominalist historicist (narrativist) terms. This makes recontextualization combined with circumvention sound more like seduction than conversation.

There is little in the relaxed candor of Rorty's writings to suggest that he would be at all comfortable with the role of seducer. Then again, he appears no more sanguine about the aims of the utopian prophet which, I have argued, he reluctantly pursues. As is so often the case with philosophers, Rorty seems, at least on the surface, to be personally at odds with many of the consequences of his thinking.

ARS CONTEXTUALIS

When Rorty claims he prefers a "pragmatism without method,"[12] he could hardly be objecting to William James' characterization of pragmatism as "a method only . . . [as] only an attitude of orientation . . . the attitude of looking away from first things, principles, 'categories,' supposed necessities; and of looking towards last things, fruits, consequences, facts."[13] Rorty is thinking of the Heideggerian strictures against method as a "mathematical procedure" which "lays down" (ta mathemata) that which is already-known.

As I argued in chapter 1, the ad hoc taxonomies which frame Rorty's self-justifying narratives render his thinking far more methodological than he would wish to acknowledge. For even if these taxonomies do not "lay down" that which must be known forever in advance, they do "set up" the narrative Rorty intends to provide.[14] We need to look more closely at Rorty's antiheuristic method, the name of which—"inquiry"—is familiar to all good pragmatists. As might be expected, Rorty provides some significant new content for the term "inquiry."

Inquiry is carried on by an inquirer, so let's begin with a picture of the inquirer. As we have seen, a person is for Rorty a set of sentential attitudes, a centerless web of beliefs.[15] And this web is dynamic. In the course of her life an individual is confronted by new candidates for beliefs which will either conform to or be in tension with beliefs in her present inventory. If the tension is great enough, we speak of contradictions.

Beliefs in conformity with one's present inventory may lead to a relatively smooth incorporation, or they may allow a reweaving into more satisfying patterns. Beliefs in tension will often require a more radical reweaving of the sort that leads to the rejection of old beliefs through active disbelief or through simple abandonment. At the minimal level such reweaving is routine and instinctive and can be associated with Dewey's understanding of "habit." The correction of a simple mistake, such as misdialing a familiar telephone number, or choosing the pepper container rather than the salt, is close enough to the routine to fall within the range of habit. When the reweaving takes place on a significant scale, however, we approach the level of inquiry. If one reaches for the salt and discovers a container of rat poison in its place, one might be led to speculate on the motives of one's formerly trusted spouse. Such speculations could require a dramatic reshaping of one's attitudes.

The greater the number of beliefs added, subtracted, or raised or lowered in priority, the farther along in the direction of inquiry we are. Rorty claims that "at a certain point in this process it becomes useful to speak of 'recontextualization'."[16] The new context acquired or constructed may be a new theory accounting for novel or past beliefs or a radical new vision leading one to exclaim, "I once was lost, but now am found; once blind, but now I see!"

Rorty distinguishes two sorts of contexts, which parallel the distinctions of habit and inquiry (and of philosophical and literary moments). One context is constituted by a new set of attitudes toward sentences already in one's vocabulary, the other by the acquisition of attitudes toward sentences towards which no attitudes previously existed. These contexts match those of inference and imagination, respectively.

> Paradigms of inference are adding up a column of figures, or running through a sorites, or down a flowchart. Paradigms of imagination are the new metaphorical uses of old words (e.g., *gravitas*), the invention of neologisms (e.g., "gene") and the colligation of hitherto unrelated texts (e.g., Hegel and Genet [Derrida] . . . Aristotle and the Scriptures [the Schoolmen].[17]

The distinction between inference and imagination, like the distinction between literary and philosophic moments, is a matter of degree. No good post-Kuhnian thinker would confidently claim that what scientists do, even and especially normal scientists operating within a fresh dominant paradigm, is simply follow the method of science as approved by that paradigm. From the beginning, every community is reweaving and reconstituting beliefs vis-à-vis nonrational factors. It is only when the fresh metaphors that have given the new community its vitality begin to grow stale and literal that anything like a rational method might be developed. But by then, the vitality has waned sufficiently to make operations within the old tradition rather unproductive.

The identification of these two contexts may vary from one person to another. Often, we may encounter theories which are old hat to many others but which function as revolutionary transformations for us. Philosophy teachers are often in the position of providing what for them and their colleagues is rather mundane fare ("All Cretans are liars" or "When does the arrow move?" or *Cogito ergo sum*) but which can have a rather dramatic effect on at least some beginning students.

The evaluation of intellectual projects may be quite disparate, of course. Is Richard Rorty's attempt to "adapt pragmatism to a changed intellectual environment," a dramatic recontextualization, as his supporters believe, or, as some of his detractors hold, a muddled form of skepticism and relativism, a malignant nihilism which, by reducing logic and scientific inquiry to the Protagorean principle, makes pragmatism a merely sophistic exercise?

Imaginative contextualizations through metaphorical operations produce the material from which later inferential contexts will emerge. Rorty can deny resort to method since the production of imaginative contexts is inexplicable. Neither the novel metaphors nor the character of the genius that produces them can be accounted for.

By virtue of the breadth of his reading and his conversational model of philosophizing, Rorty has taken the exercise of the colligation of hitherto unrelated texts quite seriously. Consider how he has paired John Dewey with alternative thinkers such as Heidegger or Wittgenstein. Such colligations, when successful, lead to a rapid reweaving in which the two sets of beliefs "become warp and woof of a new, vividly polychrome, fabric."[18] Citing Donald Davidson's oft quoted remark, "Metaphor is the dreamwork of language," Rorty finds that the recontextualizations associated with this sort of juxtapositioning are analogous to what takes place in dreams.

If one says with Rorty that the distinction between the rational and the nonrational approximates the distinction between inference and imagination, then it is easily seen that "rational" and "scientific" become broadly synonymous. One might go farther, then, and show that "scientific" and "methodological" approximate one another as well. That a stress upon science and method, to the exclusion of imagination, is then thought to be defensible on rational grounds is a perniciously circular argument.

Recontextualization is dependent upon eliding the distinction between context and object, presuming contextualized objects to be "beliefs" and affirming that "all objects are always already contextualized."[19] The web of beliefs and desires that constitutes a self is continually being rewoven through alternative contextualizations.

Rorty claims that "the pragmatist recognizes relations of *justification* holding between beliefs and desires, and relations of *causation* holding between these beliefs and desires and other items in the universe, but no relations of *representation*."[20] Thus Rorty's pragmatism steers a course between realism, idealism, and skepticism. Against the realist Rorty argues that there is no contextless object, and that no object has a context of its own as opposed to that of the inquirer. Against the idealist the pragmatist claims that inquiry may be said to constitute its object only in the weak, horizontal sense that leads us to answer questions such as "What is your inquiry *about*?" Since all objects are already contextualized, all relations of 'aboutness' are intralinguistic. Thus, in the same manner that Homer's *Iliad* is about Achilles, Riemann's axioms are about Riemannian space.

The pragmatist allows no generalized skepticism about the external world or other minds or cultures. There may be, however, skepticism about a particular belief or set of beliefs. That is to say, there is no claim on the part of the pragmatists that beliefs per se are questionable, only that some particular beliefs may be.

When Rorty claims that beliefs are about other beliefs, not about nonbeliefs, and that all objects are already contextualized, he seems to be avoiding the hard cases associated with "pain" and "causality." These are, after all, extralinguistic. They must in some sense escape contextualization; they must, in that same sense, be the sort of thing *about which* we hold certain beliefs. Here we find the same issue we encountered in our initial elaboration of Rorty's pragmatism: those enterprises which deal "formally" with pain and causality (certain sorts of literature and certain scientific theories) ought make a greater claim upon our attention.

If we look past this ontological embarrassment and leave pain and causality to themselves, we are left with Rorty's declaration that individual sentential attitudes are the only candidates for "self-subsistent, individual entities."[21] But of course, beliefs are what they are only by virtue of their membership and placement within a set of beliefs. "A belief . . . [is] a position in a web."[22]

Thus Rorty's default nominalism leads to the claim that we inquire only about things "under a description." This means that inquiry, as recontextualization, does not treat objects outside of one context in order to place them in another. All objects are always under a description and, therefore, contextualized. Rorty's sense of knowing the whole truth about an object is the same as that of Nietzsche: the "truth" concerning an object is the sum total of interpretations which might be offered. But this is a pale assertion. The significant truth about things is established by the pragmatic import of the narratives one constructs.

An "object," as a belief in a web of beliefs, or the web itself, can be treated either as a "term" or as a "relation" depending upon one's present purposes. "You can dissolve a substance into a sequence of Whiteheadian events, but you can also treat events as relations between Aristotelian substances."[23] The power accorded description here would lead us to invert Wittgenstein's claim: *Der Fall ist alles was die Welt ist.*

Rorty's contextualism cannot be called "linguistic idealism" since, though the contextualist shares with the anti-essentialist the idealist's search for coherence among beliefs and desires, she nonetheless holds, along with the realist, that there are objects which are causally independent of these beliefs and desires.

At this point I, along with other of Rorty's critics, am troubled by the seemingly blithe manner in which Rorty brushes aside, or attempts to circumvent, the charge of being an unwitting idealist. Rorty claims that the distinction between things "as they are" and "as we describe them" is unhelpful. "We do in fact describe most objects as causally independent of us, and that is *all* that is required to satisfy our realistic intuitions."[24] But Rorty seems to employ the "as they are" and "as we describe them" distinction when he says that "pain" is extralinguistic. Rorty wouldn't see it that way. The particular web of beliefs constituting his "self" contains the "difficult-to-imagine-revising belief" that causally independent objects are causing him to have new beliefs. Thus what Rorty calls his "realistic (as opposed to 'realist') intuitions" are beliefs he holds in a particularly firm manner. Rorty's belief in causally independent objects is a belief he could not easily give up.

In Rorty's defense, the belief in causal independence is one that can be derived from common sense without any appeal to sophisticated theory. But one might question in any given instance, how common sense is formed. Common sense is sometimes determined retroductively by reading backward from our institutions, customs, and theories rather than by simply looking for a few good homely truisms that match one's bedrock beliefs.

Inquiry as the anti-essentialist method of recontextualization is applicable in every area of intellectual culture. Rorty is quick to dispense with the idea that we ought make the sort of distinction hermeneuticists make between the *Naturwissenschaften* and *Geisteswissenschaften*. It is interpretation all the way down. Thus the distinction between a physicist and a political scientist is not methodological but "sociological."

Rorty argues that Davidson (among others) has helped us dispense with the belief held by Quine (among others) to the effect that there are areas of culture such as the physical sciences which have as their subjects "facts of the matter" as opposed to those areas in which interpretation reigns. This is done in a subtle, but rather easily articulated, series of steps.

Rorty characterizes two principles the anti-essentialist rejects:[25] "Russell's principle," which states: "It is not possible to make a judgment about an object without knowing what object you are making a judgment about"; and "Parmenides' Principle," namely, "You cannot talk about what does not exist." The movement from the acceptance of the former to the expedient of appealing to the latter is accounted for in this manner: Applying Russell's principle to the strange objects encountered in history or ethnography—objects such as Aristotle's *kinesis* or the Polynesian's *mana*—may lead to the conclusion that the principle fails to apply, that these objects don't exist. But if one cannot talk about what does not exist, then one is forced to soften the term "existence," so that such "nonexisting" things might be included. One might employ terms such as "linguistic existence"—a species of which might be "fictional" existence. One has now a division between things that exist objectively and the sort of things that exist by virtue of linguistic constitution. This is the basic means whereby one can teach oneself to be hermeneutical.

Though the anti-essentialist does not buy either the Parmenidean or the Russellian principle, she is nonetheless able to account for the sort of distinction among cultural objects which the essentialist deems relevant. In anti-essentialist language the distinction is not one between things with different ontological status, but simply between "objects which cause you to have beliefs about them by fairly direct causal means and other objects."[26]

Causal explanations of these two groups of things will differ in the following manner: With respect to the one group, the causal explanations will invoke the names of things themselves. For example, beliefs about Congress or the President will be acquired by one's encounter with the President or members of Congress, with one's keeping up with news stories about them, and so on. One's belief in the relative competence, or lack thereof, of a particular president will be referenced to the behavior of the President himself. On the other hand, beliefs about "the nature of true virtue," or "inertial mass," or "the sufferings of Little Nell," will likely derive from the persuasiveness of theories or narratives which contextualize these objects. "Antiessentialists think of objects as what we find it useful to talk about in order to cope with the stimulations to which our bodies are subjected."[27] The anti-essentialist Rorty agrees with Quine that all objects are "posits."

The distinction between linguistically constituted and nonlinguistically constituted objects now may be dissolved in the following way: On the principle Rorty derives from Davidson (namely, we may be said to be talking about the same thing only if we say pretty much the same things about it) one would not be able to translate "gavagai" as "rabbit" if it became clear that those who employ the term "gavagai" attach an importantly *spiritual* significance to the term. In such a situation, a hermeneuticist would be tempted to say "gavagai" is "constituted by language." Were we to find, on the other hand, that "rabbit" and "gavagai" were almost always contained in sentences expressing the same beliefs, then we should not want to make such a claim.

According to Rorty, the distinction that parallels the *Natur-/Geisteswissenschaften* distinction for the anti-essentialists is that between controversial and noncontroversial beliefs. Thus, with respect to our intercultural example, "the interesting line is not between the human and the nonhuman, nor between material objects and emotions, but between the behavioral patterns which you and the natives share and the patterns which you do not."[28]

Thus we come again to a point made in the discussion of ethnocentrism in the last chapter: the distinction between the inter- and intracultural breaks down in practice. Attempts to communicate across cultural boundaries are no less or greater examples of the muddling through operations associated with intracultural conversation. The relevant distinction is that between the familiar and the unfamiliar. In fact, many of us have had the experience of, in one way or another, feeling more at home in a foreign country than in our own.

The subject matters of inquiry are those "unfamiliar" items encountered in interactions with others. The unfamiliar becomes familiar through recontextualization of beliefs. Whether this process of recontextualization leads to a radical transformation of one's pattern of beliefs is an open question. The unfamiliar becomes the controversial when we cannot easily incorporate the beliefs it constitutes into our own inventory of beliefs.

In chapter 2 I considered Milton Fisk's criticism of Rorty's views of "principles." Fisk's basic criticism is relevant to this discussion of Rorty's misological stance. Fisk would claim that Rorty needs to own up to the principles implicit in his suggested practices. This would involve him in distinguishing the sort of metaphysics external to, from that internal to, his practices. The latter is a properly pragmatic metaphysics which acknowledges the principles involved in its commitments even while recognizing that those commitments and the practices which elicit them may change. Pragmatic metaphysics of the sort recommended by Fisk is not based upon representation or correspondence with reality. "The truth of metaphysics has to do with the validity of a practice it makes feasible."[29]

I have expressed (qualified) agreement with Fisk's criticism of Rorty. I agree with Rorty that we should not take the principles which rationalize our practices as the *meanings* of the practices, but as *reminders* of them. But I agree with Fisk that we need to highlight more often than Rorty seems disposed to do the interpretative concepts and principles that we do in fact select (from a vague field of alternative possibilities) as our peculiar reminders. The question concerning Rorty's relationship to methodology can be focused best by asking about the character of that metaphysics internal to Rorty's practice.

The first thing to be said is that Rorty's views are *acosmological* in a sense not unlike that of Montaigne and Kant. Rorty's radical acosmology, however, involves a rejection of transcendence and of transcendentals, an affirmation of the decentered, processive self, a rejection of the radical disjunctions of logic in favor of the nominalist preference for aesthetic contrast. More specifically, Rorty substitutes propositions of the form, "p or *non-p*" for all "p or *not-p*" assertions. Along with this subordination of logic to rhetoric and poetry there is the affirmation of the need to substitute "eristic" for either the dialectic of a Plato or Hegel or the "antilogic"[30] of Jacques Derrida. Further, though he attempts to maintain at least the shadow of a naturalistic foundation in the sense that causality cuts across his understandings of the world and is held to be the very bedrock of common sense, Rorty appeals to the metaphors of self-creation and intersubjective community more often than to any strictly causal accountings.

At least in the Pickwickian sense postmodern metamentality has forced upon us, Rorty is a metaphysician still. For the metaphilosophical orientation he so clearly expresses is the form metaphysics takes in our age of hyperconsciousness. Of course, Rorty is not a traditional metaphysician discoursing in the mode of *ontologia generalis*. Nor is he even congenial to the more modest exercise known as *scientia universalis*. He is neither a cosmological nor an ontological thinker.

As a linguistic acosmologist, a poetic narrativist, a nominalist historicist, Rorty's thinking illustrates what I have in other contexts called *ars contextualis*.[31] That is to say, he employs the art of contextualization characteristic of the aesthetic rather than the strictly logical thinker. This is the method of the Jamesian Dewey who has so influenced Rorty. Further, Rorty's is an anthropocentric nominalism which is concerned with the fate of human beings rather than with "all sentient beings" or the "ecosystem." This places his thinking rather close to the sophistic and existential thinkers who make "man the measure."

It is difficult to sympathize altogether with Rorty's misology. *Methodos* names a means of moving from point to point; it is a path, a way. If one sees Rorty taking the same path more than a few times when other paths are available, then, his methodophobia aside, one is permitted, I believe, to say that he has a *method*. Nonetheless, in keeping with the tacit dimension of Rorty's *ars contextualis*, perhaps we should speak of the *tao* of pragmatism.

Rorty's new metaphorical uses of old words (e.g., "metaphor"), his endorsement of neologisms (e.g., "memes"[32]), and his colligation of hitherto unrelated texts (e.g., Heidegger and Dewey; Davidson and Derrida) are vague and allusive enough to be nonmethodological, but whenever he resorts to metaphilosophy he is working primarily at the inferential level. And the distinctions he employs in advance of these spontaneous moves are predictable enough to count as method.

The polemical aim inherent in this method is "circumvention."[33] But the motor of circumvention is recontextualization. "The method is to redescribe lots and lots of things in new ways, until you have created a pattern of linguistic behavior which will tempt the rising generation to adopt it."[34] In the less neologistic sense of method ("way," "procedure"), Rorty's narratives count as method. And insofar as the narratives seem to be permutations of one Grand Narrative of the sort rehearsed in the beginning of this book, Rorty's *methodos* is that of the narrativist who recontextualizes by telling a story, complete with "good guys" (Dewey, Davidson) and "bad guys" (Kant, Husserl).

Circumvention is *possible* because of the nominalism and poetic narrativism characteristic of Rorty's thinking. But, practically speaking, resort to circumvention is often the reactive consequence of trying to prevent being co-opted by an alien discourse. We must recall that Rorty believes that "*not every argument need[s] to be met in the terms in which it is presented.*"[35] Recontextualization aims at the isolation, encapsulation, and circumvention of philosophic concepts and issues which fall outside his self-justifying narratives. Rorty claims that Heidegger and Dewey, among many others, have employed the same sort of circumventions that he attempts. Also, Wittgenstein's ahistorical approach was focused directly upon the circumvention of the language/world contrast.

Now in one sense it is uncontroversial that he who theorizes even in the loosest sense of that term can only marginalize certain discourses in the furtherance of his own views. What distinguishes the sort of marginalization associated with circumvention is its strictly nominalistic, nontranscendental character.

AROUND AND ABOUT DERRIDA

Rorty's "method" of circumvention is offered as a viable alternative to the method of "deconstruction." In his essay entitled "Deconstruction,"[36]

Rorty provides an extremely succinct and insightful version of the emergence of the deconstructive movement in terms of the thought of three principals—Foucault, Derrida, and de Man. Derrida was responsible for the philosophical program, Foucault for the "leftward slant." The students of Paul de Man have since "formed the core of the deconstructionist movement."[37]

There are significant differences, Rorty thinks, between Derrida and de Man, the most important of which involve de Man's privileging of literature. De Man distinguishes literature from other discourses, principally philosophy, by claiming that literary texts (though not their authors, necessarily) are not undermined by the aim at univocity. He exempts literature from the destructive blindness which Derrida attributes to all writing. Thus (in a much cited phrase): "Philosophy turns out to be an endless reflection on its own destruction at the hands of literature."[38] Rorty finds that the de Man version of deconstruction leads toward the development of a method to be employed by literary critics. Indeed, in the hands of many disciples of Derrida and de Man, deconstruction has become highly formulaic and algorithmic, and thus exceedingly dull.

Rorty distinguishes a wide and a narrow sense of deconstructionism. In the wide sense deconstruction represents "a sudden infusion of Nietzschean and Heideggerian ideas into the English-speaking intellectual world"[39] which aims at a drastic destabilization in a broad array of disciplines such as philosophy, law, political science, history. In a narrow sense, the sense recognizable to most American intellectuals, it is primarily a literary critical method. As such the narrow method is comparable to other methods, such as Freudian criticism, which looks to psychoanalysis for its models and vocabulary. Deconstruction is an avowedly *philosophical* form of criticism.

Derrida developed the insights which led to the sort of critique deconstruction represents in part by reflection upon Heidegger. Heidegger had claimed Nietzsche was the last metaphysician who, by reversing the being/becoming distinction, played out the final variation on the metaphysical visions Plato had willed to the tradition. Heidegger hoped to be a post-metaphysical thinker by freeing himself from the traditional binaries. Derrida believed that Heidegger failed to do so, however, due to his obsession with the history of Being. Heidegger's notion of ontological difference construed as a "difference between a listening acceptance and a desire to schematize and control,"[40] was merely one more example of the tyrannical binary oppositions.

Derrida's use of terms such as *trace, supplement, differance* was an attempt "to mock and displace Heidegger's terminology." Heidegger reverences the ineffable, the silent, Derrida admires "the elusive, allusive, the ever-self-recontextualizing."[41] Thus Derrida was able to replace Heideggerian nostalgia expressed in the search for an escape from Platonism and a regaining of the sense of Being with forward-looking attempts to expose the metaphysical character of texts. In this manner deconstruction became "the way in which the 'accidental features' of a text can be seen as betraying, subverting, its purportedly 'essential' message."[42]

Rorty claims that Derrida subverted the vertical aspirations of Heideggerian nostalgia by recognizing that language has only a horizontal character and that words have meanings not by the presence or absence of some logos, but by "difference." This jibes with the pragmatic recognition that no word can acquire a meaning by association with anything nonlinguistic and is tantamount to saying that the existence of causal relations between language and nonlanguage ("the world") is the basis for our having beliefs, though this relation does not make these beliefs true. This view saves "what was true in idealism while eschewing Berkeley's and Kant's suggestion that the material world is the creation of the human mind."[43] Rorty wants to say that the point of deconstruction is preserved in the pragmatist's claim (à la Sellars) that "consciousness is always a linguistic affair," and the allied claim that there are no determinant meanings of texts. That is to say: There are no contextless texts.

Rorty's interpretation of Derrida's contribution to deconstruction depends upon his reading of the term "logocentrism." As used by Derrideans, this notion has an almost magical flavor defining by encapsulation the "metaphysical tradition of the West," and the "discourse of philosophy" which articulates that tradition. The philosophy of presence (that philosophy which seeks to make Being present through the beings of the world, or to make objects present through discourse) is one more target of the anti-foundationalism which Rorty claims Derrida shares with most philosophers of recent times.

Rorty's critique of Derrida depends upon a recognition that Derrida's chief dilemma is posed by his affirmation, shared with Heidegger, of the omnipresence and totalizing influence of the "discourse of philosophy." This means that Derrida, in his attempts to overcome that influence, must either perpetuate that discourse by using the tools of the enterprise against it, or attempt to change terrain and risk being ignored by that enterprise. Indeed, when Derrida plays on the grounds of the more traditional philosopher, it is easy work to show that his esoteric terminology (*differance, trace, archi-writing*) reduces itself to standard fodder to be victimized by counter-deconstructive forces. And when, as in the case of *The Postcard*,[44] he moves beyond the pale of philosophy, he can expect no attention from those who wish to maintain certain basic standards of inferential activity as minimum criteria for entrance into the community of responsible thinkers.

Derrida responds to this dilemma by implicitly invoking the Ch'an Buddhist koan, "Avoid choosing by choosing both." He weaves together the presumably literal and figural discourses—the inferential, logic-based language and the noninferential, pun-infested discourse, motored by an interest in the phonic and iconic features of language.

Rorty's refusal to distinguish between literary and philosophic, noninferential and inferential, discourse is based upon the belief that we have always resorted to multiple readings of texts. "Important, revolutionary physics, and metaphysics, has always been 'literary' in the sense that it has faced the problem of introducing new jargon and nudging aside the language-games currently in place."[45] Derrida is merely "doing brilliantly and at length something most of his readers have been doing spasmodically and awkwardly in their heads."[46] I think Rorty is quite correct in his assessment of the increased ironic distance with which readers approach texts and that the enjoyment of Derrida by those who do not seek in his writings a "rigorous method" is the enjoyment by the amateur or novice of the performances of the virtuoso.

Rorty's default nominalism leads him to undermine severe disjunctions of any kind and thus to fuzzy up the major distinctions philosophers have depended upon to get their arguments off the ground. In this way Rorty seeks to circumvent even the deconstructionists. As Rorty indicates, Derrida vacillates between two philosophical styles: one which takes philosophy seriously as the determinant of intellectual discourse, the other, the style of an idiosyncratic thinker who moves within a world of private allusions.[47] The former thinker, insofar as he employs the vocabulary of *differance*, remains methodological. The latter, though nonmethodological, moves beyond the pale of communicative discourse.

Deconstructive efforts depend upon the belief that our language is shaped by a philosophical discourse itself transcendentally conditioned by fundamental binary pairings of concepts (reality/appearance, being/not-being, literal/metaphorical, logic/rhetoric) in which the former term is privileged with respect to the latter. Such deconstruction appeals by self-referential argumentation to the fact that any polarity could easily be reversed.

Derrida implies that the importance of binary oppositions in determining the fate of philosophic argumentation and construction is a consequence of the fact that Western thought has been captured by the "dream of philosophy,"—the dream of a closed, total vocabulary. Rorty grants that distinctions such as being/non-being, reality/appearance, subject/object, language/world have wrought much havoc in Western thought, but he claims that binary oppositions are not per se distinctive of philosophy itself, but of all thinking[48] and "the fact that two contrasting terms get their meaning by reciprocal definability, and in that sense 'presuppose' each other, does nothing to cast doubt on their utility."[49]

Rorty's anti-foundationalism entails the view that no hierarchical relationship between binaries can be based upon any authentic privilege accorded one term over the other. God and the world, man and nature, male and female, are all binaries the first term of which has been in our tradition accorded greater reality than the second. But this is a problem, not of the "discourse of philosophy" but of the biases of the language users. We do not, says Rorty, need to escape from philosophy or the structure of thinking, we only need to practice a continual "reweaving of our web of linguistic usage"[50] in order to overcome the perceived deficiencies of former usages. Rorty suggests we can avoid the consequences of hierarchical binaries by the method of "pointing out that the oppositions are there, and then not taking them very seriously."[51]

There are two questions here: first, whether we should identify binaries with specifically philosophic discourse, and, second, whether we can, as easily as Rorty suggests, avoid the consequences of the binaries. Is Rorty correct in taking such a lightminded attitude toward the presumed binary structure of language?

According to Barbara Herrnstein Smith, "'the metaphysics of Western thought' is thought, all of it, root and branch, everywhere and always."[52] This certainly raises an interesting question. For much work has recently been done on the difference between metaphysical and nonmetaphysical traditions.[53] If we look, for example, at the development of Chinese and Western classical orthodoxies, it does appear that though there is little by way of "metaphysical discourse" in China, binary oppositions play an equally important and even more explicit role in the development of thought. For example, one would be hard pressed to show that Taoists are objectivists either in the sense that they appeal to a ground of Being or to objective principles, yet the role of the yin/yang contrarieties is central to the rhetoric of Taoism. But these binaries are nominalized in precisely the manner that Rorty suggests.

The Chinese pairing of Being (*yu*) and Not-Being (*wu*) is a perfect illustration of this point. Contrary to the Parmenidean contrast which privileges the existential meaning of the copula, *wu* and *yu* suggest mere contrast in the sense of the absence or presence of *x* rather than the existence or nonexistence of *x*. In Chinese, the sense of "being" overlaps that of "having" rather than "existing." *To be* is *to be around*. The Chinese lack the copula.

The *yu* and *wu* problematic yields a vague supplement not only to modern Western notions of reason but to the postmodern critique of reason as well. For there is no need to overcome the "logocentrism" of a "language of presence" grounded in "ontological difference" if no distinction between Being and beings is urged by the classical Chinese language. A Chinese "language of presence" is a language of "making present" the item itself, not its essence.

Language which does not tempt one to posit an ontological difference between Being and beings, but only a difference between one being and another, suggests a decentered world whose centers and circumferences are always defined in an ad hoc manner. The mass of classical Chinese philosophical discourse, then, is already deconstructed. In its traditionally evolved form, the Chinese language is immune to deconstruction.

The Chinese, guided by the strains of their language, as we were in opposite manners, developed alternative approaches to thought and language. One of the strongest arguments in favor of Rorty's nominalistic lightmindedness is that such has already shaped the structure of a civilization which has lasted longer than any other on the face of the planet.

It seems, then, that Rorty might have good reason to question the perhaps overly profound respect of the deconstructionists for binary contrasts. Were one performing historical or rational reconstructions, these could, of course, be considered central. But, after Hegel, philosophy seems to have declined in cultural import such that what is central to philosophy may not be central to the culture, and a fortiori, given the contemporary trend toward nominalist, pragmatist, pluralist stances (not to mention the demystification of philosophical categories that attends the hyperconsciousness of the contemporary intellectual), these contrasts have lost their hold on philosophers as well. The pragmatic tactic of circumvention Rorty employs involves ignoring the binary tensions among those terms not specifically relevant to one's personal and public praxis.

In the West two sorts of language have dominated the tradition.

The first, the language of ontological presence, is that against which the postmodern thinkers have revolted. Besides the language of presence, however, our tradition also allows the employment of language in a mystical or mythopoetic way. In this usage, language advertises the absence of the referent. This is the language of the mystical *via negativa*, or the language of the poet who holds metaphor to be constitutive of discourse rather than merely parasitical upon a literal ground. We may call such expression *the language of absence*.

A language of presence is grounded upon the possibility of univocal or unambiguous propositional expressions. This possibility requires criteria for determining the literalness of a proposition. For this to be so, literal language must have precedence over figurative or metaphorical language. This means that in addition to richly vague sorts of language associated with images and metaphors, there must be concepts as candidates for univocal meaning.

Derrida's well-rehearsed neologism, *differance*,[54] is meant to suggest that the differences investigated with respect to language have both an active and a passive dimension. Meaning is always deferred. It cannot be present in language as *structure*, when that is the focus—for that omits the meanings associated with the use of the language. But focusing upon language as *event*, language as constituted by speech acts, does not solve the problem because, once more, the supplemental character of language—this time its structure—has been shifted to an inaccessible background.

Derrida might wish to accept an emendation to his notion of *differance* which would enrich the meaning of the deferring function. If one introduces the homonymic "defer," meaning "to yield," then the resultant notion of difference, as connoting both active and passive senses of differing and of deferring, accords better with Rorty's *ars contextualis*. We have here a striking resonance with Rortyan thought. We can "defer" or refuse to "defer" to opposition—or any other feature of the language in the context in which we encounter it. In homogeneous cultures, if such there be, these deference patterns are set up by ritualized role relationships. In an individualistic, democratic society these patterns are functions of conversation, debate, and the revolutionary impact of new metaphors.

The contrast of individualistic and communal cultures renders problematic Barbara Herrnstein Smith's point that "there is no reason to believe that the metaphysics of Western thought is distinct from that of Eastern thought, or tribal thought, or the thought of illiterates or of preverbal or of as yet unacculturated children."[55] If our only acceptable meaning of metaphysics is "the metaphysics of presence," this is truistic. Whoever does that sort of thing is doing that sort of thing. That sort of thing is very often (though not always) done in mainstream Western thought and very rarely (but sometimes) done in, say, classical China and the nominalized, postmodern West.

On the whole, I don't see why we can't accept Rorty's dissolution of Derrida as transcendentalist philosopher while reckoning that the latter still might have a lot of playful work to do. Those (such as Rorty and others) already equipped from other battles with sufficient irony will not need the comforts of a method to be able to see texts as tapestries which may be woven and rewoven from the warp of inference and the woof of noninferential threads. Accepting Rorty's recommendation would lead us finally beyond the false comforts of a guiding absolute. I see no reason why this is not possible. The fading of the Cheshire smile will then be in direct proportion to our refusal to smile along with it.

Rorty finds that those who would make of Derrida a transcendentalist philosopher searching out the conditions for the possibility (or impossibility) of philosophic discourse are influenced by de Man's use of deconstruction. It is the claim that literary and philosophic discourses are distinct, and that literary discourse points up the failures of philosophic discourse, that leads to the belief that Derrida has transcendentalist aspirations. But Rorty claims that Derrida is in fact problematizing argumentative discourse per se insofar as it has foundationalist pretensions, thus making a certain kind of philosophic discourse "so enigmatic as to be no longer [available for] argumentative use."[56]

I believe Rorty has a genius, not unlike that of Derrida himself, for discovering the stresses and faultlines in the theories of his fellow philosophers. For clearly, in our time of hyperconsciousness, the aim for anything like inclusiveness or adequacy of thought tends to place great strain upon the consistency of one's ideational constructs. It is this that creates the dramatic ironies besetting many of our contemporary thinkers. Irony dwells upon the both-and character of one's thinking. The philosopher becomes victim by being shown that, against his intuitions and aspirations, though he *must* have it both ways, he cannot. Only through a complete capitulation to the ironic sense will one be saved.

Derrida can't both be playful and argue. If he wants to deconstruct discourse based on privileged hierarchies, he can do this by a playful ambiguation of that discourse. If he then wishes to argue that this discourse is inescapable, the essentialism associated with such claims opens him to playful deconstruction of the sort that Rorty among others is willing to direct against his transcendentalist arguments. "The quarrel about whether Derrida has arguments thus gets linked to a quarrel about whether he is a private writer . . . or rather a writer with a public mission."[57]

Rorty thinks we can account for the belief that deconstruction (along with other techniques of examining the workings of language) has real political implications by appeal to the waning influence of Marxism and the rise of feminism. Marxism had heretofore sapped much of our critical energies; now we are looking for a novel outlet. Feminism has demonstrated the "phallocentric" nature of Enlightenment discourse shaped by the logic of power and domination; now we are looking for a purified language. Thus deconstruction can have a significance not unlike that of socialism as the name for a movement with the broadest and potentially most pervasive influence.

Rorty is aware of the charges made by several of his critics[58] to the effect that deconstruction has radical implications for political institutions while pragmatism "simply reaffirms the self-image of 'North Atlantic bourgeois liberal culture.'"[59] The disciples of Derrida who criticize Rorty's self-conscious attempts to co-opt Derrida for the pragmatic cause have two sorts of vested interests. One group (the de Manians), seek a method with which to deflate the pretensions of philosophic discourse and apotheosize the *littérateur*. Others, those closer to Derrida's (sometime) intention, wish a method with which to advertise the effects of logocentrism on all kinds of discourses. It is the latter group in particular which holds to the radical potential of deconstruction, and criticizes Rorty's attempts to pragmatize Derrida.

I believe Rorty provides a viable reading of Derrida, one which matches quite well his later efforts in particular, and I think he is justified in urging Derrida in the pragmatic direction. The first point is defended by noting actual movements in Derrida's later writings. The second point is reinforced in the following way: Rorty may be right in thinking that theory has little political potential and, in any case, it is simply not true that Rorty's position entails political conservatism.

As mentioned above, the device of dividing thinkers into early and late provides Rorty a means of designating what in their thinking he praises and what he censures. This technique enables him to effectively bypass later tendencies in a thinker, such as Heidegger, whose early work he prizes, and to ignore early tendencies which persist into the later phases of a thinker, such as Derrida, whose later thought he prefers.

Whether we take Rorty's ruminations on Derrida[60] as in many ways prophetic of the path that Derrida will actually take, or simply as a divining of one sort of strategy present in Derrida's arsenal (the alternative being the more systematic, methodological Derrida prized by many American literary critics), depends on where Derrida goes from here. But Rorty's analysis of Derrida's later work[61] seems right on target in its emphasis upon his invention of a new philosophical genre.

Comparing Derrida to Proust, Rorty claims that just as the latter's *Remembrance of Things Past* was unique, so Derrida's approach to the art of recontextualization is totally without precedent. Derrida has rejected the rules that permit argument in favor of a free play of associations which employ not only the semantics and syntactics of the discourse but the accidental features of words—their sound and shapes.

Rorty contends that by playing "all the authority figures, and all the descriptions of himself these figures might be imagined as giving, off against one another [Derrida insures that] the very notion of 'authority' loses application in reference to his work."[62] Rorty is willing to call this philosophy even though there is no argument since it presupposes the sort of in-group knowledge philosophers must own.

I agree with Rorty that, turned into a method, one could expect little by way of political consequences from deconstruction. It is difficult enough to see the relations between a specifically political and economic theory such as Marxism or capitalist theorizing and the actual Marxian and capitalist praxis, much less draw political consequences from something as abstract as deconstructionism. On the other hand, I have little difficulty seeing the revolutionary potential of Derridean prose. Derrida has provided, not a principle or set of principles, but a *model* of self-creation. Surely, there is little by way of paradox in believing that it is the later writings that portend institutional revolution. Nonetheless, Rorty is probably correct in noting that Derrida's textualism adds nothing to Romanticism and pragmatism but a new metaphor.[63]

THE SEARCH FOR PRIVATE PERFECTION

In one of his autobiographical pieces, Bertrand Russell tells of once giving a talk on the subject of solipsism which occasioned a subsequent query from an earnest lady writing him to the effect that his remarks had converted her to solipsism and that she would now like to be put in touch with some other solipsists so that they might organize a society! In another context Russell recounts how he himself was saved from solipsism by reading his erstwhile collaborator's *Process and Reality*.

Solipsism, he realized, was fallacious since he reckoned he could certainly not have written that work!

Some readers of this book, sympathetic with the kind of interpretation I have been giving Rorty, might believe these (doubtless apocryphal) stories quite relevant. Rorty's views on the relations of language and the world, the minimalist ontology associated with his default nominalism, the tenuousness of his hold even upon the extralinguistic data of pain and causality, might lead one to suspect that Rorty is as close to solipsism as one can get without the stars (in all but his sky) beginning to blink out.

Read in the light of this admittedly extreme interpretation, Rorty's call for solidarity as a means of "clinging together against the dark" carries something of the skewed poignancy of the new convert's desire to start a society of solipsists. We must, however, assume that Rorty is saved from solipsism in much the same manner as was Bertrand Russell: faced with the mass of foundationalist, objectivist, philosophical work, Rorty knows full well that he could not have produced it.

The most important reason why Rorty does not yield himself up to solipsism lies in the fact that he suffers, as so many creative thinkers before him, from "the last infirmity of noble mind"—the desire for fame. Reading Rorty, one gets the feeling that he has opted into the form of upmanship practiced by Nietzsche on Socrates, Heidegger on Nietzsche, and Derrida on Heidegger. His attempt to circumvent the Grand Deconstructor is an attempt to position himself with respect to the last best exemplars of creative thought in such a manner as to win the mantle.

The real aim is not merely fame but the sort of lasting, incorrigible fame we know as immortality. This is the desire shared by all sorts of would-be greats. For example, "Nabokov shared Heidegger's hope of eventually coming up with words and books which were so unclassifiable, fell so clearly outside any known way of grouping resemblances and differences, that they would not suffer . . . banalization."[64] Rorty ruefully admits that the best one can hope for is to make such banalization, the incorporation into common discourse, enormously difficult to achieve.

By out-nominalizing the nominalists, Rorty has played his trump card. Whether it will win for him a place in the thinker's Hall of Fame is yet to be seen. The one thing left to be said is that it is through the strong poet's aim at private self-perfection that Rorty must finally achieve prominence. A scholar's vague fame is hardly enough for anyone with the ambition to tempt the rising generation with his words, and the role of "utopian revolutionary" seems distasteful to Rorty.

Rorty is a generous contributor of novelty to the pool of metaphors from which this and future generations may draw. Also, as a critic of objectivist rationality, he is attempting to sweep away outdated metaphors which burden our common sense. Further, his narratives concerning the contemporary outworkings of liberal democracy attempt to set a context for the implementation (literalization) of novel metaphors as tools of public praxis. Oddly, therefore, though the bite of Rorty's pragmatism is every bit as bad as its bark, he seems disposed to remain more the muzzled ironist involved in self-creation than the moral hero seeking to transform the sphere of public praxis. Rorty seems to have willfully and self-consciously walled himself up in his own wine cellar by insisting upon the only indirect relevance of philosophical thinking to the public life. As we have stressed before, one doesn't have to return to the discredited modes of *Ideologiekritik* to support the contention that there are some (at least locally significant) social and political issues the confrontation of which is not optional for the thinker who responsibly seeks solidarity with others.

If what we share is the common fate of risking pain and humiliation, then public discourse serves us well only if it aims at the alleviation of these evils. For Rorty, irony expresses its value, not through direct application to the sphere of public praxis, but by detaching itself from the public weal and providing private lessons on the pain of physical violence and the humiliation of forced redescription. Thus "the metaphysician's association of theory with social hope and of literature with private perfection is, in an ironist liberal culture, reversed."[65] The liberal ironist is free to treat both metaphysicians and novelists as heroes of their own books. But one sort of hero (the metaphysician) is now treated as a hero of the private life and the other (the novelist) as a public hero.

Surely a pernicious, dramatic irony lurks somewhere in Rorty's insistence upon a "firm distinction between the private and the public."[66] For a consequence of this distinction is that "if one holds the view of the self as centerless . . . , one will be prepared to find the relation between the intellectual and the moral virtues, and the relation between a writer's books and other parts of his life, contingent."[67]

The disjunctions between intellectual and moral virtues, and between the private and the public spheres, and between ironism and liberal hope, are rather questionably consonant with the pragmatist stance that Rorty claims to maintain. The relationship between the intellectual and moral virtues cannot be read as *essentially* separate without threatening the purity of Rorty's nominalism. One must decide on a case by case basis. Rorty recognizes this in practice.

> The pursuit of private perfection is a perfectly reasonable aim for some writers—writers like Plato, Heidegger, Proust, and Nabokov, who share certain talents. Serving human liberty is a perfectly reasonable aim for other writers—people like Dickens, Mill, Dewey, Orwell, Habermas, and Rawls, who share others.[68]

Obviously, sensitizing us to pain and humiliation is not solely the task of those who have been called novelists and poets. It is equally true that, according to Rorty's underlaborer view, service to the public sphere involves more than such direct sensitizing. But it seems true as well that philosophers such as Mill, Dewey, and Habermas serve as more than mere "underlaborers" for the poets and revolutionaries. Certainly Mill and Habermas, and John Dewey as well,[69] sank their teeth into more than just other philosophers.

The shift (by way of updating pragmatism) from experience to language involves a shift from Dewey's worldly experience to the bookish experience of Rorty. Thus, the linguistic turn has become a *literary* turn. As Robert Musil, so Richard Rorty: "to live as one reads," to recognize "life as literature" is the most pleasurable state of affairs.[70] But the pragmatist strain in Rorty calls him to the tasks of social engineering. He must address the problems of the public.

It is a mistake, according to Rorty, to project, as does Michel Foucault, the desire for private autonomy onto society at large since "societies are not quasi-persons, they are (at their liberal, social democratic best) compromises between persons."[71] But one needs some clarification here. For what can "decentered" mean but that an ostensive individual is a compromise between persons, between, that is to say, sets of relatively coherent beliefs and desires? Or alternatively, one could claim that a society during its moments of relative consensus is the voice of one (reasonably coherent) set of beliefs and desires standing out amidst many possible voices.

The private/public distinction seems a resort to a deus ex machina. The distinction between an individual as a society of selves and a society as a society of such societies must remain vague in order to shore up Rorty's understanding of human beings as complexes of sentential attitudes whose beliefs are recontextualized through interactions with other individuals. A causal theory of changes in beliefs permits no sharp delineation between private and public for the same reason that it will not sustain a distinction between literary and philosophical discourse. For just as it is not for the writer but his readers to decide when "the words stand out as words," so it is not for the princes and privy counselors, but the specific parties to a supposedly private or public interaction, to decide when such exists.

The point of these remarks is that there is a suspicious downside to Rorty's circumventing strategies. While his default nominalism permits him to trade in the grandiose resort to transcendental method for the apparently more modest attempts at circumvention, his insistence upon a disjunction between private and public, combined with his self-justifying narratives, transform his proposed circumventions (which are ostensibly aimed at finding a way around the "useless lumber that blocks our highways of thought") into *circumlocutions*—personal, self-encapsulating stories which permit Rorty to avoid having to meet a conversant on his terms.

I assume that Rorty's advice to Derrida, that he continue his pursuit of private perfection by following the path of creative idiosyncrasy, to be advice that Rorty, with some inner qualms perhaps, would himself like to follow. There is, as I tried to indicate while discussing the theme of loneliness in chapter 4, a brooding desire for solitude expressed throughout the pages of Rorty's work.[72]

But Rorty is by no means settled in his views. Hopping from one lily pad to another and back again (between imagination and inference, between poetry and philosophy, between coherent narratives and the nagging, insistent particularities which coexist in no single narrative or family of narratives, between the fantasy of an encapsulated public world run by recourse to the banal morality shoring up beliefs in justice as fairness and the fantasy of an encapsulated private world closed to anyone but himself), Rorty dances the dance of the ambiguated individual.

There is little by way of true solidarity possible if any of the following obtain: (*a*) if each of us must construct her own self-justifying narrative and circumvent any attempts to play by someone else's rules, or (*b*) if all (or most) of us must buy into someone else's narrative, or (*c*) our society is a mishmash of midrange narratives which account for this or that institution, discipline, or movement. In the first instance we have a complex of windowless monads whose only social relations are with other elements of their ambiguated selves; in the second, a union of self-alienated *public-ized* individuals, humiliated by the acceptance of a set of alien descriptors. In the last instance, we are confronted with a multiplicity of publics only slightly less incoherent than the myriad private spheres illustrated by a hotchpotch of solipsists unable to give credence to the existence of others "out there." If those equipped for intellectual interactions resort to circumvention (read "circumlocution"), we have ships passing in the night; if a number of them substitute direct engagement for circumvention, we have ships colliding in a storm. Either way the Great Conversation is lost.

Responding to Joseph Singer's charge that he has "marginalized" the enterprise of philosophy, thereby depriving pragmatism of its critical bite, Rorty claims "pragmatism bites other philosophies, but not social problems as such."[73] But when pragmatic philosophers bite foundational philosophers they do so as watchdogs in service of the strong poets and revolutionaries whose task it is to sensitize us to pain and humiliation.

Rorty may be giving away a bit too much here. One might suspect him of a wistful ambivalence toward the more praxis-oriented philosophers. Certainly his attempts to read Dewey as an underlaborer, ignoring the very practical hands-on character of his public activity, is strained. Nonetheless, Rorty's disinclination to engage practical issues is consistent with his apparently strong belief in the trickle-down theory of meaning and value. If social changes are linguistically rooted and result from the effect of novel metaphors which bring about recontextualization of beliefs and desires, then one can serve the public quite well either by clearing away dead metaphors no longer relevant to the needs of private self-creation, or by the alleviation of pain and humiliation, or by the literalizing of new metaphors in order to make them into socially beneficial instruments.

One can become very frustrated with the attempt to discover whether Rorty is primarily a poet or a philosopher, whether he is more inclined toward the production of novel metaphors or their consumption on behalf of the aims of public praxis. As a metathinker and critic of alternative philosophies he is clearly performing the philosophic task as he defines it. But his "strong misreadings" of his predecessors, his creative juxtaposition of philosophic and/or literary texts, and his belief in the importance of self-creation, all point to a poetic disposition. Indeed, Rorty must acknowledge that a person, as a nexus of beliefs and desires, can only be what he *does*. This means that there isn't a single Rorty acting in two different roles—the poetic and the mundanely philosophic; there are instead (at least) *two* Rortys—Rorty$_1$ is inferential; Rorty$_2$ imaginative.

Rorty's idiosyncratic narratives are charming, disarming, and often most profound. But when all is said and (little) done, one realizes that his self-encapsulating strategies privatize his language to the extent that what he provides us is broadly irrelevant to interactive public discourse. What we are finally offered are obiter dicta . . . Richard Rorty's tabletalk.

Why is this snide word not the last one? It cannot be since so many of us, often in despite of our own understandings of what we are really supposed to be up to, remain seated at Rorty's table, waiting for what comes next . . .

EPITEXT:
GUIDE FOR THOSE STILL PERPLEXED

IMPORTANT ESSAYS KEYED TO THE CHAPTERS

The following is a selection of essays from Rorty's *Philosophical Papers*. These essays may be consulted for clarification and elaboration of the issues discussed in the various chapters of this book.

Chapter 1: Holding One's Time in Thought

1. "Philosophy as Science, as Metaphor, and as Politics" (II, 9-26)
2. "The Priority of Democracy to Philosophy" (I, 175-96)
3. "Habermas and Lyotard on Postmodernity" (II, 164-76)

Chapter 2: An Old Name for Some New Ways of Thinking

4. "Texts and Lumps (I, 78-92)
5. "Non-Reductive Physicalism" (I, 113-25)
6. "Unfamiliar Noises: Hesse and Davidson on Metaphor" (I, 162-72)

Chapter 3: Irony's Master, Irony's Slave

Chapter 4: Excursus ad Hominem

Chapter 5: Circumvention and Circumlocution

RORTY'S FINAL VOCABULARY

I have provided below a partial index to Rorty's "final vocabulary." One of the best ways of reinforcing one's understanding of the
New Pragmatism is by keeping the Rortyan meanings of these terms in
mind.

BELIEF
CAUSALITY
CENTERLESS WEB OF BELIEFS AND DESIRES
CIRCUMVENTION
DECONSTRUCTION
EDIFYING PHILOSOPHERS
ETHNOCENTRISM
FOUNDATIONALISTS
GEISTESGESCHICHTE
HISTORICISM
HUMILIATION
JUSTICE
LIBERAL
LUMPS (AND TEXTS)
METAPHORS

MORAL IDENTITY
NARRATIVES
NATURAL KIND
NOMINALISM
OBJECTIVITY
PAIN
PIECEMEAL NUDGES
PRAGMATISM
PRIVATE AND PUBLIC
PRIVATE PERFECTION
RECONTEXTUALIZATION
RELATIVISM
REPRESENTATION
SCIENCE
SOLIDARITY
SYSTEMATIC PHILOSOPHERS
TEXTS (AND LUMPS)

SOLIDARITY GROUPINGS

An important implication of Rorty's substitution of "solidarity" for "objectivity" is that he clarifies his ideas by appeals to real and imagined rhetorical communities. The following is a selection (by no means exhaustive) of the "solidarity groupings" endorsed by Rorty. As odd as it might seem, one may learn a great deal about the direction of Rorty's thinking by looking at the contemporary intellectual scene from the perspective of these communities.

EDIFYING THINKERS
ANTI-FOUNDATIONALISTS
FREELOADING ATHEISTS
LIBERAL IRONISTS
NEW FUZZIES
NOMINALIST HISTORICISTS
NONREDUCTIVE PHYSICALISTS
PIECEMEAL NUDGERS
POST-METAPHYSICAL NOMINALISTS
POSTMODERNIST BOURGEOIS LIBERALS
UNFAMILIAR NOISEMAKERS
WITTGENSTEINIAN THERAPISTS

HEROES AND VILLAINS

The fact that Rorty often provides narratives in place of arguments means that his most and least favored thinkers are identified primarily as *dramatis personae*. In the same manner that familiarity with the principal characters of a play enhances one's grasp of the dramatic events, so the recollection of the principal heroes and villains of Rorty's narratives will deepen one's understanding of the New Pragmatism.

Heroes

BACON, FRANCIS
BLOOM, HAROLD
BLUMENBERG, HANS
CASTORIADIS, CORNELIUS
DAVIDSON, DONALD
DERRIDA, JACQUES
DEWEY, JOHN
DICKENS, CHARLES
EMERSON, RALPH WALDO
FREUD, SIGMUND
HEGEL, G. W. F.
HEIDEGGER, MARTIN (EARLY)
JAMES, WILLIAM
KUHN, THOMAS
NABOKOV, VLADIMIR
NIETZSCHE, FRIEDRICH
ORWELL, GEORGE
PROUST, MARCEL
PUTNAM, HILARY
QUINE, W. V.O.
RAWLS, JOHN
SELLARS, WILFRID
UNGER, ROBERTO MANGABEIRA
WHITMAN, WALT
WITTGENSTEIN, LUDWIG (LATE)

Villains

DESCARTES, RENE
FOUCAULT, MICHEL
HABERMAS, JÜRGEN

HEIDEGGER, MARTIN (LATE)
HUSSERL, EDMUND
KANT, IMMANUEL
PEIRCE, CHARLES SANDERS
PLATO
RUSSELL, BERTRAND
WEBER, MAX
WHITEHEAD, A. N.
WITTGENSTEIN, LUDWIG (EARLY)

THE TEN COMMANDMENTS OF THE NEW PRAGMATISM

Finally, I have listed below the principal injunctions of Rorty's pragmatism.

1. THOU SHALT CLING TOGETHER WITH OTHERS AGAINST THE DARK.
2. THOU SHALT NOT FORCIBLY REDESCRIBE.
3. THOU SHALT COVET NEITHER A THEORY NOR A PLAN.
4. THOU SHALT NUDGE ONLY IN A PIECEMEAL FASHION.
5. THOU SHALT HONOR ABOVE ALL THINE OWN ETHNOCENTRIC BELIEFS.
6. THOU SHALT NOT CONFUSE THE PUBLIC AND THE PRIVATE REALMS.
7. THOU SHALT NOT WRAP THY BELIEFS AND DESIRES TOO TIGHTLY.
8. THOU SHALT SEEK TO MAKE AN UNFAMILIAR NOISE UNTO THE LORD.
9. THOU SHALT SEEK ALWAYS, WHEN IN DOUBT, TO CIRCUMVENT.
10. THOU SHALT TEMPT THE RISING GENERATION WITH THY WORDS.

NOTES

The majority of Rorty's writings are occasional in the best sense of that term. His most effective medium is the essay, and the essays he writes are, as often as not, responses to critics, friendly and otherwise. Now that most of his major essays have been published in book form in *Consequences of Pragmatism* and the two volumes of his *Philosophical Papers*, we have easy access to his principal writings. Because of the relative independence of his various papers, however, I have often deemed it important when using collections of Rorty's writings to mention the title of the essay from which a citation is given—either in the text itself, or in the notes. This should assist the reader in contextualizing Rorty's arguments. With respect to *Philosophy and the Mirror of Nature* and *Contingency, Irony, and Solidarity*, I have given only the page references.

PRETEXT

1. This remark does not imply that there are not many solid pragmatist philosophers out there who are producing potentially significant work. I only mean to suggest that the scholarly and popular *import* of the pragmatic movement has waned to the extent that traditional pragmatists seem to be writing for an increasingly smaller audience. Hopefully, Rorty's notoriety will stimulate interest in the entire spectrum of pragmatic thinking.

2. *Rorty's Humanistic Pragmatism—Philosophy Democratized* (Tampa: University of South Florida Press, 1990).

3. Critical assessments of Rorty suffer as well. A book of essays entitled *Reading Rorty*, eds. Alan Malachowski and Jo Burrows (Cambridge, Mass.: B. Blackwell, 1990) is almost unreadable due to the overly specialized, often picayunish, interests of the contributors. By their insistence upon showing off their shiny new hobbyhorses, the majority of the essayists subvert any general understanding of Rorty's thinking. C. G. Prado offers an insightful, and partially supportive, account of Rorty's thinking (*The Limits of Pragmatism* [Atlantic Highlands, N.J.: Humanities Press, 1987]), but his Peirceian insistence upon "retrospective objectivity" for theoretical discourse renders the praise faint enough to finally damn Rorty. Prado's exceptionally solid book was written before the publication of much of Rorty's latest work and is, therefore, in serious need of updating. Kai Nielsen's *After the Demise of the Tradition: Rorty, Critical Theory, and the Fate of Philosophy* (Boulder: Westview Press, 1991) focuses upon the "end of philosophy" issue, thereby under-mining many of the richer veins of Rorty's philosophy. John Smith has provided an interesting assessment of Rorty's thinking in the introduction to his *America's Philosophical Vision* (Chicago: The University of Chicago Press, 1992), but his insightful critique begins to appear rather dismissive in the light of his failure to engage Rorty's thinking at all in the body of the text.

4. *Philosophy and the Mirror of Nature* (Princeton, N.J.: Princeton University Press, 1979), 12.

5. Ibid.

6. See Bernstein's *Beyond Objectivism and Relativism* (Philadelphia: The University of Pennsylvania Press, 1983), 18.

Alan Malachowski, the editor of *Reading Rorty*, in discussing strategies for teaching *Philosophy and the Mirror of Nature*, recognizes that undergraduate students are neither familiar with nor practitioners of the sort of thinking Rorty assaults, nor do they suffer from Cartesian Anxiety. The suggestion endorsed by Malachowski, however, is that a teacher might wish to rehearse the tradition Rorty critiques in order to "give muscles to the ghosts" exorcised by *Philosophy and the Mirror of Nature*. Otherwise the power of the critique might not be properly appreciated.

Though such a strategy makes some sense when using *Mirror* as a primary text, I believe it to be misguided if one employs Rorty's later essays. In this instance the philosophical naiveté of the students actually stands them in good stead since a shift in the "climate of opinion" in contemporary intellectual culture per se, a shift for which Rorty is in part responsible, obviates the necessity to wrestle with those old ghosts. Quite apart from the fact that one is ill advised to fatten ghosts before busting them, a teacher needs to recognize that often the failure of her students to be haunted by the same ghosts as is she is less due to her students' insensitivity to poltergeists and more to the fact that those spirits have long since fled.

7. See "Posties," *London Review of Books*, 3 September 1987, 11.

8. Ibid.

9. Ibid.

10. Ibid.

11. See the introduction to his *What Is Philosophy?* (New York: W. W. Norton, 1961).

12. I am perfectly sanguine about the implication that my criticisms of the method of recontextualization might be applied to my own use of that method in exposing Rorty's ideas.

13. "Comments on Sleeper and Edel," in *Transactions of the C. S. Peirce Society* 21, no. 1 (Winter 1985): 47.

14. The Heidegger of *Sein und Zeit* is early, the author of *Zur Sache des Denkens* late; the *Tractatus* is an early work, *Philosophical Investigations* late; *Experience and Nature* is early Dewey; *Art as Experience* is late; the early Whitehead of *Principia Mathematica* is contrasted with the late Whitehead of *Process and Reality* and *Adventures of Ideas*.

15. "One Step Forward, Two Steps Backward—Richard Rorty on Liberal Democracy and Philosophy," *Political Theory* 15, no. 4 (November 1987): 557. This essay is reprinted in *The New Constellation* (Cambridge, Mass.: MIT Press, 1992), 230-57.

16. Chicago: The University of Chicago Press, 1967, 1-39.

17. In the preface to this work, Rorty says that he began thinking out the plot of the book in 1969-70, only two years after the publication of *The Linguistic Turn*. See p. xiv.

18. *The Linguistic Turn*, 39 n. 75.

19. Rorty was directly exposed to the work of two of the arch metaphilosophers of American thought—Richard McKeon at Chicago and Robert Brumbaugh (himself a former student of McKeon) at Yale. Receiving thereby both an Aristotelian and a Platonic rendering of metatheoretical approaches could not but infuse (or infect) Rorty with the metamentality characteristic of these philosophers of philosophy. This influence is reflected in the title of the introduction to *The Linguistic Turn*,

"Metaphilosophical Difficulties of Linguistic Philosophy." It is, in fact, evidenced much earlier in a review article published in *The Review of Metaphysics* entitled "Recent Metaphilosophy" (vol. 15 [December 1961]: 299-318).

In fairness to Rorty, I should say that he has not, as far as I know, explicitly acknowledged in print any substantive influence from the metaphilosophers. For Rorty's own treatment of his early psychological, sociological, and philosophical influences, see his "Trotsky and the Wild Orchids," in *Wild Orchids and Trotsky—Messages from American Universities,* ed. Mark Edmundson (New York: Viking, 1993).

I do, nonetheless, stand by my belief in the influence of, in particular, Richard McKeon. I will briefly discuss the presumed impact of the metatheorists on Rorty's thinking in chapter 2.

20. In denying a Rortyan *Kehre* I may be in the uncomfortable position of disagreeing with Rorty himself. In an essay entitled, "Twenty Five Years After," written in 1990 for the Spanish translation of *The Linguistic Turn* (*El Giro Linguistico,* trans. G. Bello [Barcelona: Ediciones Paidos, 1990]), Rorty discusses changes in his views since the initial publication of that work. He chides his former self for the vestiges of representationalism he retained in 1965. On my reading, however, the weight of these remarks is to tell how the inevitable conclusions to which his thinking was drawn from the beginning had not come completely to light in 1965. It might have been difficult for Rorty to see the 1990 version of himself in 1965, but I find that, from my post-1990 vantage point, it is difficult not to see the strict continuity between the two Rortys. It is because he discounts the early notable influences of the metaphilosophical pluralism and pragmatism of Richard McKeon and his ilk that Rorty is able to provide the *Bildungserzählung* that he does.

CHAPTER 1: HOLDING ONE'S TIME IN THOUGHT

1. CIS, 55.

2. The implications are slightly different, though only in degree, with respect to the history of science. There is, on the whole, less controversy here since during periods of so-called normal science most scientific colleagues agree on who is or is not a scientist, and what constitutes a legitimate scientific problem. Rorty's historicist approach to science is one of the more controversial elements of his thought. The question whether science has any stronger claim to realism and objectivity than any other discipline will be one of the questions we must consider at various places throughout this work. See especially chapter 2, passim.

3. "The Historiography of Philosophy: Four Genres," in *Philosophy in History,* ed. Richard Rorty et. al. (Cambridge, Mass.: Cambridge University Press, 1984), 73-74.

4. Ibid., 73.

5. Bernstein, "One Step Forward, Two Steps Backward—Rorty on Liberal Democracy and Philosophy," 248.

6. We will postpone for now addressing the question of how he comes to identify his time with "the modern age."

7. The term, of course, belongs to Harold Bloom, whose *Anxiety of Influence* (New York: Oxford University Press, 1973) has significantly influenced the shape of Rorty's arguments regarding the character of the intellectual landscape of a culture. I confess to a worry whether Rorty's strong poet and revolutionary, if allowed to join forces, would not become the functional equivalent of Heidegger's "creative statesman"—a type which has recently, and rightly so I believe, fallen under a cloud. But, as we shall see, there is in Rorty's rather severe (if somewhat problematic) disjunction between the public and the private realms some attempt to guard against this occurrence.

8. See note 7.

9. But there is another vision of social and cultural change associated with traditional cultures. In such societies novelty is masked by claims of continuity. The Father is made to live on as the immanent transmitter of cultural value. Confucianism is the best example of this vision.

   Both versions amount to much the same thing when it comes to the issue of novelty. It appears that agonal, historical cultures promote the claim to novelty while traditional cultures prize the demonstration of sameness. But there is likely an upper and lower limit to the introduction of novel circumstances and if a not a happy, then at least an acceptable, medium. China could not have survived for two thousand plus years without a great deal of flexibility. The Oedipal/agonal version of the emergence of novelty shares with the Confucian/nurtural version the conviction that the weight of the past must be shifted, part of the past elided, if room for novelty is to exist. But that end is achieved whether we attempt to cancel or at least subordinate the past to us through a violent struggle, or simply invest the past with the authority of our own novelty. Thus, traditional cultures such as China have masked a vast amount of individual creativity under the guise of "The Master (or Chairman Mao) said . . .". The West has masked a great deal of sameness under the guise of "At long last I have gotten it right . . .". But both sorts of culture always maintain a connection with the past such that its authority devolves upon a successor-present. Novelty tends to be overrated in agonal cultures and underrated in traditional societies. But there is always novelty.

10. CIS, 45.

11. CIS, 53.

12. CIS, 37.

13. Cambridge, Mass.: MIT Press, 1983.

14. See *Papers* (1), 33 n. 16.

15. *Proceedings and Addresses of the American Philosophical Association* 59 (1986): 747-53.

16. Trans. John Macquarrie and Edward Robinson (New York: Harper and Row, 1962).

17. We should not overlook, in this regard, Robert Musil's expression of this same movement in literary form. See his *Man without Qualities*.

18. Rorty sees Cassirer's *Philosophy of Symbolic Forms*, Whitehead's *Process and Reality*, Charles Hartshorne's *Divine Relativity*, C. I. Lewis' *Mind and the World Order*, Rudolf Carnap's *Logische Aufbau der Welt*, Langer's *Philosophy in a New Key*, Hilary Putnam's *Reason, Truth and History*, Donald Davidson's *Essays in Truth and Interpretation*, Nelson Goodman's *Ways of Worldmaking* and *Language and Art* as expressions of this new spirit.

19. "From Logic to Language to Play," 751.

20. Ibid., 752.

21. See his "Professionalized Philosophy and Transcendentalist Culture," in CP, 60-71.

22. "Habermas and Lyotard on Postmodernity," *Papers* (2), 164-76.

23. CP, 139-59.

24. CP, 146.

25. CP, 150.

26. Robert Neville, "Sketch of a System" in *New Essays in Metaphysics*, ed. Robert Neville (Albany: SUNY Press, 1989), 272 n. 3.

27. We may think, for example, of Alasdair's MacIntyre's critique of modernity beginning in *After Virtue* (Notre Dame, Ind.: University of Notre Dame Press, 1981; second edition, 1984) and continuing through his recent *Three Rival Traditions of Moral Enquiry* (Notre Dame, Ind.: University of Notre Dame Press, 1990).

28. See my *Uncertain Phoenix—Adventures Toward a Post-cultural Sensibility* (New York: Fordham University Press, 1982), passim, for an account of the relation of the notion of the tripartite structure of the psyche to cultural self-understanding.

29. See ibid., passim, for a discussion of the rise and fall of "the cultural paradigm."

30. See his *The Legitimacy of the Modern Age*. A principal virtue of Blumenberg's work lies in its recognition of both the Cartesian and Baconian strands of modernity.

31. See *City of God*, XII. 7. Here Augustine argues that the evil will of fallen angels has no efficient cause. See also XIV. 1.12-14 which deals with the original sin.

    Blumenberg does not explicitly consider the invention or discovery of the will by Augustine. But before there could be self-assertion there had to be a volitionally equipped self. MacIntyre, following Albrecht Dihle (*The Theory of the Will in Classical Antiquity* [Berkeley: The University of California Press, 1982]), has acknowledged Augustine's importance in the "discovery" or "invention" of the concept of "will." On Blumenberg's terms, it would have to be something like an invention—an originary act of self-assertion which produced that which would serve as the means of further acts of self-assertion. For a discussion of the consequences of Augustine's construction of the concept of "willing" for moral theory, see Alasdair MacIntyre's *Whose Justice? Which Rationality?* (Notre Dame, Ind.: University of Notre Dame Press, 1988), 146-63.

32. *Legitimacy*, 173, 184.

33. See "Philosophy as Science, as Metaphor, and as Politics," *Papers* (2), 9-26.

34. "Habermas and Lyotard on Postmodernity," *Papers* (2), 169.

35. See chapter 2 below for a discussion of Peirce's more successful attempt to bypass Kant on this issue.

36. See his *Five Faces of Modernity* (Durham: Duke University Press, 1987). These five "faces" are modernism, the avant-garde, decadence, kitsch, and postmodernism. With regard to the "idea of modernity" his basic distinction is between the two modernities—the *bourgeois*, a chronological mode, related to scientific and technological progress, and the "aesthetic idea of modernity" originating with Baudelaire and associated with antibourgeois attitudes of the artist who promoted *l'art pour l'art*.

37. See his *Fragments of Modernity* (Cambridge: MIT Press, 1986).

38. There are a number of attempts at a comprehensive investigation of the phenomenon of modernity. All share a more or less self-consciously reductive approach. Among the better of these interpretations are: Hans Blumenberg's *The Legitimacy of the Modern Age* (Cambridge: The MIT Press, 1976); David Kolb's *The Critique of Pure Modernity—Hegel, Heidegger and After* (Chicago: The University of Chicago Press, 1986); Jürgen Habermas'

The Philosophical Discourse of Modernity, trans. Frederick Lawrence (Cambridge: The MIT Press, 1987), and *Postmetaphysical Thinking: Philosophical Essays* trans. William Mark Hohengarten (Cambridge, Mass.: The MIT Press, 1992); Lawrence Cahoone's *The Crisis of Modernity* (Albany: SUNY Press, 1988); Stephen Toulmin's *Cosmopolis—The Hidden Agenda of Modernity* (Glencoe, Ill.: The Free Press, 1991); Anthony J. Cascardi's *The Subject of Modernity* (New York: Cambridge University Press, 1992); and Robert Neville's *The High Road around Modernism* (Albany: SUNY Press, 1992).

39. See David Kolb, *Critique of Pure Modernity*, 7-17.

40. *The Theory of the Avant Garde* (Cambridge: Harvard University Press, 1968), 217.

41. Gassendi's name is a convenient one to associate with the rediscovery of classical atomism which captured the thought of numerous intellectuals of the period. Besides Descartes, one might list Boyle, Hobbes, Locke, Newton, Harvey, and many lesser lights.

42. Nonetheless, Kant's separation of religion from the other value spheres did promote its becoming a *Fach*, a specialized discipline. And Rudolf Otto's defense of the autonomy of "the Holy" would hardly have been possible without Kant's initial speculations. See Otto's *The Idea of The Holy: An Inquiry into the Nonrational Factor in the Idea of the Divine and Its Relation to the Rational* (New York: Galaxy Books, 1958), trans. J. W. Harvey.

43. Hegel's interpretation of modernity is scattered throughout his writings, particularly *The Philosophy of Right* and *The Encyclopedia*. For summaries and critical interpretations of Hegel's understanding of "modernity," see Kolb, *Critique of Pure Modernity*, 20-117 passim and Habermas *The Philosophical Discourse of Modernity*, 23-44.

44. See Habermas' *The Philosophical Discourse of Modernity*.

45. "Habermas and Lyotard on Postmodernity," *Papers* (2), 172.

46. Ibid.

47. "Idealism and Textualism," CP, 148.

48. Both MacIntyre and Habermas, with quite different aims in mind, have criticized Weber's understanding of value choices. What MacIntyre calls Weber's "emotivism" is termed by Habermas "decisionism." The meaning is the same: rationality is grounded in value choices the reasonableness of which cannot be defended. See Alasdair MacIntyre, *After Virtue*, and Jürgen Habermas, *Toward a Rational Society*, trans. Jeremy J. Shapiro (Boston: Beacon Press, 1970), 62-69.

49. See Weber's *Protestant Ethic and the Spirit of Capitalism* (New York: Scribners, 1958), passim for discussions of the peculiarly "occidental" character of the rationalization and secularization of tradition.

50. "The Priority of Democracy to Philosophy," *Papers* (1), 194.

51. "Idealism and Textualism," CP, 148.

52. Ed. Bruce Wilshire, *Romanticism and Evolution* (New York: University Press of America, 1985), "Introduction," 15.

53. "The Painter of Modern Life," in *Selected Writings on Art and Artists* (New York: Penguin Books, 1972), 403.

54. Ibid.

55. Ibid.

56. CIS, 43.

57. *Of Civil Government*, Second Treatise, chapter V, section 27 (Chicago: Henry Regnery, 1955), 22.

58. *A Treatise of Human Nature*, ed. L. A. Selby-Bigge (Oxford, 1896). See especially Book II, i-ii, passim.

59. *Treatise*, II, part I, section i, pp. 276-77.

60. Ibid., 277.

61. Ibid., II, part I, section x, p. 309.

62. Ibid., 365.

63. Ibid., II, part II, section ii, p. 489.

64. Ibid., I, part IV, section vi, p. 253.

65. *An Inquiry Into the Nature and Causes of the Wealth of Nations* (Chicago: Encyclopedia Britannica, Inc., 1952), 52.

66. Ibid., 3.

67. Ibid., 6.

68. Ibid., 107.

69. Ibid., 138.

70. Ibid., 107.

71. Ed. Derk Struik, *The Economic and Philosophic Manuscripts of 1844* (New York: International Publishers, 1964), 108.

72. For a discussion of these themes in a succinct but extremely wise form, see Nicholas Xenos' *Scarcity and Modernity* (New York: Routledge, 1989). To understand the success of the capitalist discourse against its Marxist counterdiscourse, see trans. Sheilagh C. Ogilvie, Henri Lepage, *Tomorrow, Capitalism* (La Salle, Ill: Open Court, 1982).

73. *Symposium*, 203-04.

74. *All That Is Solid Melts into Air—The Experience of Modernity* (New York: Penguin Books, 1988). Recall the founders of the Chinese Communist party who sought to import a "Western heresy to use against the West."

75. Ibid., 102.

76. Ibid., 118-19.

77. The best example of this sort of analysis is to be found in Foucault's *Discipline and Punish: The Birth of the Prison*, trans. Alan Sheridan (New York: Vintage/Random House, 1979).

78. See C. N. Cochrane's *Christianity and Classical Culture* (New York: Oxford University Press, 1940), 456-74 for a discussion of the classical Greek historiography which demonstrates the distinctively philosophical character of Herodotus and of Thucydides.

79. There is, of course, an echo of this still in the English title, *History of Animals*, naming a biological treatise of Aristotle.

80. "The Higher Nominalism in a Nutshell: A Reply to Henry Staten," *Critical Inquiry* 12 (Winter 1986): 463.

81. "Solidarity or Objectivity?," *Papers* (1), 21ff.

82. "Pragmatism without Method," *Papers* (1), 63ff.

83. "Pragmatism, Relativism, and Irrationalism," CP, 160ff.

84. "Philosophy as Science, as Metaphor, and as Politics," *Papers* (2), 12.

85. See P. K. Feyerabend, *Farewell to Reason* (New York: Routledge, Chapman & Hall, 1989), 112-15 and passim for the role of lists, examples, and classificatory schemes in the development of early Greek and modern scientific argumentation. Feyerabend also discusses the role of parabolic, historical, and dramatic narratives in classifying items across time.

86. See "Philosophy as Science, as Metaphor, and as Politics," 24-25.

87. See Rorty's criticism of Habermas' transcendentalist impulse in "Habermas and Lyotard on Postmodernity," 171-75.

88. I will address this issue in more detail below.

89. Anthony J. Cascardi, in *Redrawing the Lines: Analytic Philosophy, Deconstruction, and Literary Theory*, ed. Reed Way Dasenbrock, 219-20. See also "On Ethnocentrism," in *Papers* (1), 203-10 in which Rorty claims that it is ethnographers, not historians (nor, a fortiori, historicist philosophers), who have maintained the concern for diversity.

90. Trans. Linda Asher (New York: Grove Press, 1986). See part 2, "Dialogue on the Art of the Novel."

91. See *Poetics*, 1451b.

CHAPTER 2: AN OLD NAME FOR SOME NEW WAYS OF THINKING

1. Here I will consider only the classical American thinkers. I will discuss the influence of later thinkers such as W. V. O. Quine, Wilfrid Sellars, Donald Davidson, etc. in the last section of this chapter.

2. *The Nature of True Virtue* (Ann Arbor: The University of Michigan Press, 1960), 15.

3. *Religious Affections*, ed. John Smith (New Haven: Yale University Press, 1959), 298.

4. "Miscellanies," no. 293, Yale Library Collection of Edwards Manuscripts (Sterling Library, Yale University). Quoted in Roland Delattre (New Haven: Yale University Press, 1968), 183.

5. New Haven: Yale University Press, 1968, 28, note.

6. "Miscellanies," 117.

7. Though I don't want to make too much of this point, it is true that Rorty has read both Whitehead and Paul Tillich with some care, and the existential mood of their religiousness seems to have influenced him to some degree.

8. See his *Jonathan Edwards* (Cleveland: World Publishing Co., 1959), 240.

9. "The American Scholar," from *The Complete Essays and Other Writings of Ralph Waldo Emerson* (New York: Modern Library, 1950), 61.

10. Ibid.

11. "The American Scholar," 62.

12. Emerson, *Essays*, 152.

13. Ibid., 148. My italics.

14. See "The Priority of Democracy to Philosophy," *Papers* (1), 194-95.

15. See *Collected Papers*, II, par. 198.

16. Ibid., par. 199.

17. "Pragmatism, Relativism, and Irrationalism," CP, 161.

18. *Collected Papers* (Cambridge, MA: Harvard University Press, 1965), vol 1., par. 377.

19. Ibid., par. 380.

20. See "Comments on Sleeper and Edel." Once, when challenged on his understanding of Dewey, Rorty responded that, as an undergraduate he much preferred James to Dewey, that he only began to study Dewey rather late and then only because in his later thinking he has continually been led back to Dewey to find resonance with the sorts of things he wants to say. In fact, Rorty has a much stronger point when he indicates, in this same paper, that internal conflicts in the development of analytic philosophy in America led it to contradict its founders and to begin to sound more like James and Dewey.

21. *A Pluralistic Universe* (Cambridge, Mass.: Harvard University Press, 1977), 145.

22. *Principles of Psychology* (New York: Dover, 1950), vol. 2, 673.

23. Rorty's Ph.D. dissertation was on Whitehead and Aristotle.

24. For Whitehead's discussion of logical and aesthetic order, see chapter three of his *Modes of Thought* (New York: Capricorn Books, 1938). I have elaborated upon this distinction in my *Eros and Irony* (Albany: SUNY Press, 1982), chapter four ("The Ambiguity of Order").

25. See "The Subjectivist Principle and the Linguistic Turn," in *Alfred North Whitehead: Essays on His Philosophy* (Englewood Cliffs, N.J.: Prentice-Hall, Inc., 1963), 153. In conjunction with this essay, see Rorty's comparison of Whitehead and Aristotle: "Matter and Event," in *Explorations of Whitehead's Philosophy*, eds. Lewis Ford and George Kline (New York: Fordham University Press, 1983), 68-103. This essay was also written in 1963.

26. Ibid., 153.

27. *Process and Reality* (corrected edition), eds. David Ray Griffin and Donald Sherburne (New York: The Free Press, 1978), 337.

28. Berkeley: The University of California Press, 1942. This taxonomy was worked out over many years concluding with his *Concept and Quality: A World Hypothesis* (La Salle, Ill.: Open Court Press, 1967).

29. See McKeon's "Philosophic Semantics and Philosophic Inquiry," in *Freedom and History and Other Essays: An Introduction to the Thought of Richard McKeon* (Chicago: The University of Chicago Press, 1990), 242-56. Indeed, Robert Brumbaugh, a student of McKeon's, translated his teacher's pluralistic insights along more constructive, Platonic lines. See Robert Brumbaugh's, "Preface to Cosmography," "Cosmography," and "Cosmography: The Problem of Modern Systems" in *The Review of Metaphysics* 7:53-63, 25:337-47, and 26:511-21, respectively. See also Robert Brumbaugh and Newton Stallknecht, *The Compass of Philosophy* (Albany: SUNY Press, 1990).

30. See my *Uncertain Phoenix*, 12-19 and passim for an articulation of the development of metatheory from the early Platonic and Aristotelian models.

31. See *The Postcard from Socrates to Freud and Beyond*, trans. Alan Bass (Chicago: University of Chicago Press, 1987).

32. For a discussion of this distinction see the special issue on "Systematic Pluralism" *Monist*, vol. 73, no. 3 (July, 1990), 337.

33. Walter Watson, one of the more doctrinaire of the systematic pluralists, provides just this when he places Nicholas Rescher's "perspectival pluralism" alongside Stephen Pepper's "pluralism of hypotheses," Richard McKeon's "archic pluralism," and the "methodological pluralism" of Wayne Booth, completing a systematic classification of the types of pluralism (See Watson's contribution to ibid., "Types of Pluralism," 350-66).

   Watson doesn't seem in the least chary about the implication that he is suggesting not only a typology of pluralisms but a classification of types of classifications of pluralism. He recognizes that his "archic" classification could be supplemented by the three alternative approaches.

   It is difficult to take this seriously, once one realizes that there need be no end to the hierarchical organization of types of types. Now we run the risk of developing a variety of comparative methodologies. Little is left but to try to chart the ways of thinking and to provide a guide to the assumptions of the philosophic schools. This is a mode of hyperconsciousness which threatens to degenerate right away into reductio ad absurdum arguments directed against the sheer subtlety of the enterprise.

34. See Nicholas Rescher's defense of his liberal mode of orientational pluralism against the self-defeating consequences of a pernicious relativism in his *Strife of Systems—An Essay on the Grounds and Implications of Philosophical Diversity* (Pittsburgh: University of Pittsburgh Press, 1985), 173-201.

35. Rorty was an undergraduate at the University of Chicago when McKeon was at the peak of his influence. Though Rorty himself might wish to dismiss the pervasiveness of the early influence of McKeon, I am unable to avoid the suspicion that his views have been profoundly shaped by his

reaction to that early training. Thus I disagree with C.G. Prado when he remarks in *The Limits of Pragmatism* (p. 41) that the views of McKeon (and Brumbaugh) were "inspirational for Rorty, rather than methodologically influential."

36. Many of McKeon's students found his taxonomic approach to the history of philosophy, though providing a powerful set of tools for textual analysis, somewhat stultifying. They have often found it difficult to escape the typological mentality and have become bedazzled curators of other's thoughts rather than original thinkers in their own right. Rorty is clearly one of the "survivors."

I grant the fact that McKeon's students have often taken what I believe to be the sterile, purely taxonomic route. But I hold that to be a failing of the less imaginative of his students, those who have settled for becoming his disciples. These followers have associated him too closely with the scholasticism of his colleague, Mortimer Adler, and the "Great Books" approach to education developed in the Hutchins era at Chicago. My own reading of McKeon leads me to believe that the single most important philosophical influence on McKeon's pedagogical method is his one-time teacher, John Dewey. I take seriously, therefore, McKeon's statement, "From Dewey I learned to seek the significance of philosophic positions in the problems they were constructed to solve." (See McKeon's "Spiritual Autobiography," in ed. Zahava K. McKeon *Freedom and History and Other Essays—An Introduction to the Thought of Richard McKeon* [Chicago: The University of Chicago Press, 1990], 8.)

McKeon is an interpretative pluralist who supports the solid pragmatic credo that thinking is, above all, problem-oriented. Moreover, it is easy enough to see the shadow, or reflection, of McKeon in Rorty's metaphilosophical writings.

37. See "Recent Metaphilosophy," in *Review of Metaphysics* 15 (December 1961): 299-318. This article, written more than thirty years ago, sounds very like the contemporary Rorty. So much for those who believe in a Rortyan *Kehre*.

38. Ibid., 301.

39. Ibid., 301-2.

40. Ibid., 302.

41. See "Pragmatism, Relativism, and Irrationalism," CP, 167-69.

42. I will briefly discuss some of these influences in the following chapter.

43. Emerson, "Self-Reliance," in *Essays*, 152.

44. See the preface to the 1948 enlarged edition (Boston: The Beacon Press, 1957), v.

45. Ibid., xl.

46. *Art as Experience* (New York: Capricorn Books, 1958), 22-23. First published in 1934 as an enlarged version of the 1931 William James lectures at Harvard.

47. "Comments on Sleeper and Edel," 40. Rorty is here responding to criticisms of his interpretation of Dewey. For other such criticisms, see Garry Brodsky, *Transactions of the Charles S. Peirce Society*, 18, no. 4 (Fall 1982): 311-27. In this latter article, Brodsky claims that Dewey's experimentalism and naturalism would have prevented his acceptance of historicism in any relevant sense.

48. Unpublished ms.

49. Ibid., ms. page 4.

50. Ibid.

51. See Rorty's "That Old Time Philosophy," *The New Republic*, 4 April 1988, pp. 28-33, and the response to Rorty's essay by Harvey C. Mansfield, Jr., "Democracy and the Great Books," in ibid., pp. 33-37. The quotation is from Mansfield's reply, p. 36.

52. The "broker" image is used effectively by Robert Schwartz in his 1983 review of Rorty's *Philosophy and the Mirror of Nature* [PMN]. See *The Journal of Philosophy* 80, no. 1 (1983): 66-67.

53. See "The Historiography of Philosophy: Four Genres," in *Philosophy in History*, 64ff.

54. Rorty's narrative of professionalization is complex. In a review of *Philosophy and the Mirror of Nature* [PMN], ("Is the End in Sight for Epistemology?," *The Journal of Philosophy* 77, no. 10 [October 1980]: 579-88), Ian Hacking chastises Rorty for, among other things, accusing Kant of professionalizing philosophy when in fact American thought was professionalized without a Kantian influence. But, of course, Rorty had, at about the same time, written two essays ("Professionalized Philosophy and Transcendentalist Culture" and "Philosophy in America Today") both reprinted in CP, neither of which mentioned Kant. While Hacking may be right that professionalized philosophy in America was not the fault of Kant, it is, nonetheless, true that appeal to the indigenous American tradition, in the absence of any absorption of German philosophy, would have made professionalized philosophy hard to defend.

55. Quoted in Richard Rorty, "Unfamiliar Noises: Davidson and Hesse on Metaphor," *Papers* (1), 165. See Davidson's "A Nice Derangement of Epitaphs," in ed. Ernest LePore *Truth and Interpretation: Perspectives on the Philosophy of Donald Davidson* (Oxford: Blackwell, 1986).

56. CIS, 17.

57. CIS, 5.

58. Ibid.

59. "The World Well Lost," CP, 14.

60. CIS, 17.

61. C. G. Prado would qualify the extent to which Rorty's understanding of language could be said to be Davidsonian. See his *The Limits of Pragmatism*, 53-55.

62. CIS, 5.

63. CIS, 6.

64. Although, with respect to the Aristotle-Newton shift, Tom Sorrell has criticized Rorty. See his "The World from its Own Point of View," in *Reading Rorty*, 18-19.

65. CIS, 48.

66. CIS, 50.

67. CIS, 30.

68. CIS, 43.

69. CP, 19-36.

70. There is a problem with respect to Rorty's avowed materialism. His "atoms and the void" beliefs could lead to a stronger interpretation of nominalism than his more literary efforts suggest. I will take up the issue of the relation of Rorty's nominalist language to his physicalist language below.

71. "The Higher Nominalism in a Nutshell: A Reply to Henry Staten," *Critical Inquiry* 12 (Winter 1986): 463.

72. See *Papers* (1), 78-92.

73. *Papers* (1), 84.

74. *Papers* (1), 87.

75. *Papers* (1), 82.

76. *Papers* (1), 81.

77. *Papers* (1), 84.

78. *Papers* (1), 81.

79. CIS, 88.

80. CIS, 92.

81. *Papers* (1), 113-25.

82. *Papers* (1), 114.

83. *Papers* (1), 115.

84. PMN, 389.

85. *Papers* (1), 92.

86. CP, 15.

87. See "Philosophy as Science, as Metaphor, and as Politics," *Papers* (2), 9-26.

88. See "Davidson's "Paradoxes of Irrationality," in eds. B. Wollheim and J. Hopkins *Philosophical Essays on Freud* (Cambridge: Cambridge University Press, 1982).

89. "Freud and Moral Reflection," *Papers* (2), 147.

90. Ibid.

91. *Papers* (2), 152.

92. See Rorty's "The Banality of Pragmatism and the Poetry of Justice," in *Pragmatism in Law and Society*, eds. Michael Brint and William Weaver (Boulder, Colo.: Westview Press, 1991), 89-97, for a discussion of the distinctiveness of the New Pragmatism and its relevance to legal theory.

93. See "Postmodernist Bourgeois Liberalism," *Papers* (1), 197-202.

94. See, for example, Alasdair MacIntyre's *After Virtue* and *Whose Justice? Which Rationality?*

95. *After Virtue* (second edition), 25-31.

96. "Freud and Moral Reflection," *Papers* (2), 159.

97. "The Priority of Democracy to Philosophy," *Papers* (1), 195.

98. Quoted in Milton Fisk, "The Instability of Pragmatism," *New Literary History* 17 (1985): 23-30.

99. I am using the concept of vagueness in the general way that Peirce used the term—"open to rich articulation."

100. Often a term may be vague in both senses. Thomas Kuhn's notion of "paradigm" has been rendered in numerous ways by both Kuhn and his

discussants; most of the meanings were a part of the traditional cultural inventory, others were apparently new uses of the term.

101. Questions of synonymy do not begin with the query whether different verbal locutions have the same meaning. The more primitive question is whether two utterances of the putatively same locution carry the same sense. As the mainstream analysts would have it, two individuals do not mean the same thing by x ostensively recognized if they say quite different things about x.

102. I discuss these types of vagueness in "Reason and its Rhyme," *The Journal of the Indian Council of Philosophical Research* 9, no. 2: 25-46.

103. See *Steps Toward an Ecology of Mind* (New York: Ballentine Books, 1972), 279-303.

104. Ibid., 29.

105. Ibid.

106. Ibid., 27.

107. In the *Analects* (5.13), a disciple of Confucius, Tzu-kung, complains: "One cannot get to hear the Master's views on human nature and the Way of Heaven." Confucius was noted for his reticence to speak about things we should call metaphysical. It is not that one could not deduce a set of onto-logical and cosmological commitments from Confucius' sayings, but it would be considered by the Master to be rather bad form to insist upon doing so.

108. See Jeffrey Stout "Liberal Society and the Languages of Morals," *Soundings* 69, no. 1-2 (Spring/Summer 1986): 40-41 for a brief characterization of the loose consensus on the good maintained in a liberal society.

109. I recall the complaint of an older student in one of my philosophy classes to the effect that, after learning of the various meanings of "love" in the Western philosophic tradition, he had a serious argument with his wife of thirty-plus years when they learned that they had "totally different mean-ings of love." Their mutual devotion, I argued, should not be undermined by the questionable idea that incommensurable meanings of "love" at the level of theory must lead to incommensurable practices.

110. Later, we shall address the important issue as to whether Rorty is guilty of a kind of smugness which leads him to ignore the legitimate demands of critics of liberal society that he articulate the principles suggested by his practice. See chapter 5, "Circumvention and Circumlocution."

111. "Justice as Fairness: Political Not Metaphysical," *Philosophy and Public Affairs* 14 (1985): 225.

112. "The Priority of Democracy to Philosophy," *Papers* (1), 189.

113. *Papers* (1), 190. This statement embodies the principle of "circumvention," a form of "recontextualization"—the activity which serves as the surrogate for philosophical method in Rorty's thought. See chapter 5 below for a discussion of this "method."

114. *Papers* (1), 190.

115. CIS, xiv.

116. "Postmodernist Bourgeois Liberalism," *Papers* (1), 198.

117. *Papers* (1), 199.

118. CIS, 68.

119. CIS, xv.

120. Ibid.

121. Ibid. Rorty's conception of philosophy is very close to that of his hero, Francis Bacon, at least as Macaulay conceived him: "The true philosophical temperament may . . . be described in four words: much hope, little faith."

122. In his article, "Unger, Castoriadis, and the Romance of a National Future," *Papers* (2), 177-92, Rorty draws principally upon Unger's three-volume *Politics: A Work in Constructive Social Theory* (Cambridge: Cambridge University Press, 1987) and Castoriadis' *The Imaginary Institution of Society*, trans. Kathleen Blamey (Cambridge, Mass.: MIT Press, 1987) and *Crossroads in the Labyrinth*, trans. K. Soper and M. Ryle (Cambridge, Mass.: MIT Press, 1984).

123. *Social Theory*, vol. 2 of Unger's *Politics*, 223-24. Quoted by Rorty in *Papers* (2), 181.

124. *The Imaginary Institution of Society*, 200.

125. *Papers* (2), 186.

126. *Papers* (2), 189.

127. PMN, 369.

128. See *Metaphysics*, V. 1.

129. PMN, 371.

130. PMN, 372.

131. One might argue, in fact, that the received Aristotle is closer to the foundationalist position than is Plato. His doctrine of the four causes has led to an orgy of taxonomic foundationalism for the last two millennia.

132. *Process and Reality*, 3.

133. I confess that I have been very much influenced by the thought of Whitehead without once believing him to have found the truth about things or to have believed that his language constitutes a final metaphysical vocabulary. Certainly many of Whitehead's disciples have been guilty of really poor taste, and a failure of tact, in their misguided attempts to squeeze a dogmatic system from Whitehead's thought. But this says little against Whitehead; it only argues for the truth of the pragmatist Giovanni Papini's observation (in his *Life of Christ*) to the effect that the only thing wrong with messiahs is that they must have disciples.

134. See PMN, chapter 3.

135. See PMN, chapter 4, "Privileged Representations," pp. 165-212, for a discussion of Sellars and Quine.

136. *Science, Perception, and Reality* (New York, 1963), 160.

137. Putnam is one of Rorty's respected, if flawed, philosophical heroes. Like Kuhn, and others, Putnam abjures any attempt to move outside theories to attain "a God's-eye view," but this "internalism" which he opposes to the realist and relativists (Rorty being included among the latter) still allows him to ask the question, "Is there a *true* conception of rationality, an ideal morality, even if all we ever have are our conceptions of these?" (*Reason, Truth, and History* [Cambridge: Cambridge University Press, 1981], 216).

138. *Papers* (1), 1.

139. See, for example, C. G. Prado, *The Limits of Pragmatism*, passim. But see Davidson's remarks in *Reading Rorty*, which begin "Where Rorty and I disagree, if we do . . ." Doubtless, a small cottage industry could revolve around answering the question as to what extent Davidson retreats from Rorty's advances. On the whole, Davidson seems rather coy about the issue. Perhaps he is waiting to see which way the winds will blow. In fairness to Davidson, however, the fact of the matter is that it isn't as easy as one might think to understand the more arcane implications of one's own thinking. More often than we would like, we know not what we mean . . .

140. *Papers* (1), 160.

141. CP, xli.

142. CP, 149.

143. CP, 153.

144. See PMN, chapter 7, 215-56.

145. PMN, 316.

146. PMN, 332.

147. CP, 155.

148. CP, 151.

149. See his *The Art of the Novel*.

150. Ibid., 159.

151. "Heidegger, Kundera, and Dickens," *Papers* (2), 70.

152. See *Papers* (2), 77.

153. *Papers* (2), 75.

154. Ibid.

155. *Papers* (2), 78.

156. CIS, 146.

157. CIS, 157.

158. Ibid.

159. See the afterword to *Lolita*.

160. CIS, 164.

161. CIS, 173.

162. CIS, 182.

163. CIS, 185.

164. This is Rorty's definition of "humiliation."

165. CIS, 102, 103.

166. CIS, 105.

167. Ibid.

CHAPTER 3: IRONY'S MASTER, IRONY'S SLAVE

1. CIS, 73.

2. CIS, 87.

3. Ibid.

4. CIS, 75.

5. *Well Wrought Urn* (New York: Harcourt, Brace and World, 1975), 209.

6. CIS, 79.

7. Rorty's failure to recognize the constitutive irony of Plato is a rather dramatic instance of the manner his Grand Narrative allows him to exclude data relevant to his discussion. By failing to appreciate Plato's irony, Rorty extends himself the privilege of reading Plato as arch-foundationalist.

8. See Emerson's "Plato, or, The Philosopher" in *The Writings of Ralph Waldo Emerson*, ed. Brooks Atkinson (New York: The Modern Library, 1950), 488.

9. See my *Eros and Irony* (Albany: SUNY Press, 1982), 211ff for a discussion of "Platocratic" irony.

10. From the preface to *Skepticism and Animal Faith* (New York: Dover, 1955), v. Rorty has some sympathy with Santayana's denial that he is a metaphysician, metaphysics being (for Santayana) little more than "dialectical physics." But in his ontological period, certainly, Santayana could fairly be deemed a systematic rather than edifying philosopher. For Rorty's sympathetic treatment of Santayana, see "Professionalized Philosophy and Transcendentalist Culture," in CP, 60-71.

11. *Process and Reality*, 337, 338.

12. CIS, 87. Contrary to Rorty, I find it hard to imagine a culture which socialized its youth to be nominalist and historicist without thereby causing them to be ironic as well. I'm not sure how one would go about settling this issue at the normative, or theoretical, level.

13. CIS, 83.

14. See "The Priority of Democracy to Philosophy," *Papers* (1), 194-95.

15. Later on, we shall see that Rorty claims Dewey to be a liberal ironist. Given the public focus of Dewey's writings, and the practical engagement of Dewey with the social and political problems of his time, it is difficult to see how Rorty would claim that irony is always harmful if made public.

16. CIS, 79.

17. CIS, 89.

18. *The Apology*, trans. Benjamin Jowett (New York: Random House, 1937), 41-42.

19. In the final chapter we shall examine the consequences of Rorty's attempt to use irony as a means of avoiding methodological commitments.

20. Donald Davidson and John Rawls are exceptions. Rorty does seem to have had some influence upon both of these thinkers. But for the most part it is the great dead thinkers who are being redescribed, or intransigent thinkers such as Quine, Sellars, Derrida, even Habermas, who are self-consciously being made to serve Rorty's purposes.

21. CIS, 79.

22. Quoted in the introduction to *Thus Spoke Zarathustra*, trans. and ed. Walter Kaufmann (New York: Penguin Books, 1978).

23. I don't recall who said this.

24. CIS, 61.

25. CIS, 68.

26. Others may be found who employ this return to Aristotle. See Michael McCarthy's *The Crisis of Philosophy* (Albany: SUNY Press, 1990).

27. *The Philosophical Discourse of Modernity*, trans. Frederick G. Lawrence (Cambridge: MIT Press, 1990), 56.

28. Ibid., 207.

29. In an essay entitled "Philosophy and Science as Literature" (*Postmetaphysical Thinking—Philosophical Essays* [Cambridge, Mass: MIT Press, 1992], 205-27), Habermas elaborates the discussions of the functions of language.

30. For a most succinct and profound presentation of his relationship to Peirce see his recent essay, "Peirce and Communication" in *Postmetaphysical Thinking—Philosophical Essays*, 88-112.

31. CIS, 67.

32. CIS, 67-68.

33. See "Philosophy as Stand-In and Interpreter" in *After Philosophy*, eds. K. Baynes, J. Bohman, and T. McCarthy (Cambridge: Cambridge University Press, 1987), 296-318.

34. Ibid., 298.

35. Ibid., 297.

36. Ibid., 313.

37. See Habermas' "Toward a Critique of the Theory of Meaning," *Postmetaphysical Thinking—Philosophical Essays*, 57-87.

38. See CIS, 64 n. 24.

39. *Discipline and Punishment—The Birth of the Prison*, trans. Alan Sheridan (New York: Penguin Books, 1977).

40. CIS, 94.

41. CIS, 65.

42. *Language, Counter-Memory, Practice*, ed. Donald Bouchard (Ithaca, N.Y.: Cornell University Press, 1977), 230.

43. "Heidegger, Contingency, and Pragmatism," *Papers* (2), 32.

44. Ibid., 40.

45. *Papers* (2), 37-38.

46. *Papers* (2), 46.

47. I insist that I am not simply joining in the currently fashionable exercise of Heidegger bashing. Long before the current stir over Heidegger's Nazi connections, I argued for the totalitarian implications of some of the arguments in *Introduction to Metaphysics*. See my *The Civilization of Experience* (New York: Fordham University Press, 1973), 4-5, and *Eros and Irony* (Albany: SUNY Press, 1982), 90-95. I am in essential agreement with Habermas' views expressed in his *Philosophical Discourse of Modernity*, trans. Frederick Lawrence (Cambridge: MIT Press, 1990), 156-60.

48. *Introduction to Metaphysics* (New York: Doubleday, 1961), 42.

49. "Philosophy as Science, as Metaphor, and as Politics," *Papers* (2), 19.

50. *The Philosophical Discourse of Modernity*, 158-59.

51. See her remarks in *Heidegger and Modern Philosophy*, ed. Michael Murray (New Haven: Yale University Press, 1978), 298-303.

52. Ibid., 303.

53. Victor Farías, *Heidegger and Nazism*, ed. Joseph Margolis and Tom Rockmore; trans. from the French by Paul Burrell, and from the German by Gabriel Ricci (Philadelphia: Temple University Press, 1989); Philippe Lacoue-Labarthe, *Heidegger, Art and Politics*, trans. Chris Turner (Oxford:

Blackwell, 1990); Jacques Derrida, *Of Spirit: Heidegger and the Question,* trans. Geoffrey Bennington and Rachel Bowlby (Chicago: University of Chicago Press, 1989); Luc Ferry and Alain Renaut, *Heidegger and Modernity,* trans. from the French by Franklin Philip (Chicago: University of Chicago Press, 1990). This is but a small fraction and the list gets longer as each intellectual is called to account either by conscience or public demand.

54. See his review of Farías' book, "Taking Philosophy Seriously," *The New Republic,* 11 April 1988, and his reflections entitled "Diary" in *The London Review of Books,* 8 February 1990, 21.

55. "Diary," 21.

56. Ibid.

57. Ibid.

58. "Taking Philosophy Seriously," 34.

59. "Diary," 21.

60. CIS, 111 n. 11.

61. *Papers* (2), 19 n. 27.

CHAPTER 4: EXCURSUS AD HOMINEM

1. See "Philosophy as Science, as Metaphor, and as Politics," *Papers* (2), 12ff.

2. "Solidarity or Objectivity?," *Papers* (1), 30.

3. CP, xlii.

4. "Pragmatism, Relativism, and Irrationalism," CP, 166.

5. CIS, 93.

6. CIS, 185.

7. CIS, 186.

8. *Papers* (1), 13.

9. See *Religion in the Making* (New York: Meridian Books, 1960). My emphasis.

10. See Paul Tillich's discussion of this contrast in *Systematic Theology* (Chicago: The University of Chicago Press, 1967), vols. 1 and 2, passim.

11. One may say that it is in this sense, rather than the sense of Bernstein quoted above, that Rorty might be said to be a "one-time true believer who has lost his faith."

12. CP, xlii-xliii.

13. "The Priority of Democracy to Philosophy," *Papers* (1), 192.

14. The description is A. N. Whitehead's. See his *Process and Reality*, part V, section VII.

15. "Solidarity or Objectivity," *Papers* (1), 31.

16. See chapter 1 above.

17. *Papers* (1), 33.

18. Ibid.

19. CIS, 94.

20. "Freud and Moral Reflection," *Papers* (2), 159.

21. *Papers* (2), 160.

22. "On Ethnocentrism: A Reply to Clifford Geertz," *Papers* (1), 205.

23. "Solidarity or Objectivity?," *Papers* (1), 31.

24. "One Step Forward, Two Steps Backward," *The New Constellation*, 244.

25. "The Priority of Democracy to Philosophy," *Papers* (1), 195.

26. "Two Cheers for the Cultural Left," in *The South Atlantic Quarterly* 89 (Winter 1990): 230.

27. Ibid., 234 n. 5.

28. "On Ethnocentrism: A Reply to Clifford Geertz," *Papers* (1), 206.

29. See Peirce's "On Detached Ideas in General and On Vitally Important Topics as Such," in *Collected Papers*, MS 435 (1898).

30. "Liberals, Communitarians, and the Tasks of Political Theory," *Political Theory* 15, no. 4. (1987): 600.

31. "From Logic to Language to Play," 753.

32. "Solidarity or Objectivity?," *Papers* (1), 26.

33. Rorty is not conservative in any fundamental sense. It is true, however, that a "clotted liberal" may sometimes be mistaken for a conservative of sorts.

34. But it is difficult not to sympathize with Rorty when he derides *Ideologiekritik* as "a dreadful, pompous, useless, mishmash of Marx, Adorno, Derrida, Foucault, and Lacan," and calls Marxism an "amiable,

but fruitless, exercise in nostalgia." See Rorty's "Thugs and Theorists: Reply to Richard Bernstein," *Political Theory* 15, no. 4: 570.

35. There is an illustration of this in the recent protest movements in China. The Chinese have traditionally not employed conceptions of "natural law" or "human rights" as transcendent norms in accordance with which to judge their society. The poets and revolutionaries in China suffer precisely the sort of immanent alienation that would urge them to move their society closer to its image of itself. Recent attempts to import Western liberal democratic slogans into China, as in the case of the Tiananmen protests, failed largely because of the strong ethnocentrism of Chinese culture. The Chinese ethos cannot easily resonate with appeals to transcendent norms.

36. See his "A Pragmatist View of Rationality and Cultural Difference," *Philosophy East and West* 42, no. 4 (October 1992): 581-96. See also his "Heidegger, Kundera, and Dickens," *Papers* (2), 66-82. This essay was also published in *Culture and Modernity—East-West Philosophic Perspectives*, ed. Eliot Deutsch (Honolulu: The University of Hawaii Press, 1991) under the title "Philosophers, Novelists, and Intercultural Comparisons: Heidegger, Kundera, and Dickens," 3-20.

37. Here Rorty echoes a theme discussed at some length in Whitehead's *Adventures of Ideas*—namely, how the irrationalities of technological and political developments interacted with Christianity and democratic pluralism to create an environment characterized by "wide intellectual tolerance."

38. "A Pragmatist View of Rationality and Cultural Difference," 585.

39. In "A Pragmatist View of Rationality and Cultural Difference," Rorty discusses Ashish Nandy's *Traditions, Tyranny and Utopias* (Oxford: Oxford University Press, 1987), which argues for the need for religious transcendence.

40. See, for example, V. S. Naipaul's *India—A Million Mutinies Now* (New York: Viking Press, 1991) for a set of reflections on India as a model for a pluralistic society. See, also, the conclusion of Stephen Toulmin's *Cosmopolis—The Hidden Agenda of Modernity* for a brief discussion of India as "adaptively disarticulated."

41. "A Pragmatist View of Rationality and Cultural Difference," 593.

42. "Heidegger, Kundera, and Dickens," *Papers* (2), 73.

43. Nothing begins and ends
    which is not paid with moan.
    We are born in another's pain
    and perish in our own.
                    Francis Thompson

44. "Detested sport that owes its pleasures to another's pain."
                                        William Cowper

45. *Treatise on Human Nature*, Book II, part III, section IX, 439.

46. "Dewey Between Hegel and Darwin," unpublished manuscript, 7.

47. CIS, 55.

48. CIS, 16.

49. *The Phenomenology of Mind*, trans J. B. Baillie (New York: Humanities Press, 1964), 250-51.

50. This use of so-called romantic irony goes as far back at least as Sterne's *Tristram Shandy* and Byron's *Don Juan*.

51. "Freud and Moral Reflection," *Papers* (2), 154.

52. Ibid.

53. *Papers* (2), 154-55.

54. *Papers* (2), 155.

55. See section 2 of that chapter.

56. *Papers* (2), 162.

57. Ibid.

58. See *Papers* (2), 154.

59. See chapters 7 and 8 of CIS.

60. See chapter 5 below on "Recontextualization."

61. See "The Banality of Pragmatism and the Poetry of Justice," *Pragmatism in Law and Society*, eds. Michael Brint and William Weaver (Boulder, Colo.: Westview Press, 1991), 89-97.

62. Ibid., 92.

63. "The Philosopher and the Prophet," *Transition*, no. 52: 74.

64. Ibid.

65. John Dewey, "From Absolutism to Experimentalism," in *Later Works of John Dewey*, vol. 5 (Carbondale: Southern Illinois University Press, 1984), 160. Quoted in Rorty's November 1990 Tanner Lecture, "Feminism and Pragmatism," *Michigan Quarterly Review* (Spring 1991), p. 255 n. 26.

66. "The Philosopher and the Prophet," 73.

67. Ibid.

68. Ibid., 75.

69. See "The Banality of Pragmatism and the Poetry of Justice," 93.

70. "Feminism and Pragmatism," 231-58.

71. *Feminism Unmodified: Discourses on Life and Law* (Cambridge, Mass: Harvard University Press, 1987).

72. *The Politics of Reality: Essays in Feminist Theory* (Trumansburg, N.Y.: Crossing Press, 1983).

73. "Feminism and Pragmatism," 234.

74. "Feminism, Ideology, and Deconstruction," to appear in *Hypatia*, unpublished ms. p. 11.

75. Ibid., 12.

76. As I have said, we might leave this issue to be settled empirically. In chapter 5, I will challenge the view that binary opposition has a deep metaphysical character by contrasting its absence in the structure of the Chinese language, while noting its (nominalized) importance in China's political and philosophical traditions. See section 3 of that chapter.

77. "Feminism and Pragmatism," 247.

78. "On Ethnocentrism: A Reply to Clifford Geertz," *Papers* (1), 209.

79. "Philosophy without Principles," *Critical Inquiry* 11 (March 1985): 462.

80. "Feminism and Pragmatism," 244.

81. Ibid.

82. "Philosophy as Science, as Metaphor, and as Politics," *Papers* (2), 17.

83. See "Inquiry as Recontextualization: An Antidualist Account of Interpretation," *Papers* (1), 93ff.

84. Geoffrey Hartman, *Saving the Text: Literature, Derrida and Philosophy* (Baltimore: Johns Hopkins University Press, 1981) quoted in *Papers* (2), 88.

85. "Moral Identity and Private Autonomy: The Case of Foucault," *Papers* (2), 198.

86. Ibid.

87. The term "dryness" is Iris Murdoch's.

88. *Papers* (2), 195.

89. *Papers* (2), 196.

90. *Papers* (2), 195-96.

91. CIS, 44.

92. CIS, 53.

93. CIS, 54.

94. CIS, 61.

95. CIS, 60-61.

CHAPTER 5: CIRCUMVENTION AND CIRCUMLOCUTION

1. 344b (L. A. Post translation).

2. *Phaedo*, 89d (Hugh Tredennick translation).

3. The term, of course, belongs to Jacques Derrida.

4. See my *The Civilization of Experience*, 11-21, for a discussion of Whitehead's mode of analogical argumentation and his use of five sources of evidence.

5. Note that any of the three methods of argument (analysis, dialectic, or analogy) can be employed rhetorically—that is, they may be used to accommodate pathos and ethos. Analytic appeals to common sense, or dialectical examinations of opposing doctrines, or suggestions of analogies among contrasting elements of experience, may be rhetorical as long as they are not strictly delimited by the strictures of a single logical or semantic system (or by appeal to ontological least units—atoms, and so forth).

6. "Pragmatism without Method," *Papers* (1), 67.

7. CIS, 5.

8. CIS, 54.

9. CIS, p. 54 n. 8.

10. "The Priority of Democracy to Philosophy," *Papers* (1), 194.

11. "Philosophy without Principles," *Critical Inquiry* 11 (March 1985): 461.

12. See Rorty's "Pragmatism without Method," *Papers* (1), 63-77.

13. *Pragmatism* (New York: Meridian Books, 1955), 46, 47.

14. Rorty could justifiably say that his metanarratives and taxonomies are so many vessels which may be set adrift once we reach the far shore. That's essentially what Plato said about his dialectical method. "Benevolent disputation by the use of question and answer without jealousy . . ." seems no more confining than such disputation carried on among nominalist, poetic narrativists. Plato may indeed have believed the end of the journey a quite different place than Rorty, but the mode and means of transportation seem strikingly similar.

15. We may, as Rorty suggests, dispense with the locution "and desires" since the belief "It would be better that *y* than not-*y*" incorporates the desire, "I want *y* to be the case!"

16. "Inquiry as Recontextualization: An Antidualist Account of Interpretation," *Papers* (1), 94.

17. *Papers* (1), 94.

18. *Papers* (1), 95 n. 1.

19. *Papers* (1), 97.

20. Ibid.

21. *Papers* (1), 98.

22. Ibid.

23. *Papers* (1), 100.

24. *Papers* (1), 101.

25. See *Papers* (1), 105.

26. *Papers* (1), 106.

27. *Papers* (1), 107.

28. *Papers* (1), 104.

29. "The Instability of Pragmatism," 29.

30. See G. B. Kerford's discussion of these modes of argumentation in *The Sophistic Movement* (Cambridge: Cambridge University Press, 1981), 59-67.

31. For an elaboration of the meaning of *ars contextualis*, see my "Logos, Mythos, Chaos: Metaphysics as the Quest For Diversity," in ed. Robert Neville *New Essays in Metaphysics* (Albany: SUNY Press, 1987), 1-24, passim and *Thinking through Confucius* (Albany: SUNY Press, 1987), chapter four, passim. Contrary to Rorty's preference for avoiding terminology, I believe

that clarity and candor are gained by encapsulating in a term the sense of a regular practice. In this I am again expressing agreement with Milton Fisk.

32. "Memes" are the linguistic equivalents of "genes."

33. See "Deconstruction and Circumvention," in *Papers* (2), 85-106.

34. CIS, 9.

35. *Papers* (1), 190. Emphasis mine.

36. Forthcoming as a chapter in volume 8 of the *Cambridge History of Literary Criticism*. Citations are from the unpublished manuscript.

37. Ibid., 2.

38. *Allegories of Reading: Figurative Language in Rousseau, Nietzsche, Rilke and Proust* (New Haven: Yale University Press, 1979), 115.

39. "Deconstruction," 2.

40. Ibid., 5.

41. Ibid.

42. Ibid., 6.

43. Ibid., 10.

44. *The Postcard from Socrates to Freud and Beyond*, trans. Alan Bass (Chicago: The University of Chicago Press, 1987).

45. "Deconstruction and Circumvention," *Papers* (2), 99.

46. *Papers* (2), 100.

47. Rorty also astutely observes that the writings of Paul de Man have given the distinctive shape to American versions of deconstruction. See Rorty's "Two Meanings of 'Logocentrism': A Reply to Norris," in *Papers* (2), 107-18, and "Deconstruction." See also "Philosophy as a Kind of Writing: An Essay on Derrida," in CP, 90-109, and chapter 6 of CIS entitled "From Ironist Theory to Private Allusions: Derrida," 123-37.

48. Here Rorty is in agreement with Barbara Herrnstein Smith in *Contingencies of Value* (Cambridge, Mass.: Harvard University Press, 1988), 118ff.

49. "Two Meanings of Logocentrism: A Reply to Norris," *Papers* (2), 111.

50. *Papers* (2), 109.

51. "Deconstruction and Circumvention," *Papers* (2), 103.

52. Quoted from *Contingencies of Value*, 118. Cited in Rorty "Two Meanings of 'Logocentrism': A Reply to Norris," 109.

53. See A. C. Graham's *Unreason Within Reason—Essays on the Outskirts of Rationality* (La Salle, Ill: Open Court, 1992) and David L. Hall and Roger T. Ames *Anticipating China: The Circle and the Square* (Albany: SUNY Press, 1994).

54. See Derrida's *Writing and Difference*, trans. Alan Bass (Chicago: The University of Chicago Press, 1978), passim.

55. *Contingencies of Value*, 118.

56. *Papers* (2), 118.

57. "Is Derrida a Transcendental Philosopher?," *Papers* (2), 120.

58. Notably Jonathan Culler, *On Deconstruction*; Richard Bernstein, "One Step Forward, Two Steps Backward," and Christopher Norris, *Contest of the Faculties* (London: Methuen, 1985). See chapter 6 of the latter work: "Philosophy as a Kind of Narrative: Rorty on Post-Modern Liberal Culture." See also Norris' *Derrida* (Cambridge, Mass.: Harvard University Press, 1987), passim.

59. Norris, *Derrida*, 157.

60. See "Philosophy as a Kind of Writing: An Essay on Derrida," in CP, 90-109.

61. See, for example, *The Postcard*. The book was originally published in 1980. Rorty discusses this work in CIS, chapter 6, "From Ironist Theory to Private Allusions: Derrida."

62. CIS, 137.

63. CP, 154-55.

64. CIS, 161 n. 26.

65. CIS, 94.

66. CIS, 83.

67. CIS, 111 n. 11.

68. CIS, 145.

69. In "The Philosopher and the Prophet," 74, Rorty qualifies his interpretation of Dewey as an underlaborer: "James and Dewey, I admit, were lucky enough to combine, to some extent, the roles of professor and of prophet."

70. See Musil's magnificent (uncompleted) send-up of European culture at the end of its tether, *The Man without Qualities*.

71. *Papers* (2), 196.

72. I refer readers to Rorty's recent autobiographical piece, "Trotsky and the Wild Orchids." Here, in an uncharacteristically open and personal manner, Rorty tells of his childhood and adolescent development. The single most important impression one receives from reading this piece is just how important to Rorty were the satisfactions of solitude.

73. See "Feminism and Pragmatism," 253 n. 23. Singer's remarks are quoted from "Should Lawyers Care About Philosophy?," *Duke Law Journal* (1989): 17-52.

NAME INDEX

277

SUBJECT INDEX

Aesthetic pluralism: and American philosophy, 66-80, 108, 180; Dewey and, 71, 81-85; Edwards and, 66-67; James and, 70-71; McKeon and, 74, 77, 79, 80; Peirce and, 68-70; Pepper and, 73-74; Whitehead and, 71-72. *See also* Pluralism

Belatedness, 123; Heideggerian, 162-63

Beliefs: agencies of change in, 97-100, 210-12; and common sense, 130-31, 176-77; and ethnocentrism, 178-83; and final vocabularies, 129-35, 170-71; inertia of, 193-94; as positions in a web, 216; and recontextualization, 213-21; as rules for action, 209; as

substance of self, 213, 217, 233-35. *See also* Self

Capitalist/marxist dialectic, 34, 41-46, 157, 230, 252n. 72

Cartesian Anxiety, 4, 244n. 6

Causality: and common sense, 220; as extra-linguistic, 90-93, 101, 216, 231; as subject matter of science, 95

Circumvention: and circumlocution, 234-36; and deconstruction, 221-30; and recontextualization, 221-22, 261n. 113. *See also* Deconstruction; Recontextualization

Common sense, 130-31, 134-35, 137, 232; and belief in causality, 217, 220; metaphysics as extension of, 131; and reasonableness, 206

283